ISBN: 978-1-4834-5391-0 (sc)
ISBN: 978-1-4834-5392-7 (e)

Lulu Publishing Services rev. date: 9/9/2016

WAR ON THE MIDDLELINE

*The Founding of a Community in the
Kayaderosseras Patent in the Midst
of the American Revolution*

JAMES E. RICHMON

Contents

Dramatis Personae

Arnold	Benedict	Rebel American general. Attacked Quebec 1775. Led American Navy at Valcour Island 1776. Led charge at Saratoga 1777. Traitor 1780.
Ball	Eliphalet	Minister, Bedford, NY. Recruited settlers to Ball's Town. First Minister of Ballston Presbyterian Church.
Ball	John	Son of Eliphalet. Husband of Mary Collins. Captain, Revolutionary War.
Beekman	Johannis	One of the 13 original Proprietors of the Patent. Merchant – Albany.
Benedict	Elisha	Middleline Road pioneer. Captured in October 1780 raid.
Benedict	Calib	Middleline Road pioneer. Son of Elisha. Captured in October 1780 raid.
Benedict	Elias	Middleline Road pioneer. Son of Elisha. Captured in October 1780 raid.
Benedict	Felix	Middleline Road pioneer. Son of Elisha. Captured in October 1780 raid.
Benedict	Dublin	Middleline Road pioneer. Slave of Elisha. Captured in October 1780 raid.
Bettys	Joseph	American sailor at Valcour Island 1776. Later Loyalist spy and raider from Ballston. Son of Joseph, Sr., Ballston tavern keeper.

Bickley	May	One of the 13 original Proprietors of the Patent. Attorney General – New York City.
Brant	Joseph	Mohawk Warrior. Led raids on American settlements in Schoharie and Mohawk Valleys. aka, Thayendanegea.
Bridges	Ann	One of the 13 original Proprietors of the Patent. Wife of Attorney General – New York City.
Broughton	Sampson	One of the 13 original Proprietors of the Patent. Son of Attorney General – New York City.
Butler	John	Loyalist. Captain of Butler's Rangers. Led raids on American settlements in Schoharie, Cherry, and Mohawk Valleys.
Carleton	Christopher	Major 29th British Regiment. Led October 1780 raid on Fort Ann and Fort George.
Clopper	Cornelius	Trustee of the Patent. NYC businessman. Member of the Provincial Assembly.
Colden	Cadwallader	Surveyor General. Scientist. Lt. Governor. Loyalist.
Collins	Tyrannus	Captain, 12th Albany County Militia. Led company against Loyalists. Captured in October 1780 raid.
Collins	Manasseh	Middleline Road pioneer. Son of Tyrannus Collins. Avoided capture in October 1780 raid.
Davis	John	Middleline Road pioneer. Captured in October 1780 raid.
Fauconnier	Peter	One of the 13 original Proprietors of the Patent. Receiver General – New York City.
Filer	Jonathan	Middleline Road pioneer. Avoided Capture in October 1780 raid.
Fillmore	Cyrus	Middleline Road pioneer. Servant of Enoch Wood. Captured in October 1780 raid. Escaped October 17.

Fisher	Johannis	One of the 13 original Proprietors of the Patent. Merchant – Albany.
Fraser	William	Loyalist from Ballston. Captain in McAlpin's American Volunteers. Led Loyalist company in October 1780 raid on Ballston.
Galbraith	Jack	Middleline Road pioneer. Servant of James Gordon. Captured in October 1780 raid.
Gordon	James	Arrived from Ireland, 1758. Trader during French and Indian War. Leading settler of Middleline Road. Lt. Col. 12th Albany County militia. Captured in 1780 raid. Escaped from Canada. Congressman 1791-1795.
Gordon	James, Jr	Middleline Road pioneer. Son of James Gordon. Captured in October 1780 raid.
Gordon	Nero	Middleline Road pioneer. Slave of James Gordon. Captured in October 1780 raid. Sold. Escaped from Canada.
Gordon	Jacob	Middleline Road pioneer. Slave of James Gordon. Captured in October 1780 raid. Sold in Canada.
Gordon	Ann	Middleline Road pioneer. Slave of James Gordon. Captured in October 1780 raid. Sold in Canada.
Haldimand	Frederick	Governor General of the Province of Quebec. Authorized 1780 raids.
Harmanse	Nanning	One of the 13 original Proprietors of the Patent. Merchant — Albany.
Hendrick	King	Mohawk sachem. Disputed Kayaderosseras land grant. aka Theyanoguin.
Higby	John	Middleline Road pioneer. Captured in October 1780 raid.
Higby	Lewis	Middleline Road pioneer. Son of John. Captured in October 1780 raid.

Hollister	Josiah	Middleline Road pioneer. Captured in October 1780 raid. Wrote journal.
Hooglandt	Adrian	One of the 13 original Proprietors of the Patent. Merchant — New York City.
Hooglandt	Joris	One of the 13 original Proprietors of the Patent. Merchant — New York City.
Hyde	Edward	Lord Cornbury. Governor of New York 1702-1708. Granted Kayaderosseras Patent in 1708 in name of Queen Anne.
Jessup	Edward	Loyalist. Captain of King's Loyal Americans (Jessup's Rangers).
Jessup	Ebenezer	Loyalist. Brother of Edward. Served in King's Loyal Americans.
Johnson	Sir William	Commissioner of Indian Affairs. Leading British land owner in the Mohawk Valley. Negotiated Patent settlement.
Johnson	Sir John	Loyalist. Son of Sir William. Colonel, King's Royal Regiment. Led October 1780 raid through Schoharie and Mohawk Valleys.
Kennedy	George	Middleline Road pioneer. Emigrated from Ireland. Captured in October 1780 raid. Released October 18.
Kennedy	Thomas	Middleline Road pioneer. Emigrated from Ireland. Brother of George and John. Captured in October 1780 raid.
Kennedy	John	Middleline Road pioneer. Emigrated from Ireland. Brother of George and Thomas. Avoided capture in October 1780 raid.
Kissam	Benjamin	Trustee of the Patent. NYC Lawyer. Served in colonial & provincial Assembly.
Lefferts	Dirck	Trustee of the Patent. NYC businessman. Agent for the Patent.

Low	Isaac	Trustee of the Patent. NYC businessman. Served in First Continental Congress. Later Loyalist.
McAlpin	Daniel	Loyalist. British half-pay officer. Colonel American Volunteers.
Munro	John	Loyalist. British half-pay officer. Captain, King's Royal Regiment. Led October 1780 raid on Ballston.
Myers	John W.	Loyalist spy and raider from Albany County.
Palmatier	Isaac	Middleline Road pioneer. Captured in October 1780 raid with John Shew.
Palmer	Thomas	Commissioner of the Kayaderosseras Patent. Cartographer. Resided in Dutchess County.
Palmer	Beriah	Surveyor and lawyer. Brother of Thomas. Local agent for the Patent. Congressman 1803-1805.
Parlow	John	Middleline Road pioneer. Servant of James Gordon. Captured in October 1780 Raid. Released in Canada.
Patchin	Jabez	Middleline Road pioneer. Captured in October 1780 raid.
Patchin	Samuel	Middleline Road pioneer. Son of Jabez. Captured in 1781 raid on Ballston.
Pierson	Paul	Middleline Road pioneer. Captured in October 1780 raid. Released October 18.
Pierson	John	Middleline Road pioneer. Son of Paul. Captured in October 1780 raid. Released October 18.
Schuyler	Phillip	Rebel general in American Revolution. Commander of Northern Department.
Scott	George	Middleline Road pioneer. Emigrated from Ireland 1774. Brother-in-law of James Gordon. Wounded in October 1780 raid.

Shew	John	Fish House pioneer. First person killed in Ballston raid
Smith	William, Jr	Lawyer. Chief Justice of the New York Supreme Court. Author. Loyalist.
Sprague	Ebenezer	Middleline Road pioneer. Captured in October 1780 raid. Released October 18.
Sprague	John	Middleline Road pioneer. Son of Ebenezer. Captured in October 1780 raid. Escaped from Canada.
Sprague	Elisha	Middleline Road pioneer. Son of Ebenezer. Captured in October 1780 raid.
Stephens	John	One of the 13 original Proprietors of the Patent. Lawyer—New York City.
Stow	Isaac	Middleline Road pioneer. Miller for James Gordon. Nephew of Tyrannus Collins. Killed in October 1780 raid.
Tatham	John	One of the 13 original Proprietors of the Patent. Lawyer—New York City.
Tudor	John	One of the 13 original Proprietors of the Patent. Provincial Recorder— New York City.
Van Dam	Rip	One of the 13 original Proprietors of the Patent. Governor's Council— New York City.
Watrous	Edward	Middleline Road pioneer. Captured in October 1780 raid.
Webb	Charles	Chief Surveyor of the Patent. Stamford, Connecticut.
Wood	Enoch	Middleline Road pioneer. Captured in October 1780 raid.

Preface & Acknowledgements

This book began as a follow-on project to a brief history I had done on Rowland's Hollow mills in the Town of Milton, Saratoga County, New York. I live just down the road and through the woods from the abandoned mill and, with my children, have often scrambled around the rock pile remains of the old stone buildings. A paper for a class at Schenectady Community College on Industrial Archeology led to a pamphlet focusing on people of the mill, where they came from, whom they knew and how they came to this small hamlet.

My interest in local history grew and I soon became interested in the 1780 British Raid along Middleline Road in Ballston, a town on the frontier in the newly partitioned Kayaderosseras Patent. Occurring three years after the Battles of Saratoga, its story has receded in time and has become a faint memory for some, an unknown event for most. What triggered my interest were the detailed accounts about the raid itself, each slightly different, but all naming the settlers who were caught up in the raid. The Tories and their Indian allies scooped up the settlers and drove the men north to Canada, leaving their families behind to gaze on their burned-out homes. Especially interesting to me was the fact that the narratives provided a house-by-house record of the residents, almost reading like a city directory. So I started out to tell their tale, following the Rowland's Hollow approach-where they came from, why they came, and with whom. For this, I have relied on my long-term interest in genealogy.

Focusing on the people of the Middleline begged the larger question. Who were the twelve men and one woman first receiving the Kayaderosseras land grant from Lord Cornbury, the Royal Governor of

New York, in 1708? How was it that this area, which lies within 20 miles of Albany and Schenectady, communities founded more than 100 years earlier, was still a wilderness in the 1760's? What was the role of the local Indian tribe, the Mohawks, and the Iroquois Confederation, in delaying this settlement? To answer these questions, I had to push back the time horizon to the first years of the 18th century (80 years before the raid) and explore the history of this grant. Middleline Road was indeed the middle line of a much larger tract of land known as the Kayaderosseras Patent.

The conclusion of the story is an account of the 1780 Raid and the subsequent experience of the captives in Canada. This narrative can only be told in the context of the revolutionary struggle which often took on the characteristics of a civil war. Locally, the conflict did not end with Burgoyne's invasion of 1777 and the battles at Saratoga. As the war continued year after year, it became a much more personal conflict among newly arrived farmers, tradesmen, merchants and land speculators. It is a story of those families that rose up against the King and his government and embraced the revolution vs. those that remained loyal to the Crown and paid the price for their decision. This small raid on a frontier community was but one example of how the American Revolution disrupted the lives of people dealing with the reality of the new world the war created.

You will see that this is not a comprehensive history of the Patent, the Revolution, or the founding of the Town of Ballston. Its focus narrows as we move from chapter to chapter. Starting out with the major players in colonial New York politics, a succeeding chapter concentrates on the politics surrounding the Patent. Later chapters focus on the local story, first to the settlement of the Five-Mile Square that became Ballston, then to the area's revolutionary travails and finally to the lives forever changed along the narrow, dusty path called the Middleline. One further consideration. This account is densely packed with names and citations in the desire to provide enough information to those who would consider extending the research begun here. It is hoped that the story comes through to the reader amidst the factual details. Appendix Two is meant to assist the reader in following the genealogical path of the families involved. Appendix Three traces the journey of the captives after the raid.

Regarding the application of place names, the Town of Ballston began life as Ball's Town in honor of its first resident promoter, Eliphalet Ball. In

1775 it became the Balls Town District and increasingly became referred to as Ballston during the Revolutionary War. In this book, I have referred to the community as Ball's Town until the beginning of the war, and Ballston thereafter. I have used the same approach in citing Long Lake in the pre-war period and Ballston Lake in later years. Finally, the line that divided the Five-Mile Square, was often referred to as "The Middleline" in early deeds. I have mostly referred to it as Middleline Road in this book.

This project has connected me with many people who share my interest in history and were a joy to work with and learn from. First, I want to thank Lorie Weis and Don Carpenter who know more about the Kayaderosseras Patent than I ever will and were happy to share their knowledge. It was so exciting to mention some of the obscure proprietors of the patent, and actually find someone who knew who I was talking about! For the revolutionary struggle, no one could ask for more than the two historians who shared their work, insights and humor with me – Gavin Watt, author of several books on the Revolution, and Nicholas Westbrook, Director Emeritus of Fort Ticonderoga. Nick exceeded all expectations in taking an active interest in working with me on this, my initial foray into a book-length project. Remaining faults are all mine, but they are certainly less than they would have been without Nick's fastidious zeal. Beth Finch McCarthy, a gifted genealogist, also was quick to provide finding aids that allowed me to dig deeper into the lives of the captured Tyrannus Collins and his family.

Among the local friends I have made that provided their time and insights were Lauren Roberts, the Saratoga County Historian, who always had something new to share. John Cromie's insights into the history of Ballston were invaluable. David Fiske helped guide me through the tortious path to publication. Kathleen Coleman and Anne Clothier from the Saratoga County Historical Society at Brookside assisted me in exploring their extensive archives. For local editorial assistance, Kim McCartney, Milton Town Historian, Dr. Ethel Lesh, a lady of multiple talents and passions, and Dr. Tim Sommerer took the time to turn this rough manuscript into something resembling the English language. My friend Matt Grumo and I spent hours together sifting through the old records of Ballston, sharing our findings. Matt is working on his own history of Uriah Gregory, the original owner of his current home in Ballston. But the best part of our friendship was our trips to Virginia. We took a break from the Revolutionary War era and enjoyed the pageantry of several Civil War 150th Anniversary gatherings. Rick Reynolds, Ballston Town Historian, opened up his files to us, gave Matt and me unlimited access to the old town records, and read my early drafts with a critical eye. Thanks to all of you for this great experience!

PROLOGUE
Milton Center – October 17 1780

Rebel Lieutenant Colonel James Gordon sat shivering in the cold of an early October morning. The sky was just beginning to brighten, but it had not taken away the cold and it could not take away the pain. Surveying the scene, he could just make out the faces of those around him. He did not know the Indian and the German sitting closest to him, but he would get to know them and many other of his captors in the coming days. The party of British Tories and Mohawk Indians and their thirty-one captives had waded across the Kayaderosseras Creek and stopped to regroup on the orders of their commander, Captain John Munro. He had concluded that they were safe, at least for a while, from the militia that was sure to be on their trail. Looking south, all could see and smell the smoke from the burned cabins and barns. The Tories had done their work well. It was likely that not a person remained along the Middleline, the path cut out of the forest to divide the new lots of the Kayaderosseras Patent. The thirty-one captives had left behind wives and children and several men lucky enough to escape the sudden calamity that had burst in upon them in the dead of night. They almost surely had fled to the safety of the stockade, or were cowering in the woods. The lives of all had been changed forever.

Looking around, Gordon knew every one of the twenty-nine other men and one woman sitting quietly, uncomprehending. The shock of their capture, the uncertainty of the fate of their loved ones, the realization that all their meager worldly possessions were gone, pillaged or burned, had not yet hit home. Six of those faces belonged to his own household. Jack Galbraith and John Parlow labored for him on his farm and mills along the Mourning Kill. Jacob, Ann and Nero also served, but as slaves. Gordon had four slaves, but he was unsure what had happened to Liz. She was his wife's servant and he hoped she had escaped with them to safety. The sixth face was his first-born son, James Gordon, Jr.

Eighteen of the others he knew in a different way, the special relationships that bond men together in a time of war. They all served in the 12th Albany County Militia. Together they had been called out on numerous alarms over the last five years. They often chased after neighbors whose allegiance to the British Crown was stronger than the pleas and threats from their former friends to pledge allegiance to a new flag. They had fought together in October, 1777, in the second Battle of Saratoga, and many had stayed on to witness the surrender of General John Burgoyne - a triumph for the new nation. As the Lt.Col. of the regiment, Gordon was their leader and protector. But he knew he did not protect them from the devastation visited upon them and their families last night and that he could not protect them now.

As they resumed their march northward, Gordon prayed that his wife Mary and their four-year old daughter, Melinda, would do as he had instructed them – go to the stockade and tell the local militia not to follow and not to seek retribution for the raid. Hopefully one of the officers, Mary's brother John Ball, would ensure that that advice was followed. Captain Munro had made it clear that any attempt to rescue the captives could result in their death, instantly cut down by the raiders, Tories and Indians. The line of march made such a threat easy to carry out. Each captive was preceded and followed by one of the attackers - Gordon himself was being led by a Tory soldier and followed by an Indian, whom he imagined would use any excuse to do him in.

Walking on now, ahead of that Tory soldier, Gordon could make out the bloody hunched back of Captain Tyrannus Collins, blood stains covering his nightshirt. While Gordon himself had been so completely surprised by the raid that he had been taken without incident, Collins had resisted and it had cost him. Pressing his back against the door, trying to keep out the invaders he had taken a blow from an Indian's tomahawk crashing through the thin cabin door. Gordon and Collins, serving together in the Militia, neighbors and friends, had become the first men captured. The Tory raiders had continued up the Middleline, plundering, burning and herding their prisoners and their cattle, until they had come to the end of the settlement and crossed the Kayaderosseras at dawn.

As they trudged along, Gordon glanced eastward toward the woods. Undetected by those who passed by, but known to him, resting against a tree were two millstones. As a businessman as well as a soldier, he had already erected several mills in the vicinity. This was to be his next venture, here along the banks of the Kayaderosseras. He knew then that he would be back to continue the work he had started. Somehow he would survive and the men with him would survive too.

CHAPTER 1
Anne, by the Grace of God

Ninety years before Gordon sat shivering alongside the Kayaderosseras there had been a larger, more deadly raid twenty miles to the south at the Town of Schenectady. Indians were involved in that attack as well. Eighty members of the Mohawk tribe of the Iroquois Confederacy were joined by sixteen Algonquins. The Europeans with them however were not English, but one hundred-fourteen French soldiers. They had traveled down from Canada following a water route as much as possible, passing a few miles east of the future Middleline Road, then a dark forest. The Mohawks knew this land well – it was their summer hunting ground. From Canada they had moved swiftly over the large frozen expanse of Lake Champlain and Lac Saint Sacrement (Lake George), south along the North (Hudson) River and then up Fish Creek to Saratoga Lake. Following the shoreline, they entered the narrow Kayaderosseras Creek moving upstream before heading south over a two-mile portage to Long Lake, across the burnt hills to Alplaus Kill to its mouth on the Mohawk River. From there it was a short, easy walk to the stockaded walls of Corlaer (Schenectady).[1] They struck in the dark of a cold February night, and the results were devastating. The event was reported by Jacob Leisler, the insurgent governor of New York, in various dispatches to other provincial leaders.

> To our great griefe I must acquaint you of the sad and deplorable massacre which happened at Skenectady near Albany by the French and their Indians the 19th day of

February last betwixt Saturday and Sunday at eleven of
the clock in the night 200 men fell upon them and most
barbarously murdered sixty two men women and children and burned the place left but 5 or 6 houses unburned
and carried away captive 27.[2]

Forever after known as the Schenectady Massacre of 1690, this was the
opening attack of King William's War, the initial conflict in a seventy-year
struggle between the French and English for control of North America.
The war in America was just a small side show of a much larger war in
Europe that had been precipitated by the Glorious Revolution of 1688.
Protestant leaders in England invited William of Orange to cross the
channel and depose King James II, their Catholic-leaning monarch. Faced
with defeat by the invaders, James abdicated and fled to refuge in France,
precipitating the conflict known as the Nine-Years-War in which France,
led by Louis XIV, faced off against a Grand Alliance of European powers,
including England, Spain, and The Holy Roman Empire.

In Canada, French strategy against the English was orchestrated by
Louis Frontenac, Governor of New France. He surmised that controlling
the important corridor between Montreal and New York City that was to
become known as the Great Warpath, was the key to success against the
English. Without the resources to launch a major invasion, he devised a
plan to launch raids against English settlements on the frontier. His goal
in doing so was to keep them on the defensive, employing their resources
to protect their settlements, rather than launching an invasion against
lightly defended French Canada. This same strategy was to be employed
ninety years later by the British during the latter years of the American
Revolution.[3]

That Leisler was the New York governor who communicated the
results of the Schenectady raid was a direct consequence of this Glorious
Revolution. He was the short-term beneficiary of the ripple effect of
William and Mary's ascendency to the British Crown. Colonists in Boston
had seized this opportunity to depose Edmund Andros, the unpopular
governor of the Dominion of New England. The Dominion had been
an ill-fated attempt by James II to consolidate New York and the New
England colonies into one entity. The high-handed tactics of Andros

offended the sensibilities of the colonists in New England, long protective of their local autonomy. When his King and benefactor was deposed, Andros was arrested and shipped back to England.

The upheaval spread to New York City where Leisler, a German-American merchant and militia captain, wrestled control from the old regime. He exposed a split among the people of the Royal Colony of New York that had existed before, and would continue long after, his execution for treason in 1691. Leisler's Rebellion was more than just a political or religious revolt. It was an economic upheaval as well. He represented the middling planters, traders and merchants. They had long chafed under the dominance of the well-entrenched elites who held a monopoly of political and economic power in New York.[4] These elites were a powerful alliance of Dutch and English interests and they would not be denied. With the support of the new monarch, Leisler's short-lived rebellion was quashed. The men of property and wealth had beaten back this early attempt by the middling class to redress the balance of power in the colony. They would parlay their connections with the representatives of the British Crown to further enrich themselves by seeking the most precious and potentially lucrative commodity of all in colonial America—land grants.

Ten years later, in 1701, Edward Hyde, titled Lord Cornbury, arrived to assume the joint governorship of New York and New Jersey. This appointment was bestowed on him by King William for Hyde's early allegiance to him during the Glorious Revolution of 1688. He had brought his regiment into William's camp at the start of William's invasion of England. This action may have turned the tide in the struggle against King James.[5] For Cornbury it may have been personal. His cousin Mary, the wife of William, became Queen. Cornbury began his term as a well-respected representative of the English aristocracy, but soon came under criticism for his lavish lifestyle and questionable financial practices. These issues, as well as the accusation that he dressed as a woman to impersonate his cousin Queen Anne, have recently been questioned. Stories of his malfeasance in office were cited by several historians starting as early as 1757 in William Smith's *History of the Province of New York*.[6]

By 1708 Cornbury was constantly under attack by Lewis Morris, his political opponent in the New Jersey Assembly. The Assembly's refusal to pay his salary caused the governor to borrow funds to support his expenses. He was subsequently arrested for debts, removed from office and sent back to England.[7] It is still uncertain if Cornbury illustrated "the worst form of the English aristocracy's arrogance, joined to intellectual imbecility" as 19th century historian George Bancroft had claimed, or if he was just a victim of his political enemies.[8] Maybe not a moral pillar of the community, but certainly a person that could be useful to well-connected New Yorkers.

In 1708, during what proved to be the last year of his governorship, Lord Cornbury issued a land patent to thirteen influential men. It had

taken many petitions and much lobbying, but thought by them to be well worth the effort, to secure several hundred thousand acres of virgin lands called Kayaderosseras. However, not even the rich and powerful can control the future. None of them would live to see the partition and settlement of this land, but for most of them it was enrichment they were seeking, not developing and presiding over a vast landed estate. It was the prospect of selling these lands for a profit that motivated them.

Edward Hyde, Lord Cornbury 1661-1713

It is beyond the scope of this story to present the intricacies and machinations involved in the land grants awarded in the early colonial period in New York. But most of these transactions involved three different constituencies - the natives, the patricians and the politicians - who had different motives and different understandings of the process.

As a result of differences in culture and different concepts of land ownership, Native Americans were often unaware of the implications of their agreement to sell their land. Their approach to land ownership was based on what is referred to as Usufruct Rights. They believed the land was owned in common by the tribe, but may be used by individuals or families. If the land was not occupied or used, they lost their rights to it.[9] Absentee ownership was not a concept understood by the Indians.

As a consequence, their increased dependence on trade goods provided by the Europeans often resulted in their agreement to permit usage of vast lands in exchange for a few trinkets. The legendary "selling" of Manhattan for the equivalent of $24 is often cited as an example of this unequal exchange.

The second set of players was the influential and powerful patricians. They were land owners and merchants who had initially prospered for forty years under the unbridled capitalism of the Dutch of the New Amsterdam colony. Long after the British took over in 1664, Dutch entrepreneurs continued to play a major role in the economic and political life of New York. Over the years they had been joined by Englishmen whose wealth and influence often could be traced to relationships with the monarchy and with politicians back in England. As the early records indicate, these men used these relationships to exert influence on the third group of players: the colonial officials who represented the British Crown. While conflict often erupted between these two groups in the constant battle for control and power, they often agreed on the common objective: to take advantage of the opportunities available in the new world to enrich themselves and provide financial security for their descendants. The story of the Kayaderosseras Patent is a story of these two groups working in concert to achieve these objectives, often at the expense of the Native Americans. But to be successful, they had to follow the rules.

While these rules of the game could be modified to ensure a successful outcome for the elite, there were rules, established soon after the British takeover of the colony from the Dutch in 1664. The first rule was that the land in fact belonged to the natives. You could not just take it, at least not without the approval of the Governor. The Duke of York was given control over the colony by Charles II, and under the Duke of York's Laws this was made clear early on.

> No purchase of lands from the Indians after the first day of March 1664 shall be esteemed a good title without out leave first had been obtained from the Governor, and after leave so obtained, the purchasers shall bring the Sachem (tribal leader) and right owner of such lands before the Governor to acknowledge satisfaction and

payment for the said lands whereupon they shall obtain
a grant from the Governor.[10]

This procedure was followed for the first substantial purchase made
north of Albany in 1683, twenty-five years prior to the Kayaderosseras
Patent. In that year the Mohawks sold land along both sides of the
Hudson River, extending twenty-two miles north to the present village
of Schuylerville and six miles into the woods on either side of the river.
Included in the purchase price were two half casks of beer and two
small casks of wine. Following the law, the patent was then awarded
by Governor Thomas Donegan in 1684. This acquisition was called the
Saratoga Patent, and established an English presence along that vital
waterway, the first major land grant in what was later to be Saratoga
County.[11]

Two of the proprietors of that patent were from the most influential
families in Albany. Pieter Schuyler was the eldest son of Dutch emigrant
Phillip Schuyler, and was soon to become the first mayor of Albany under
the Donegan Charter authored by Robert Livingston, the Scottish son of
a Calvinist minister. Livingston was a master of business and trade, and
became one of the wealthiest men in Albany. It did not hurt Livingston's
standing at all when he married Alida Schuyler, Pieter's sister. She was the
widow of Nicholas Van Rensselaer, the proprietor of Rensselaerswyck,
the largest patroonship in New York.[12] This pattern of wealth, political
influence and family ties was to be repeated again in the history of the
Kayaderosseras Patent, a much larger transaction, with implications that
would affect its partition and settlement.

Appointed by King William in 1700 to be the Attorney General for the
Colony of New York, Sampson Shelton Broughton was certainly an influential member of the Governors' Council. He petitioned Lord Cornbury
in April 1703 to be allowed to purchase "on behalf of himself and company a tract of vacant land in the county of Albany known by the Indian
name of Kayaderosseras, adjoining to the north bounds of Schenectady."[13]
The petition was granted, for one year, but the purchase was apparently
not so easily accomplished, and Sampson came back in November 1704,
requesting a year's extension to conclude the acquisition. It seems this
request was to provide the cover needed to legitimize his purchase after

the original petition had expired – four days later he was back again, this time to ask for a patent for the same tract of land.[14] Indeed, the purchase had been made a month earlier from three Mohawk sachems, known as Joseph, Cornelius and Hendrick for sixty pounds.[15]

Only Hendrick is known to us. He was one of four Mohawk Indians who accompanied Pieter Schuyler to England in 1710 in an attempt to encourage the Iroquois to align with the British against the French during Queen Ann's War. When he was introduced to Queen Anne, Hendrick was not aware that the huge Kayaderosseras patent issued in her name two years earlier had been based on his approval of the sale of what he understood to be a small parcel of land.[16] This seems to be confirmed by the wording of the deed which conveyed the land to Broughton.

> All that certain tract or parcel of Wood Land situate ly-
> ing and being in the County of Albany called or known
> by the name of Kayaderosseras adjoining to the North
> Bounds of the Schoneghtade (Schenectady) Patent to-
> gether with a vacancy that lies between the ael Place
> (Alplause Creek) down along the river about one mile
> more or less on the east side thereof to the West Bounds
> of the Saratoga Patent on the north side thereof to the
> Albany (Hudson) River.[17]

While the exact location of this land may be difficult to discern from this deed, it seems consistent with later Indian claims that the parcel sold was for "three small farms." The scale of the boundaries is telling. In 1704 the only distance mentioned was "down along the river one mile, more or less." Four years later when the Patent was issued the distances multiplied to five miles by fourteen miles by eight miles by twenty miles! This discrepancy, along with who among the Mohawks actually agreed to the sale, would come back to haunt the heirs of the purchasers over fifty years later.

It is unlikely that these concerns caused Lord Cornbury to delay acting on Sampson's request for the patent. The four-year delay was more about politics than propriety. During this time Broughton died and his widow and then his son Sampson continued to ask the Governor to

consummate the grant. Cornbury seemed to ignore these requests probably because of his own disputes with Broughton, Jr. The Governor had refused to recognize the son's appointment to succeed his father as Attorney
General, appointing May Bickley instead. It may have been to overcome
this roadblock that another prospective proprietor stepped into the process. Nanning Harmense, a wealthy Albany fur trader, was very active in
seeking land grants in the northern areas of the Colony. He had already
been involved in at least three other transactions in Albany County,
including one called Shanondehaway, better known as the Clifton Park
patent, in 1707.

So it was that on September 27, 1708, Nanning Harmanse filed a petition which reads in part:

> That the said Naning Hermanse out of good will to-
> wards Sampson Shelton Broughton, Esq then Attorney
> Gen of this Province after a license first obtained from
> your Excellency in council in said Broughtons name to
> purchase vacant and unappropriated land in the County
> of Albany did really purchase a certain track of land
> called by the Indians Kayaderossos, situate lying and be-
> ing on Schenectady and Hudsons river above Albany
> the Indian Deed whereof duely made and executed as
> the Law directs and paid by him and Peter Fauconnier
> alone, he did put in the hands of the said late Sampson
> Sheldon Broughton to solicit and obtain a patent for the
> same although the said Broughton never did pay one
> farthing towards the same, that the said Naning and
> his Associates were promised by said Sampson Shelton
> Broughton and since by his son Mr Sampson Broughton
> that a patent should be obtained by them yet none having
> been granted, Your petitioner after so long a stay hoping
> that your Excellency will be favorably pleased to grant
> the same now.[18]

Apparently Nanning had connections, or was willing to pay more
to the Governor for the patent than Broughton, for little more than

a month later his petition was granted in the name of Queen Anne. The long-sought-after grant of land was now in the hands of thirteen well-established patricians of the Colony whose names would be associated with the Kayaderosseras Patent long after their deaths. The patent was drawn up by Attorney General Bickley, one of the thirteen purchasers, and issued on November 2, 1708. The twelve men and one woman listed at the beginning of the document were an who's-who of New York's influential citizens.

> ANN, by the Grace of God, of Great Britain, France and Ireland Queen Defender of the faith, To all to whom these presents may come or in any wise concern sends greeting. Whereas our loving subjects Nanning Harmanse, Johannes Beekman, Rip Van Dam, Ann Bridges, May Bickley, Peter Fauconnier, Adrian Hooglandt, Johannes Fisher, John Tudor, Joris Hooglandt, John Stevens, John Tatham and Sampson Broughton by their petition presented to our right trusty and well beloved cousin Edward Viscount Cornbury Capt General and Governor in chief of our province of New York in council have prayed our grant and confirmation for all that tract of land scituate lying and being in the County of Albany called Kayadorosseras...to have and to hold one thirteenth part of the tract of land and premises aforesaid... [and] shall within the space of seven years after the date hereof settle, clear and make improvement of or upon some part of the parcel thereof.[19]

The tract laid out in the Patent was vast. It contained upwards of 800,000 acres, and encompassed the major part of what is today Saratoga County as well as parcels in Warren and Fulton Counties. These thirteen people appeared to have won an 18th century version of the lottery, but who were they?

Probably one of the most prominent among them was Rip Van Dam. Although born into a middle-class Dutch merchant family in Albany in 1660, he became a prosperous merchant in New York City in the decade before the arrival of Lord Cornbury. He was involved in shipbuilding and the transatlantic trade of both wine and Africans.[20] In 1702 he was appointed a member of the Governor's Council, a position he held for the next 30 years.

By 1703 he was among the wealthiest of New Yorkers, living in a mansion on Sloat Lane adjacent to Wall Street, with a large family of nine along with six slaves.[21] As an Anti-Leislerian who supported the property

Rip Van Dam 1660-1749

rights of the aristocratic class, he proceeded to involve himself in the politics of the Colony parlaying economic influence into political power. One of the primary methods that politicians used to extend their wealth was to take an active role in seeking land grants and Van Dam availed himself of that opportunity as well. As a member of the Council he was often involved in decisions involving these grants, recommending against some, and advocating for others. We can only surmise that self-interest played a role in his recommendations.[22] Van Dam capped his career with a short term as Acting Governor of New York in 1731, when the previous governor, John Montgomery, died in office.

A second proprietor of high rank and influence was surprisingly neither Dutch nor English, but a French Huguenot. Peter Fauconnier arrived in England in 1685, found success as a London merchant and supplier to the government, and became the private secretary to Lord Cornbury, traveling with him to New York in 1702.[23] He was appointed as the Receiver-General for New York and New Jersey, and oversaw the collection of duties on imports to the colony. As was common practice in colonial New York, he used this position to great personal advantage. Between 1702 and 1708 he acquired land in at least twelve major patents issued during Cornbury's tenure as Governor. In addition to the Kayaderosseras, Fauconnier was a partner in the adjacent Clifton Park Patent, and the Nine Partners and Pauling Patents in Dutchess County. This last grant, situated on the east side of the Hudson River covered

4000 acres. Fauconnier's one-fifth share became known as the Hyde Park Patent in honor of his benefactor Edward Hyde, Lord Cornbury. This relatively small acquisition became famous 200 years later as the home of both the Vanderbilts and the Roosevelts.[24]

As a protégé of Lord Cornbury, Fauconnier was a victim of political attacks from the same people who had made life so difficult for the Governor. In 1708 he was removed from his position as Receiver General when he refused the request of the Assembly for a full accounting of his activities in that lucrative post.[25] Lamenting his loss of position, he complained in a letter to Cornbury that his downfall was the result of "inveterate hatred against him, and tend to the entire ruine of your petitioners credit and reputation".[26] It was too late for the Governor to come to the assistance of his lieutenant since he himself was in the final days of his own term. Both men were victims of their own excesses, and their enemy's ability to capitalize on them.

Among the other proprietors were the current Attorney General, May Bickley as well as the wife of the former Attorney General, Ann Bridges. The original petitioner Sampson Broughton, who had lost out in his quest for the Attorney General position to Bickley after the death of his father, was also listed in the Patent. It seems that politics could be set aside in the interest of financial gain. It is interesting that Broughton was brought in on the land deal, despite his many failed attempts to secure the patent on behalf of his parents and himself. He was the last proprietor listed, maybe as an afterthought. There is speculation that his inclusion was to assuage his ire at losing the Attorney General post.

Several merchants were among the thirteen, among them Adrian and Joris Hooghlandt of New York City. The Hooghlandt family had arrived in New Netherlands as early as 1638 when their grandfather Cornelius operated a ferry service between Brooklyn and New Amsterdam. Known as a middling merchant, Adrian was successful enough to engage in transatlantic trade by 1701, and in 1703 was credited with four slaves. His brother Joris was in a similar financial position, with two slaves.[27] The slaves proved to be Adrian's undoing. One of his slaves, named Robin, rose up and killed him with a knife thrust to the back during the New York City slave revolt of 1712.[28] The Hooghlandts may not have been of the stature of a Van Dam and Fauconnier, but all three families owned slaves who participated in this revolt and ended up paying for it with their lives. Four slaves of these three patentees were convicted and hanged for their offense, while a fifth received a reprieve.[29] Although the Hooghlandt name disappears from the story of the Kayaderosseras Patent, this family held on to their shares longer than most of the other original patentees. Joris died in the same year as Adrian, and in 1723 his children sold their share of the patent to Adrian's widow.[30] Adrian and his wife had three daughters whose own children would claim the families' legacy sixty years later when this grant was finally surveyed and partitioned. Evert Bancker, Helena Rutgers and Adrian Renandet together received two of the thirteen patent shares in 1770, the largest single distribution that can be traced back to an original proprietor.[31]

While the Hooghlandts kept their shares within the family, several others may have had a different motivation for their participation among the thirteen original proprietors. To understand their motivation we have to take a look at colonial New York politics at the turn of the 18th century and introduce other players into the story of the Kayaderosseras Patent.

Tracing the real benefactors of land grants in colonial America is always a challenge, but even more so in New York where the legacy of the mercantile Dutch establishment carried over into the years of English rule. Unencumbered by the Puritan religious constraints of their neighbors to the east in New England, or the Quakers to their west in Pennsylvania, they lived in a culture more focused on financial gain than their neighboring colonies. However, all colonial officials commonly took advantage of their position to become wealthy, often returning to England enriched by their years of service in the New World.

One way these officials were able to line their pockets was the result of the process of land acquisition. A person or group so inclined had to seek warrants from the governor to purchase land from the natives, another to survey it, then another to actually receive the patent. At each step the prospective proprietors remitted fees to the governor or other colonial leaders. Even more important, these officials often ended up with large tracts of land in these patents, although they were not named in the patent itself. To overcome the restrictions in place to limit grants to any individual to 2,000 acres, influential members of the government often sought out proxies named in the patent, who surreptitiously sold or gave their shares to the officials after the patents were issued.[32]

An example may help explain how this process worked. In 1730 Captain Walter Butler, the commanding officer at Fort Hunter near the Indian village of Tiononderoge on the Mohawk River petitioned the Governor for the right to purchase 12,000 acres. He and five associates were named, as required by the law. The next year he upped the ante. Fifteen petitioners sought 30,000 acres. These requests were not granted, but in 1733 a new Governor, William Cosby proved more amenable. By this time, the consortium had grown to 43 men, seeking 86,000 acres, and they guaranteed Cosby a one-third share of the grant if he would approve the petition. He did. The petitioners turned their attention to a conference with the Mohawks and were able to purchase 150,000 acres for £368. This large grant came to be known as Butler's Purchase. Whether or not the Indian signatories to the deed were aware of the extent of this transaction, they had forfeited most of their land in the Mohawk Valley. Much of this land was transferred from the original petitioners to others. They had fulfilled their role as straw men for the real purchasers. For example, four years later 36,000 acres was sold to the newly named Governor George Clark for £50.[33]

Clarke stands out as one of the most successful officials in playing this game. He arrived in the Colony in 1703 as an auditor representing the Crown's Treasurer and soon became engaged in the conflict with Lord Cornbury over his expense accounts, as related above.[34] This dispute may have insured that Clarke was not one of the thirteen proprietors, but he subsequently became the largest landowner of the Kayaderosseras Patent. Within two years he held title to almost 31,000 acres by acquiring partial rights of several original proprietors.[35] For Clarke this was one of his first forays in the land business, but he obviously became good at it. Over a long career that included a term as acting Governor of New York from 1736-1747 he owned over 120,000 acres in twenty-seven separate patents, including Butler's Purchase.[36] Twenty-two of these tracts amounting to over 100,000 acres, were acquired through these "trustees."[37]

As was the case with many of these grants, they languished without sufficient settlers to make them profitable. However, one land acquisition that was an exception to this rule was the Cherry Valley Patent.

Clarke was able to establish a settlement there by making a deal with Reverend Samuel Dunlap. He would give him 400 acres if within twenty years Dunlap could secure settlers for 2,000 acres of Clarke's land, either by sale or lease. This model was applied twenty-five years later in the Kayaderosseras Patent, when another minister acting as an agent for the landowners was granted free land and the legacy of a town named after him, Ball's Town.

Not all the land transactions may have been as blatant as Butler's Purchase, but many were just as convoluted. Many of the original pro-prietors of the Kayaderosseras Patent divested their interests over the years, some through outright sales or sham transfers and others through bequests or gifts to family members of succeeding generations.

John Tudor's share may have been the first to be passed on. He died in November 1708, just as the Patent was being issued. Arriving in New York in 1674, after being ordered out of Boston upon conviction for fornication with his future wife, he became a lawyer and eventually the Recorder for the City of New York. Leaving no will, his estate transferred to his wife. She later sold her rights to Richard Bradley, Attorney-General of the Colony for almost thirty years.[38] Bradley served as the Attorney General during both the 1735 Peter Zenger trial, known for its landmark decision on freedom of the press, and the 1741 Negro Plot trial, which resulted in the execution of thirty slaves.[39] When he died in 1751 he left "1/13 part of the Patent of Kayaderosseras, said to contain upwards of 20,000 acres," to his creditors in England.[40] In 1768 John Tudor's grandson, also named John, sold the same share to William Smith, Jr, Chief Justice of New York, and William Kelly, a New York City merchant. They were identified as the owners of one-half share each when the Patent was divided a few years later. How this land was transferred from Bradley's creditors in England to John Tudor's grandson remains a mystery.[41]

John Tatham was the second proprietor to pass from the scene when he died in 1713. He was the son of one of founders of Burlington, New Jersey, known as the "missing Governor of East Jersey", who served in 1690. John Sr. was a known Catholic, lawyer and merchant and was involved in many land deals in New Jersey in the 1690's. His home was described as that "great and stately palace of John Tatham, Esq" in Burlington.[42] He died in 1700, leaving his estate to his wife Elizabeth.

It included the mansion house valued at £1000 and seven slaves worth £202.[43] His son and heir continued to be involved in land transactions in New Jersey, selling 650 acres in 1711.[44] Upon the son's death, his wife Mary became his "sole heiress and executrix of his real and personal estate in NY, NJ and Penn."[45]

John's share of the patent is traceable through a court case 100 years later. In 1715 his wife sold his share to Elias Boudinot, who was a successful French Huguenot merchant. He in turn conveyed it to George Clarke two years later. In 1768, Clarke's son, George Jr, sold his share to Dirck Lefferts and Peter Remsen, just as these men became involved in the settlement of the Kayaderosseras.[46] These lands were later divided among them in a survey conducted in 1774.[47] Lefferts, who became one of the Trustees responsible for administering the sale of the Patent, acquired additional land from other sources as we shall see later.

Another lawyer, proprietor John Stevens migrated to New York from London in 1699. He was indentured as an apprentice to Barne Cozens. He served out his seven-year apprenticeship, during Cozens tenure as Court Register. Toward the end of his indenture he had the good fortune to marry Ann, the eldest daughter of John Campbell, one of the original proprietors of New Jersey.[48] It may have been this connection that secured him a share of the Patent, alongside several more prominent men of the Colony. In 1714 he moved to Perth Amboy and became the Port Collector in the hometown of his father-in-law. This was the same year he sold his stake in the Kayaderosseras to Patrick MacNight.[49] MacKnight, a Scots-Irish merchant in New York City, was a "dissenting Protestant" who was instrumental in founding the First Presbyterian Church in New York City in 1718.[50] He married Cornela Clopper whose cousin Cornelius also would become a trustee of the patent, along with Lefferts.[51]

The only woman among the original proprietors, Ann Bridges also quickly disposed of her stake in the Patent. That transaction led to a landmark legal case a century later, an example of the convoluted claims and counter-claims that resulted from the long time delay from original ownership to settlement. After the death of her husband, Ann remarried to Joshua Hunloke and together they sold their rights in the patent to Peter Fauconnier in 1711. One hundred years later, John Gilchrist was living on 119 acres of that land with deeds to prove ownership. By that time the land had finally been surveyed as we will see, and was designated Lot 8 of the XIII Allotment, today located in the town of Charlton. The direct descendants of Bridges claimed the right to the land, arguing the original sale was void since a woman's property could not be sold without her consent. In 1818 the State Supreme Court sided with Gilchrist who was deemed the rightful owner based on his deeds. That paved the way for disposition of many other such cases in the early 19th century.[52] An interesting side note to this case was that Gilchrist was defended by Martin Van Buren. The future president was chastised for his "enormous" fees in this case.[53]

The heirs of two other proprietors were to maintain ownership of the patent within their families for the next sixty-five years. The final disposition is an interesting study in the allocation of the land. Johannes Beekman, trained as a blacksmith, climbed the ladder of success as a merchant and businessman in Albany. He died in 1732 leaving his 1/13 share of the Kayaderosseras to his five sons. His son Johannes in turn passed the property on to his sons John and Jacob in 1756. It was this third John who much later in 1775 became involved in the division of the lands which had been assigned to the heir of Johannes Fisher.

Fisher was almost certainly the brother of Nanning Harmanse, the successful petitioner for the patent, whose proper surname was Visscher. Both were sons of Harmen Visscher who migrated from the Netherlands in the 1650's, married Hester Dircks in New York City, where their first son was born in 1652. Moving up the Hudson River to Albany, Harmen became a successful fur trader and merchant. This legacy he passed on to his five sons, including Johannes and Nanning.[54] So the two brothers along with Johannes Beekman, three successful businessmen, represented the Albany contingent among the thirteen proprietors. Some 65 years later their heirs agreed to equally divide the Visscher grant. They split each Visscher parcel into A sections, drawn to the House of Johannes "Fisher", and B sections in the name of John Beekman.[55]

But we get ahead of ourselves. Why was it that these surveys and the partition were not conducted until the 1770's? Despite all the effort put forth to secure this tract of land from the Indians, the multiple petitions to Lord Cornbury to issue the patent, the jockeying for position among the Proprietors, the bequests, sales and the behind the scenes deals to secure real ownership of the land, no progress was made to improve the land once the Patent was granted. For the next sixty years, no surveys were conducted, no attempt was made to partition the lands, few if any settlers moved onto the land, vast as it was. While later patents were soon parceled out into farms and settlements, the huge expanse of the Kayaderosseras, extending from just north of Albany and Schenectady to the foothills of the Adirondacks, remained the hunting ground of the Mohawks, the easternmost tribe of the Iroquois League. It was as if the Patent had never been granted. And the Mohawks, who viewed this vacant land as belonging to those who used it, liked it that way just fine.

CHAPTER 2
This Extravagant Grant

I n 1710, two years after the Patent was issued, Cadwallader Colden, a twenty-one-year-old Scotsman, arrived in Philadelphia. He was an ambitious young man trained in medicine at the University of Edinburg. Colden quickly rose in society and was invited to move to New York by Governor Robert Hunter, and appointed the colonies first Surveyor General in 1720. This proved to be the beginning of a fifty-year career in New York government, even though his passion was science, not politics. An associate of Benjamin Franklin and other prominent colonial men, he is one of the many colonial men of knowledge and intellect whose names are little known to us today.

In 1732 at the behest of the then-Governor of New York, William Cosby, Colden prepared a paper on the state of land patents in New York. Lamenting both the failure to settle lands long since deeded to men of influence and power in the colony, and even more importantly, the inability of His Majesty's government to collect quitrents on these lands, Colden had a ready explanation. The patents granted in the land-grab frenzy of the previous thirty years were just too big. Their size made it impossible for the proprietors to improve the land. The cost was prohibitive. One way of overcoming this problem would be to bring in tenant farmers as the old Dutch Patroons had done in the previous century. But the time when settlers would accept such an arrangement was passing quickly. New arrivals, whether from Great Britain or from just across the border in New England, were bent on owning their own land. For these reasons, much of New York remained unsettled, long after immigrants flooded into Pennsylvania and other neighboring colonies. Colden's observations applied generally to land grants throughout the colony, but easily serve as one explanation for the lack of settlement within the Kayaderosseras Patent.[1]

Kayaderosseras Patent 1708

However, other factors were at play in the failure to settle this vast land north of Albany. While the English and French had seemingly enjoyed a thirty-year truce in their struggle over supremacy in North America, the conflict was not over and the Kayaderosseras lands were in dispute throughout this period. In 1745, war broke out again. King George's War was the North American extension of the War of Austrian Succession.

During this conflict a force of 500 French and Canadian Indians attacked and destroyed the village of Saratoga, (now Schuylerville) killed more than thirty people, and carried over 100 into captivity, more than half of which were slaves. Clearly settlements north of Albany were not safe, and most of the families along the Hudson River north of Albany abandoned their farms for several years after this massacre. [2]

Finally, the Mohawks continued to use this land with its streams, lakes and habitat for an abundant variety of wildlife, as their favored hunting ground. While no permanent villages were located in the Patent, temporary hunting and fishing camps were established each year along its waterways. From these locations they were able to observe the encroachment of white settlers on their lands, land that tribal leaders con-

King Hendrick 1691-1755

tinued to believe was theirs. As the years went by, the fact that their forefathers may or may not have conveyed this tract to the English back in 1704 became lost on the Mohawks. They had seen their lands in the Mohawk Valley sold out from under them. The Kayaderosseras was in many ways their last refuge.

In 1753, Theyanoguin, a leader among the Mohawks, referred to as Chief Hendrick by the colonial officials, traveled to New York with a group of sixteen other members of his tribe to meet with Governor George Clinton

and pass on a message. He declared that the Covenant Chain, which had kept the Iroquois at peace with the Colony since 1677, was in danger of being broken.[3] The continuing failure of the colonial leaders to address Indians' concerns over land grants, chief among them the Kayaderosseras Patent, was threatening this long-term relationship. In fact, Governor Clinton may have orchestrated this event to put pressure on the colonial Assembly to address the Indian concerns that they had continually ignored.[4] This concern quickly traveled back across the Atlantic to the Lords of Trade, the British agency responsible for managing the affairs of the American colonies. They were once again becoming concerned about increasingly belligerent actions by the French in New York and farther west in the Ohio Country. Another war was on the horizon that would prove to be the ultimate conflict between the French and English in North America. The response of the Lords in England and the Governor in New York was to convene a conference with the Iroquois, along with officials from several other colonies, in an attempt to settle these disputes.

They were determined to convince the Iroquois to join them in the coming conflict, or at a minimum to maintain the neutrality policy of the
Six Nations. This had been the hallmark of British-Iroquois relations for
over fifty years.[5]

This treaty conference, referred to as the Albany Congress, met in
June 1754. This conference is mostly remembered for the Albany Plan
of Union, Benjamin Franklin's failed attempt to create a confederation
among eleven of the Colonies. However, Indian grievances over unscrupulous land deals were also an important part of the agenda. Soon after
the conference began, members of the Lower Castle of the Mohawks near
Fort Hunter brought up their main issue related to the Kayaderosseras
stating that "upon enquiry of our old men, we cannot find that it was ever
sold."[6] Upon investigation, newly appointed Lt. Governor James Delancey
came to agree with their claim. Soon after the conference ended he again
raised the issue with the Lords of Trade. He forwarded a copy of the original deed to them and compared it to the 1708 patent, "the bounds of which
seem to me to be much larger than those in the Indian Deed." He also
raised another issue that would confound the partitioning, settlement and
future sales of this land for generations.

> This tract was granted to thirteen persons as tenants in
> common, but is now by purchases and devises branched
> out in such a number, as can scarce be known or found,
> and so it is rendered extreamly difficult, if not altogether
> impracticable to divide and settle it.[7]

Delancey's solution was to scrap the patent altogether and settle the
land in townships, usurping the ownership of the patentees, their heirs
and subsequent purchasers. After mulling this over for almost two years,
the Lords of Trade dumped the problem back in the lap of the colonial government in 1756 by suggesting that the New York Assembly should pass
a law "vacating and annulling these exorbitant and fraudulent Patents."[8]
Governor Hardy, who had replaced Delancey when Delancey became
the Chief Justice, did his best to follow this policy. However, given the
fact that many of the men in the Assembly had an interest in the Patent,
there was no way they were going to vote against their own self-interests.

The politics behind the failure to take action on this issue was a result of the long-standing conflict between two factions vying for control of colonial New York from the 1740's through the 1760's. This conflict was represented by two families, the Delanceys and the Livingstons. The Delancey faction had come to power during the administration of Governor George Clinton. As Chief Justice, and with his influence in the Colonial Assembly, James Delancey was the most powerful politician in New York. His ascendency reached its zenith when he was also appointed Lt. Governor in 1747, from which position he rose to the governorship when Clinton returned to England in 1753.[9] Opposing the Delanceys was the Livingston family, led by William Livingston. He was joined by two other prominent lawyers, William Smith, Jr. and John Morin Scott. Known as the "New York Triumvirate", their long association began when they launched a partisan magazine, *The Independent Reflector,* in 1752. As Presbyterians, many of the articles written by the Triumvirate criticized the policies of the Delancey administration's support of the Anglican Church and the attempt to launch a college under its jurisdiction.[10] With the death of James Delancey in 1760, power shifted to the Livingston faction. Although it is an oversimplification, the Livingstons represented the landowners and the Whig principles of popular government, while the Delanceys supported the merchants and Tory principles of more hierarchal leadership.[11]

It appears that the Assembly's inaction during the 1760's regarding the Kayaderosseras Patent was due in part to the control of that body by the Livingston faction. It is interesting that two of the members of the Triumvirate, Smith and Scott, owned a stake in the Patent, and the third, William Livingston, continually defended his family's actions in securing the Canajoharie Patent, widely recognized as another fraudulent land grant.[12]

So no law vacating the patent was ever passed, although the Assembly felt the need to come up with some explanation for their inaction. These reasons, which included not wanting to disparage the character of the original grantor, Lord Cornbury, appeared quite a stretch to William Johnson, the Indian Commissioner to the Iroquois.[13]

Johnson, the son of Irish parents of Catholic heritage, had sailed away from that treacherous world by emigrating to New York in 1738. He was the protégé of his uncle, Admiral Peter Warren. Warren was a successful officer in the British Navy who made the most of his opportunity to become wealthy through illicit trade and his marriage into the Delancey family. He was able to acquire 14,000 acres south of the Mohawk River in the 1730's, an estate that needed managing. This was a perfect role for his nephew William even though he was only twenty-three years old at the time.[14]

Sir William Johnson 1715-1774

Johnson quickly adapted to life on the colonial frontier by positioning himself as a leading trader between the local Mohawk tribes and the merchants of Albany and New York. More than any other white man, he immersed himself in the culture of the Iroquois. He became accepted by them first as a brother and eventually as a Mohawk sachem (tribal leader) himself. His long career was not without its ups and downs. He became Indian Commissioner to the Iroquois in 1746 but resigned in 1751 after a dispute over payment for his expenses incurred during his tenure. He was reinstated in 1755 when the Six Nations demanded it as a prerequisite for their participation in the looming French and Indian War. His reinstatement was mutually beneficial. The Iroquois needed Johnson to help them restore their waning influence among tribes in the Northeast and the Ohio valley. Johnson needed them to insure his dominance of the Indian trade and peaceful settlement of the Mohawk Valley, which he oversaw from his estate at Fort Johnson.[15]

This history helps us understand Johnson's strong support of the Indian position regarding the Kayaderosseras Patent. After the failure of the Colonial Assembly to overturn the Patent, despite the efforts of several governors, Johnson would not let the issue rest. Chief Hendrick had been killed in the Battle of Lake George at the start of the French and Indian war in 1755, but at a conference at Fort Johnson in 1760, his brother Little Abraham renewed their complaint. Lamenting that "we are a poor people, having no land we can call our own," he challenged Johnson to take up their cause.

> We must beg to trouble you once more about that large Tract called Kaniadarusseras which was never honestly purchased of us, nor any consideration paid for it. You told us some time agoe that you did not doubt but it would be settled to our satisfaction, this gave us great Encouragement but hearing no farther about it, We are afraid it will be forgot, and then we must be a ruined people.[16]

Johnson promised to help them, but in his reply there is a sense that he is not convinced that he can do much, offering that, "I will make the best enquiry I can into the true state of your complaint and when I am master of it will transmit it to England." That path had been traversed before, but dutiful to his commitment, Johnson raised the issue to the Board of Trade in several letters in the coming years. In 1763 in a long letter to the Board, he laid out the specific disputes regarding the Patent: That the original sale was for a small piece of land (about enough for three farms); that the purchase money was never paid; that the ensuing patent of 800,000 acres included the most valuable part of the Mohawk hunting grounds; and that no survey or settlement had been attempted in fifty-five years.[17]

Johnson continued to do his best to state the Indian case to the Board of Trade. In another letter in 1764 he disputed the weak arguments made by the New York Assembly to justify their unwillingness to vacate the Patent. He defended the integrity of the Iroquois, stating that the legislature's claim that the Indians had a habit of denying sales agreements made by their forebears was without foundation. Their claim that it was impossible to determine the true owners of their land was also a "gross error", stating that "each nation is perfectly well acquainted with their exact original bounds." Johnson concluded his entreaty persuaded that the Lords of Trade would take the "necessary steps" to right this wrong.[18]

Apparently nothing ever came of his inquiries and over the years Johnson became more than a little frustrated with the lack of redress for the claims of the Mohawks. Often finding himself taking the side of the Indians against the landed interests of the colony, he took it personally that he been unable to resolve their complaints concerning the disposition of the Kayaderosseras lands. By 1766, more than ten years after the Albany Congress, and with no resolution in sight, his patience ran out. In a letter to the Earl of Shelburne, President of the Board of Trade, he clearly described his view of the values of the men who withheld justice from the Indians.

> That the majority of those who get lands, being persons of consequence in the Capitals... are totally ignorant of the Indians, make use of some of the lowest and most selfish of the Country Inhabitants, to seduce the Indians to their houses, where they are kept rioting in drunkenness till they have effected their bad purposes...Thus the affair of the extravagant Grant Kayaderosseras aforementioned, which has exasperated the whole Six Nations, remains still undecided and truth obliges me to add that tho' Proclamations are issued, and orders sent to the several Governours experience has shewn that both are hitherto ineffectual and will be so, whilst the Gentlemen of property and Merchants are interested in finding out evasions or points of Law against them.[19]

The month before Johnson's passionate letter, New York's Governor Henry Moore had once again clearly articulated the Indians' complaints, elaborating on the issues raised by Johnson. The Mohawk nation consisted of three groups, the Turtle, Bear and Wolf clans, but only two of them had signed the deed. The purchase price was a meagerly 60 pounds as agreed in the deed, but even that small sum had not been received by the Mohawk. The payment was to be in the form of in-kind goods that were to have been sent to Schenectady, but had been burned in a fire and were never replaced.[20]

Pressure was mounting to finally resolve the land issue. As the demand for settlement of this land increased after the end of hostilities with the French, so did the value of the shares of the proprietors. In 1760, 1/13 of the Patent had been sold for £500. Seven years later, Goldsbrow Banyar, the agent for George Clark Jr., indicated he had an offer of £2,100 for a similar share.[21] The current owners were clearly anxious to cash in on this suddenly lucrative asset. These men made a first attempt to propose a settlement as early as 1765, but nothing came of it.[22]

Governor Moore was equally determined to get this issue behind them, restore the relationship between the Iroquois and the colony, and open up this land to settlement. In his 1766 letter to the Earl of Shelburne he noted that one of the complications in resolving this problem was that the Patent land was now in the hands of over 130 people, making it exceedingly difficult to reach any sort of agreement. However, the combined efforts of Gov. Moore and Indian Agent Johnson were beginning to bear fruit thanks to the willingness of the proprietors to finally come to the table.

Early in 1767, William Johnson met with John Beekman, a representative of the proprietors, to once again lay out the issues that had been repeatedly raised by the Indians over the past fifteen years. At a March meeting, a group of these proprietors offered a settlement to release the western portion of their claim to its original native owners. Their proposal stated their willingness to give up their "rights" west of a line from the North Chuctenuda Creek, near present day Amsterdam, to the northwesternmost head of the Kayaderosseras Creek.[23] William Johnson gladly presented this offer to a gathering of the Mohawks, but because their leaders were absent, no response was received until the following year.[24]

The year 1768 proved to be pivotal. Sixty years after the patent was issued everything came together during a four-month period. Ironically, it was the proprietors who took the lead after ignoring the pleas of the Indians, William Johnson, and a host of colonial governors for years. In March they gave Peter Remsen, a New York City merchant, a Power of Attorney to settle all disputes concerning the Kayaderosseras. In the same letter to Johnson, Benjamin Kissam, the legal representative of the proprietors, put pressure on all involved to get this done. In expectation of a settlement they decided to publish legal notices in the newspapers preparatory to a partition, "just to save time."[25] The "all involved" included Governor Moore. In May 1768 Moore was able to report that representatives of the proprietors had given him "Carte blanche to settle this dispute with the Indians on such terms as I shall think proper."[26]

The stage was set for a settlement, but there proved to be one more hurdle to overcome. In June a Congress was held at Johnson Hall, orchestrated by Guy Johnson standing in for his uncle William, who was in Connecticut hoping to improve his failing health at the seashore.[27] Governor Moore was accompanied by several prominent men of the colony, including Philip Schuyler, a newly elected member of the Assembly and future rebel general. Representing the proprietors were Remsen and John McCrea, a lawyer who had settled in the Northumberland section of the Patent in 1763 and married into the Beekman family in 1766. He was to become a colonel in the 13th Albany County Militia during the Revolution, but may best be known as the brother of Jane McCrea who was killed by Indians during the Burgoyne campaign prior to the Battle of Saratoga in 1777.[28]

After days of restating positions long held by both sides, an agreement was concluded that the Patent, as claimed by the proprietors, should be reduced, with a major section of the western portion returned to the Mohawks. This had been the approach promoted by the patentees since at least 1765. The sticking point became the line of partition, specifically the location at which the boundary line crossed Kayaderosseras Creek. Abraham, spokesman for the Iroquois, insisted the line from the Mohawk River to the falls above Fort Edward pivot at the head of the nearest branch of the Kayaderosseras, while the proprietors held fast to their initial position that this point be at the northernmost head of the Creek. The different points meant that many thousands of acres remained under dispute. To make matters worse, no one seemed to be able to fix either position on their maps.[29]

This uncertainty provided an opening for Governor Moore to seize the initiative. Stating that the maps were defective and that these different points could not be fixed with any certainty, he proposed that a survey be conducted to determine the true locations. Both sides agreed to this plan and Christopher Yates was given the task of doing the survey, accompanied by several members of the Mohawk tribe.

While previous efforts to reach a settlement seemed to drag on year after year, not so now. By July the survey had been completed and the

Proprietors were anxious to return to the table. A committee of thirteen of them gave Remsen and Isaac Low, another New York City merchant, "full powers to strike a bargain with the Indians." This group of thirteen included three men—Dirck Lefferts, Cornelius Clopper and Benjamin Kissam, the group's lawyer—who were destined to play an important role in the settlement of the Kayaderosseras Patent in future years. They, along with Isaac Low, later became the Trustees responsible for administering the sale of the land once it was surveyed and partitioned.[30]

In early August, the conference reconvened at Johnson Hall. Remsen, referring to the recently completed survey, pointed out that the northern head of the Creek appeared less favorable to the patentees as it was not as far northwest as they had anticipated. In spite of this fact, they proposed setting the line at that point as now clarified on the map. After deliberations among the Indian attendees, Abraham agreed to the proposal.

The only matter left to decide was the purchase price. The Proprietors had a price in mind, but rather than offer it, they asked William Johnson to propose the amount. By making Johnson the final arbiter of the sale price, they hoped to avoid any further disputes that could delay the partition and settlement. Johnson, whose impartiality was accepted by both sides, came back the next day with the price—$5,000. This was more than the Proprietors expected to pay. They had come to the conference with $2,000.[31] Nonetheless they were not going to let the issue of cost get in the way of a final settlement. Isaac Low indicated their acceptance of Johnson's recommendation in a final address to the Indians.

> Brothers, I am very happy to find this old dispute so amicably settled. The Patentees will all be extremely obliged to you for your friendship to them on this occasion, and I am to inform you on their parts, that they will faithfully observe all that you have recommended, and will never act contrary thereto. Sensible of Sir William Johnson's interest and influence with you, they applied to him for them, and although the sum of money which is proposed to be given to you, be larger than we expected, we readily agree to it, and shall honestly pay you without delay.[32]

It was done. To cover the remaining $3,000 of the purchase price, the representatives of the Proprietors—Low, Remsen and McCrea—signed a note and passed it to Johnson as security. Mission accomplished. The next steps were already underway.

CHAPTER 3
Links and Chains

otices began appearing in New York City newspapers in the late summer and early fall of 1768 that outlined the next steps in dividing the unimproved land of the Kayaderosseras Patent into parcels that could be sold and settled. These steps had all been carefully prescribed in an Act passed by the Assembly in 1762. Many Assembly members had a personal stake in insuring that the current owners of these lands could finally cash in on their claims. The appointment of the Commissioners and the Surveyor, the method for dividing the land among the Proprietors, the setting aside of tracts within the Patent to defray the expenses of the partition, even the daily pay rates for the surveyors, chain bearers and clerks, were all clearly laid out in this Act.[1]

The subscribers to these advertisements, William Smith Jr., Benjamin Kissam and Peter Remsen referred to themselves as "being three of the Proprietors of the said tract of land." For Smith, ownership of one-half share in the Kayaderosseras Patent was a minor footnote on his resume. Son of a prominent lawyer and judge, he had followed in his father's footsteps, graduating from Yale in 1745, and was now Chief Justice of the Supreme Court of New York. A prominent attorney at an early age—he had initially turned down the Chief Justice appointment in 1763 at the age of thirty-five—Smith was also well known for his literary career. As previously mentioned, he was a cofounder, along with William Livingston and John Morin Scott, of The *Independent Reflector*, New York's first magazine. In 1757 he had published the first comprehensive history of New York, *The History of the Province of New York,* still used as a source for early colonial history. Long a defender of the landed interests, he often supported the proprietors in defense of their ill-defined estates.[2] In 1764 he had, along with William Kelley, jointly purchased the original share of John Tudor as noted above. Smith, being listed first in these advertisements, certainly would draw attention to the pending sale of this vast tract of land located in the wilderness north of Albany.

Benjamin Kissam, the Proprietors' lawyer, also had an interest in the patent through his marriage to Catherine Rutgers, great-granddaughter of Adrian Hooghlandt. Kissam had an established law firm in New York where he nurtured the legal skills of John Jay, one of the founding fathers and later the first Chief Justice of the United States. Kissam was to be one of the four trustees soon to be responsible for the distribution of the Patent land.

Peter Remsen, who had been authorized by the Proprietors to negotiate the final settlement with the Indians, had purchased one-half of John Tatham's share from George Clark, Jr. only six months earlier, in March 1768. He was part of an influential old Dutch family that included his cousin Henry Remsen, who became a strong patriot and member of the Continental Congress. Peter's political allegiance would never become an issue. Unfortunately, he died in 1771, just as the Kayaderosseras lands were finally being divided.

As part of the notices, these three Proprietors appointed three commissioners to administer the partition of the Patent. John Glen and Christopher Yates of Schenectady, along with Thomas Palmer of Orange County New York, were selected to be the next link in the chain between the Proprietors and the settlers and were charged with conducting the survey of the Kayaderosseras. As required in the 1762 law, the notice was careful to mention that these men "are in no ways interested in the said tract of land." Two of these three men may have had no interest in the Kayaderosseras but they were very active land speculators in other deals in the area.

John Glen was thirty-three at the time of his appointment. He was an Albany merchant in partnership with his great uncle, Hendrick Bleecker, until the latter's death earlier that year. Glen's father and grandfather had both died young, leaving it to the women in the family to prepare their offspring for successful careers as merchants and traders. Fortunately, his mother, Elizabeth Cuyler, and grandmother Jannetje Bleecker were both surrounded by large families who were among the mainstays of Albany economic and political life.[3] Son and grandson of Indian commissioners and traders, Glen was well positioned to join the frenzy for land in the post-war scramble during the 1760's. Serving as a quartermaster during the French and Indian War had given him the means to delve into real estate. As early as 1761, he joined Phillip Van Patten and Simon Schermerhorn in petitioning for a license to purchase 30,000 acres northwest of the Patent that he had just been appointed to survey. Earlier in 1768 they secured an Indian deed for 50,000 acres northeast of the Kayaderosseras Patent.[4] This purchase became known as the John Glen Patent, and included land surrounding the falls on the Hudson that would come to bear his name, Glens Falls. Sometime in the 1760's Glen moved to the Stockade section of Schenectady where he lived just around the corner from Christopher Yates. His home would become one of several claimed to be visited by George Washington during his visit to the area at the close of the Revolutionary War in 1783.

Yates and Glen had become friends and associates while serving together under William Johnson in the various campaigns against the French. Yates, a surveyor by profession, was a natural fit to join with his neighbor in the enterprise to partition this tract of land, lying only a few miles north of their hometown. He had already been involved in the initial survey of the boundaries that had provided the basis for the settlement with the Mohawks. Christopher, also referred to as Colonel Stoeffel Yates in recognition of his military service, was the son of Joseph Yates. Joseph had moved from Albany in 1734 and owned a large plantation just north of the Mohawk River where his son was born in 1737. Christopher was wounded at Bloody Pond near Lake George in 1755 at the age of eighteen while serving under Johnson.[5]

In 1761 Yates married Jannetje Bradt, from an old established Schenectady Dutch family. After three daughters, he and his wife were eagerly awaiting the birth of their next child when he was tapped to serve as a commissioner. In fact, his son Joseph was born just weeks before the three men convened at the Albany Courthouse to be sworn in as commissioners in November 1768. Yates could not have imagined that his newborn son would grow up to be a State Senator, Judge of the New York

Supreme Court, and Governor in 1823. Christopher himself would go on to distinguish himself in the Revolutionary War when he commanded a regiment of fatigue men responsible for delaying Burgoyne's army by felling trees along the British general's line of march to Saratoga.[6] Aside from his family lands in the vicinity of Schenectady, there is little evidence that he was a player in acquiring any of the large tracts of land that were up for grabs at the time.

Not so for the third Commissioner, Thomas Palmer of Orange County. Thomas and his brother Beriah most probably represent a family whose ties to the new world go back further than almost anyone else involved in the story of the Kayaderosseras Patent. Their great-great grandfather, William Palmer, arrived in Plymouth Colony in 1621 as a passenger on the *Fortune,* the second ship to arrive after the *Mayflower.* His family arrived two years later on the *Anne,* establishing the Palmer family in America. His son William became a public official in Duxbury and was elected a Selectman in 1674, only to lose his life a year later in King Phillip's War. It was his son that drew the attention of this author, when it was discovered that William had married Mary Richmond, establishing a connection between the Palmers and Richmonds.[7]

The Palmer family resided in eastern Massachusetts for the next 100 years until both brothers moved westward to reside along the Hudson River in Orange County. Thomas, the older brother by almost ten years, moved first. In 1758 he married Alenah Brouwer at the Rumbout Presbyterian church in Fishkill, NY. That this move may have had a religious motivation is supported by the fact that Chauncy Graham, was the minister of this church and was known to draw members from as far away as Rhode Island and eastern Massachusetts. How Thomas was named a Commissioner alongside the two men from Schenectady is still an open question. His skills as a surveyor and cartographer certainly complimented the business acumen of Glen and Yates. In any event, his appointment coincided with the arrival of his brother, Beriah, who would play a long-term role in the settlement of the Patent and the development of a community that would grow up within it.

It was older brother Thomas Palmer, whose appointment as a Commissioner reinforced his interest in the undeveloped lands north of the Patent. It may be that his exploration of the rivers, streams and lakes of the Kayaderosseras whetted his appetite for a piece of the action. In the midst of the partition process, Thomas petitioned the Governor, on behalf of himself and others, to purchase a tract of 46,000 acres northwest of the Patent he was surveying. The Governor obliged in a big way. In July 1772 an Indian deed was recorded, not for 46,000 acres but for 133,000 acres! This grant was to become known as Palmer's Purchase. The tract began on the northwest side of the Sacandaga River and extended to present day Wells and Speculator in Hamilton County. It is interesting to note that the "others" in his group of purchasers included Isaac Low and Dirck Lefferts, both with a stake in the Kayaderosseras and both set to play an important role in its settlement.[8]

True to the timetable laid out in the newspaper notices, the three newly named Commissioners held their organizational meeting on November 28, 1768 at the Courthouse in Albany where they were sworn in by Volkert Per Douw, the mayor of Albany. They immediately appointed Cornelius Cuyler as their clerk. Cuyler was a Schenectady resident, but a descendent of a prominent Albany family that had produced three mayors of that city over the previous 50 years.[9]

They next met on April 28 the following year at the tavern of Robert Clench in Schenectady to get down to the business of conducting the survey. At that meeting they received guidance from William Cockburn, Deputy Surveyor General, outlining the borders of the Patent to be considered in partitioning the land. Cockburn was relaying instructions from his boss, Alexander Colden, the surveyor general of the colony and son of the current Lt. Governor, Cadwallader Colden. Cockburn was a Scotsman who had settled in Kingston, NY. He had taught surveying and other mathematical skills in Hanover Square in New York as early as 1763.[10] He was careful to explain that the line should be drawn to the northwesternmost point of the Kayaderosseras, as agreed in the deal with the Iroquois the previous year.[11]

The commissioners then appointed Charles Webb of Stamford, Connecticut to actually conduct the survey, along with Stephen Hooper and Walter Dance as chain bearers. Although Webb has been identified as Colonel Charles Webb, it is more likely that the surveyor would have been his son Charles, born in 1750. In 1769 his 45-year-old father was already an important man of affairs in Stamford, serving as both the town Selectman and a member of the colonial legislature. He would hold these positions for more than twenty years. Charles, Sr. also had a military career, with the rank of Captain in the French and Indian War and would lead a regiment of Connecticut soldiers in the early years of the Revolutionary War. It is unlikely that a man of his position would accept a commission to tramp around the wilderness for a year on an assignment for which he had no experience. It is more reasonable to assume that his son, probably unknowingly, followed the career path of another young ambitious man - his father's soon-to-be commanding officer, George Washington. The younger Webb may have even learned his surveyor skills in the classroom of William Cockburn. During the Revolutionary War, he would serve as a lieutenant in his father's regiment, losing his life on a gunboat in Long Island Sound in 1780.[12]

The question remains concerning why the Commissioners would have chosen Webb. This choice leads us to take a closer look at the Connecticut connections that would play an important role in the settlement of the lands at the heart of the Kayaderosseras Patent. The actual survey work was now underway and would continue for the next 18 months. Behind the scenes, far away from the woodland, fields, streams and ponds being dissected by the surveyor's links and chains, others were becoming interested in the prospects of settling in this new land.

At the time that the Commissioners held their first meeting in November 1768, Reverend Eliphalet Ball was between assignments. He had been released from his position of minister of the Presbyterian Church in Bedford, New York, along the border with Connecticut. He had served that congregation for 14 years, after graduating from Yale in 1748. Ball was a native of New Haven and raised in the home of his great-grandfather Ailing Ball, a short walk down the street from Yale. Ailing had arrived in the colony of New Haven in 1643, and had managed the 600-acre farm of John Davenport, the pastor of the church and one of the founders of the Colony.[13] The Ball family had prospered in the colony in succeeding years. When John Ball, Eliphalet's father, died in 1731 at the age of forty-five, he left an estate valued at £1,204 to his wife Mary and children. His grandfather died the same year, so eight-year-old Eliphalet grew up in the household of his mother and six siblings.[14]

It may have been fortunate for him and his future career that in 1739 his mother married Deacon John Punderson who had served as Steward (administrator) of Yale. Eliphalet entered Yale in 1745 to study theology just as the Great Awakening was running it course. However, its effect on the college, its staff and students was still being felt. Thomas Clap, the "Old Light" rector of the school, had been named president in 1745, when Eliphalet began his studies there. The Old Lights generally opposed the Great Awakening and its "new lights" personified by the emotional preaching of Jonathan Edwards and Rev. George Whitefield. This upheaval had split the New Haven church into two congregations. Earlier, Clap had gone so far as to close the college for a period in 1742 because of the disruptions of the religious revival.[15]

Ball apparently embraced the New Light movement. Soon after his call from the Bedford church in 1754, his views on the subject put him at odds with the conservative members of his congregation. The Bedford Church had been founded by members of the Stamford Parish in Connecticut, and retained the strict New England approach to religious discipline in spite of the fact that their village and church had come under the authority of New York around the year 1700. They became known as a "dissenting congregation" and had come under the jurisdiction of the Presbytery of New York prior to the arrival of Reverend Ball.[16] By 1763 the Presbytery was investigating the situation and in 1764 responded to a petition of some members of the church by initially supporting Ball. The situation did not improve and in 1768 Ball himself asked that he be released from his responsibilities to the congregation. His term of service ended December 22, 1768.[17]

So it may well have been that during the winter of 1769, Rev. Ball could be found "sitting around his hearth discussing the possibilities of new lands to the north" with Colonel Charles Webb, a member of Ball's second congregation in Stamford.[18] In fact, Webb may have been explaining to Eliphalet that his son Charles Webb Jr., was about to be appointed to survey these lands, and it might be a great opportunity for a fresh start for his minister and some loyal members of his flock.[19] When spring arrived in Bedford, Eliphalet had made his decision. In April he began selling off his property in the area, including his slaves Jane and York. In November he sold his homestead and ten acres to Enos Miller, one of his parishioners. The cord had been cut.[20]

Meanwhile, work on partitioning the Patent lands continued. It is not known how many men or teams were employed to conduct the survey. Each team would have consisted of the chief surveyor using a compass, also called a circumferentor, to sight the bearing; chain bearers to position the heavy sixty-six foot Gunter's chains; a man to handle the six-foot wooden ranging rod that was used as a target for the surveyor, and chain bearers; as well as axmen to clear obstacles along the path. Each chain was divided into 100 links, each 7.92 inches long, often set off every 10 links with pieces of brass. The measurements were written down in a field book along with notes and sketches that were later transcribed into parcel maps.[21] Surveyor teams in Virginia had been known to survey 1,000 acres per day using this method. Maintaining a similar pace for the Kayaderosseras Patent, the survey could be completed in approximately 400 days, which it was. Arduous work it must have been, running their lines across the wooded wilderness, wading across swamps and streams and hauling their equipment up and down ravines, hills and mountains.[22]

The central dispatch point for all of this activity was the cabin of Michael McDonald along the west bank of Long Lake, today known as Ballston Lake. Michael and his brother Nicholas were natives of Ireland who had emigrated to America, arriving first in Philadelphia as indentured servants. They both served in the French and Indian War, which may have provided them with an opportunity to meet and come under the influence of their fellow Irishman Sir William Johnson. It may have been Johnson who in 1763 encouraged the McDonalds to settle along the banks of the lake on the Indian path leading from the Mohawk River to Lake George. Johnson himself had taken this trail in 1755 during his campaign against the French.[23] Charles Webb and his survey teams would have fanned out from McDonald's cabin establishing field camps as they progressed west, north and east from this starting point.

This survey effort was but the first of several similar exercises in converting unimproved land into partitioned lots available for sale to eager settlers during the early 1770's. As noted, the advent of peace, by removing the threat of attack by the French and their Indian allies, had increased the demand for land and its value rose significantly. Up and down the Hudson River and west along the Mohawk, landowners seized their opportunity to cash in. They used the provisions of the 1762 Act for the Collection of Quit Rents, and a later 1768 Act, to follow the same process employed by the Proprietors of the Kayaderosseras. Numerous newspaper advertisements of the time recorded the establishment of similar commissions throughout the region. In Albany County alone, surveys of the Hosak, Otsquago and Coeymans Patents were conducted during this period. In 1774 Thomas Palmer would again be appointed as a Commissioner, this time of the Coeymans Patent located on the west bank of the Hudson River south of Albany.[24]

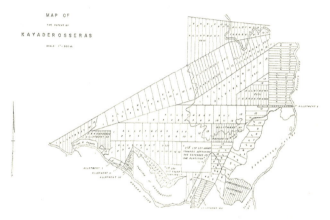

Kayaderosseras Patent Survey 1771   © *Don Carpenter*

The survey of the Kayaderosseras Patent began in the spring of 1769, and was completed by the fall of 1770. The Commissioners and the surveying team had divided the 406,000 acres of the patent into twenty-five allotments. Each allotment was further divided into thirteen great lots, one for each of the original proprietors. The lots were of various sizes, an attempt to insure that each was of equivalent value. Lots along streams that contained fertile land were generally smaller than more remote, hilly parcels. On December 20 1770 the Commissioners served notice that this part of their work was completed. Maps and two signed copies of the field books were in the hands of officials in Albany and New York. They also signaled the next step in the process.

> We do hereby appoint the twenty-second day of February next at the house of Walter Brock Inn Keeper situate in the City of New York near the city hall of the said city

to be the day and place for balloting for the said lots and allotments and do hereby require all persons interested then and there to attend.[25]

On the appointed day the Commissioners and the representatives of the Proprietors assembled at Brock's establishment. They were joined by Chief Justice Daniel Horsmanden. Horsmanden, in his late seventies, was chronically ill, living out his days without friends or respect. The high point of his career had come thirty years before when he led the prosecution of slaves accused of conspiring to burn New York and kill their masters. His unscrupulous actions during these trials contributed to the death by burning or hanging of thirty blacks. Ironically, he owned no slaves himself, but many of the Proprietors in the room with him did.[26]

Ballots were prepared and ten-year-old William Simmons drew the tickets from two boxes. One held the names of the Proprietors, the second contained the lot numbers. In this way, each of the thirteen great lots in each allotment were assigned to one of the original Proprietors.[27]

That was the easy part. The problem was that none of the thirteen people who had been granted this land in 1708 were still alive. As has been shown, their claims had been disbursed through a labyrinth of inheritances, sales and re-sales that would be extremely difficult to sort out. This would become the responsibility of another group of men, the Trustees of the Patent, charged with converting the partitioned lots into profit for the current owners of the Patent.

CHAPTER 4
The Five-Mile Square

After the balloting was complete, the Commissioners had one remaining task. The next day they authorized the sales of the lands set aside to defray the expenses associated with surveying and partitioning the land as stipulated in the 1762 Act. The sales would take place two months later, on April 23, 1771, again at Brock's Tavern in New York City. Two tracts had been designated for this purpose. One was a 5,029 acre parcel located in the future town of Charlton, the second was what was referred to as the Five-Mile Square containing 16,321 acres, now known as the Town of Ballston. So in total, about 5% of the land was set aside to reimburse the Proprietors for the expenses they had incurred for the work performed by the Commissioners, the survey teams, and the cost of their equipment.[1]

On July 15, 1771 the following advertisement appeared in the *New York Gazette*. It reads in part:

> TO BE SOLD, in lots of about 1200 or 1300 acres, A Tract of land containing 16000 acres, in the north side of the Mohawk's River, in the patent of the Kayaderosseras in the county of Albany. This tract was sold only a few weeks ago by the commissioners for defraying the charges of partition of the said patent, and is well known to be extraordinary good land...Such persons therefore who are disposed to remove from old and worn-out farms, to fertile, rich new lands, which will abundantly

compensate their owner and afford a comfortable subsistence for themselves and family; will please speedily
apply to us the subscribers, to whom the said tract is conveyed in trust to be sold for the benefit of the proprietors,
and they may agree to very reasonable terms. New York,
May 16,1771

Benjamin Kissam   Cornelius Clopper
Dirck Lefferts   Isaac Low[2]

We have encountered some of these gentlemen before and will pres-
ently explore their backgrounds and relationships further. Unlike the
Commissioners, these four men who became the Trustees of the set-aside
tracts certainly had an interest in the Kayaderosseras. All of them owned
land in the Patent, as we shall see. As Proprietors themselves, they knew
well the opportunity in front of them to reap the financial rewards of
the sale of these lands. In addition, all four were New York City men.
Three were influential merchants and one a lawyer, indicating that it
was the downstate Patentees who controlled the process. Although they
supposedly purchased the land at an open auction as prescribed in the
1762 Legislative Act, it is more than likely that their winning bid was a
foregone conclusion.

It is interesting to examine this advertisement further before proceed-
ing. Notice that the tract was to be sold in 1200 to 1300 acre lots. Their
enticement to farmers seeking to replace their "old and worn out farms"
notwithstanding, this notice was not directed to average yeoman farmers
who could not afford and could not manage such a large expanse. This
first division of these lands was meant to entice the middlemen speculators who could afford to invest in these large tracts to divide and sell, or
more likely lease, smaller lots that would be attractive for settlers to farm.

A second important aspect of this advertisement is the position of the
Trustees themselves. The tract was "conveyed in trust to be sold for the
benefit of the Proprietors." The Trustees had purchased these set-aside
tracts for £3500, the approximate costs incurred by the Commissioners to
pay the survey teams and their related expenses. The subsequent account
books of the Trustees indicate that the payments received for this land

were allocated back to the current Proprietors, less commissions paid to the four Trustees, which totaled £280 at the time of the first division.[3]

In order to ascertain how these four men came together to form a partnership to purchase these tracts it may be helpful to look into their backgrounds. Benjamin Kissam has already appeared in our narrative as one of the Proprietors in the negotiations with the Indians and was one of the signatories of the advertisement announcing the partition of the Patent. Kissam was born on Long Island in 1728, where his grandfather had emigrated to Great Neck in the mid- seventeenth century. His father, Joseph, was a farmer with some stature in the local community, serving as vestryman of the church and Justice of the Peace.[4] Benjamin moved to New York City to study law and became well respected in his field. He had acquired his stake in the Kayaderosseras Patent through his 1755 marriage to Catherine Rutgers, whose father, Peter, had married Helen Hooghlandt, daughter of Adrian Hooghlandt. Benjamin's connection to the Rutgers family propelled him into the inner circle of New York City social and political life.

Peter Rutger's other daughter, Helena, had married John Morin Scott. Scott was considered one of the leading lawyers in New York City and as a member of the New York Triumvirate was associated with the Livingston faction in colonial politics. As brothers-in-law, Benjamin and John would warm to the patriot cause and join the Provincial Congress and the Committee of One-Hundred, organized in New York City in response to British provocations in the years preceding independence. Known as moderates rather than radicals in the early years, they would be joined by another moderate, whom Benjamin knew intimately. John Jay, who later was to become the first Chief Justice of the Supreme Court, studied law under Kissam in the 1760's. Their correspondence indicates a warm personal friendship between mentor and student.[5]

A second Trustee, Isaac Low, was also well-known in New York social, commercial and political circles. Isaac's great-grandfather emigrated from Holland in 1659 and settled in Kingston, New York. His grandfather and father, both named Cornelius, became successful traders and merchants in New York City and New Jersey. Cornelius, Jr. built a home in Raritan Landing for his bride, Johanna Goveneur. Her mother was the daughter of Jacob Leisler who had been executed in 1691 during the aftermath of the

Glorious Revolution in England.[6] His son, Isaac, was born at the Raritan home in 1731. After a flood in 1738 the original house was replaced with what could only be described as a mansion. It still stands today and is on the United States National Register of Historic Places.[7]

Isaac's social status could only have been further elevated by his marriage to Margareta Cuyler in 1760. She was the daughter of Cornelius Cuyler of Albany, who had himself married into the Schuyler family. In Albany even more than New York, a few leading families formed a tight social circle that was strengthened by repeated intermarriages. Cornelius served as Mayor of Albany during the 1740's, a post his father-in-law had also held.[8]

Isaac formed a business partnership with Abraham Lott around the year 1753. Their firm remained intact for over a decade, during which time they imported and offered for sale a large assortment of European and India goods, as advertisements repeatedly attested. Their business was located in Hanover Square, the center of trade in New York, where many of the great merchants of the city were located. After severing their partnership in 1766, Isaac continued in the dry goods trade, while Abraham moved full-time into government service. The latter was appointed Treasurer of the Colony in 1767.[9]

Low himself entered the political arena during the Stamp Act crisis in 1765. He joined two hundred merchants in New York City who agreed to suspend trade with England until the Stamp Tax was repealed.[10] Low rose to leadership of these merchants when he joined with James De Lancey, William Walton and other prominent men to urge the Assembly to erect a monument to William Pitt, who was hailed by the colonists as the British leader responsible for the repeal.[11]

In 1771, while continuing his mercantile business in New York, Low joined in the foursome that would administer the sale of lands 150 miles north. At the time of his appointment as Trustee, Isaac and his father Cornelius together owned a half share in the Patent. It was one of the smaller portions among the twenty-one people and families identified as the principal owners in the division of land listed in the account books of the Trustees. His involvement in the Patent was one of his many business ventures during this time. He had emerged as one of the spokesmen for the Proprietors during the negotiations and final settlement with the

Iroquois. However, given his political engagement, it could be assumed that he did not take the lead in administering the sale of these tracts. For that, we have to look to the other two Trustees, who were close associates of Low.

Cornelius Jansen Clopper arrived in New Amsterdam sometime in the 1650's, emigrating from Bergen op Zoom in the Netherlands. A blacksmith, he established his shop at a strategic location near the shore of the East River known as De Smit's Vly, where travelers from Long Island first disembarked in their journey to the city. Doing business along the road that would later become Maiden Lane, Cornelius did very well for himself. When he died in 1693, his estate was valued at over $10,000. He was one of the richest men in New York, years before Lord Cornbury came to America. His widow Helike married Shuart Olpherts, who himself owned considerable property in what was to become the heart of New York City.[12] When Helike died in 1700 she passed on a considerable estate to her children and grandchildren, which they parlayed in various business enterprises and real estate transactions.

In 1728, her grandson, Cornelius, sold a lot to four prominent Jewish businessmen in the Dock Ward. That lot would become the location for the first Jewish synagogue in New York.[13] His son, Cornelius, Jr. the future Patent Trustee, was born in 1716 and became a successful businessman, importing goods from Holland, England and other European countries to his store in Hanover Square.[14] He also engaged in the real-estate business, selling lots in New York and property in the countyside. Among Cornelius' business interests was a bakery located behind his house on Duke Street where he apparently utilized both indentured servants and slaves.[15] In spite of his many business ventures, by 1760 there are indications that all was not well with the Clopper empire. In 1761 he put his house and bakery up for sale[16] and in 1768 a notice appeared in the *New York Gazette* requesting that "all persons having any demands against Cornelius Clopper, Jr., late an insolvent, are desired to send their accounts properly proved to Elijah Steel or Thomas Randall, assignees."[17]

So in 1771 when Clopper was appointed to his position as one of the Trustees of the Kayaderosseras Patent, it may be fair to ask how such an opportunity came his way. It turns out that the Clopper family had connections with another Dutch family on Maiden Lane, relationships that connected Cornelius to the fourth Trustee, Dirck Lefferts. Clopper and Lefferts had developed many close associations over the years. Clopper's brother Peter had married Elizabeth Lefferts, Dirck's sister, in 1743. Throughout the 1750's Cornelius and Dirck were neighbors on Maiden Lane where they both had their business establishment, and both apparently relocated to Hanover Square in the 1760's.[18]

It was Lefferts who would have the greatest and longest lasting impact on the settlement of the Patent. Descendant of another old Dutch family, his grandfather Leffert Pieterse settled in Flatbush, across the East River from New Amsterdam, in 1660 at the age of 17. Although his father died soon after their arrival, Leffert inherited his father's farm which he operated with the labor of slaves and indentured servants. In this way they were following the practice of many of the Dutch immigrants who settled in Brooklyn. Their enterprise made Brooklyn the breadbasket for the city across the river, mostly relying on slave labor. By his death in 1704 he had accumulated land in Queens, Staten Island and New Jersey in addition to the family's home farms in Flatbush and Bedford.[19]

Lefferts had 14 children, including nine sons, thus establishing the Lefferts clan's place in the early history of New York. One of his sons, Abraham, left the farm and settled in New York City. In 1713 he married Sarah Hooghlandt, daughter of Adrian, providing him with the Lefferts family's first stake in the Kayaderosseras Patent. There would be more. In 1752, Abraham purchased additional shares in the Patent from Elias Boudinot, who had been the executor of the estate of Peter Fauconnier and John Emott, Boudinot's son-in-law.[20]

Abraham Lefferts brought with him another legacy from his family across the river. Slaves were part of his household and in 1741 his "man" Pompey was indicted in the so called Negro Plot for participating in a conspiracy to take over New York. They were accused of planning to set fires and overthrow their masters. While that conspiracy appears to have been largely fabricated, the resulting trials led to the conviction and deaths by hanging or burning of thirty blacks. Pompey was spared that fate, but subsequently sold off to a much more difficult life as a slave in the Caribbean.[21] Named as a merchant in that trial, Abraham was also involved in real estate, as numerous advertisements in the New York newspapers attest. Upon his death in October, 1767, his son, Dirck, inherited two houses and a storehouse. They were located between the homes of William Walton and Jacobus Roosevelt, two of the most successful merchants in New York. In addition, he received his share of the Kayaderosseras lands of his father.[22]

This was only the first step in a process that would make Dirck Lefferts the single largest landowner in the Patent. The next year he and Peter Remsen acquired the share originally granted to John Tatham from George Clark as noted previously. He also would end up with rights to partial shares of John Stevens and May Bickely.[23] Altogether, Lefferts could claim ownership to parts of the grants of five of the original thirteen Proprietors, totaling 1 5/6 portion of the original thirteen shares.[24]

Having been assigned as Trustees for the sale of the 21,000 acres set aside to reimburse the Proprietors, these four men based in New York City needed a local agent to promote and sell this land. Fortunately, that agent was already hard at work. Rev. Eliphalet Ball, accompanied by the family of Epenetus White, a member of his former congregation, moved north soon after he sold his land in Bedford in 1770. Before the survey was completed, and before the Trustees had purchased the set-aside tracts, he had been engaged by the Commissioners or the Proprietors to promote this new land. They chose wisely. Ball had a ready source of buyers back in Bedford and Stamford. Several members of his flock, loyal to him and his ministry, were willing and able to pull up stakes and join their former pastor. Within a year, approximately twenty families had joined him and built homesteads on the shores of Long Lake, one of the most desirable tracts in the Patent.[25]

Each side of the Five-Mile Square measured 404 chains as laid out by the surveyors, and was located in the southeast quadrant of the Patent. Beginning at a point southeast of Long Lake, the southern boundary line followed a tract across the lake. There the land rises gently westward and then northward through forests that sheltered fertile soil for farmland. There were also several streams prized by settlers for their potential for sawmills and gristmills, the lifeblood of all farming communities.[26]

The Square was crossed by an old Indian path that angled northeast, linking the Mohawk River to the Hudson, and continuing on to the waterways that carried Indians and soldiers north to and from Canada during the many conflicts between the English and French. Another faint path led northward through the Patent and into the highlands beyond, finally reaching the western shores of Lake Champlain. This route would be used ten years later to forever disrupt the lives of dozens of residents located along a new path in the center of the Five-Mile Square.

The surveyors had divided the Square into thirteen great lots, much as they had done with the twenty-five allotments that surrounded this section. Unlike the other tracts these lots had not been assigned to the thirteen Proprietors. Instead, they were now in the hands of the Trustees, with the responsibility to sell them on behalf of all the Proprietors. To make these parcels accessible to the prospective buyers, the surveyors made provision for a road that would split the square in two. Running from south to north, in a straight line over ridges and streams, the road would be used both as a marker for the lots being laid out, and a path to market for the farmers. The settlers were soon building their homes on these lots and beginning the arduous work of improving their 200 acre farms, working to clear land for planting while maintaining sections for pasture land and woodlots. This road was appropriately known as "The Middleline", a name it retains today. Traveling northward along it, with its open fields and sprinkling of old farmhouses and new 20th century homes, it's easy to picture a time almost 250 years ago when this newly-laid-out dirt roadway beckoned pioneers bent on establishing new lives in their new communities.

∞

The Trustees set about their task. Their first sale was not a sale at all, but a gift in kind. In October, 1771, they recognized the services of Eliphalet Ball. This deed confirms that Ball had served the Proprietors well. For the nominal sum of ten shillings, they sold him 400 acres of prime land "for and in consideration of the many services he has done and the expenses he hath been at, in and towards advancing the settlement of said Township." That township was already informally called Ball's Town in honor of its second citizen. The McDonalds had lost the opportunity to stamp their name on the new settlement.[27] Worse, the following year Nicholas McDonald was required to secure a mortgage to keep his land, obligated to pay £85 to John Glen.[28]

The frenzy of partition and settlement of the several patents surrounding Albany led the colonial government to divide huge Albany County into more manageable civil entities. Albany County was larger than all the other counties of New York combined, and the increasing population was putting a strain of the civil administration. Accordingly, in March 1772 the Colonial Legislature formed two new counties, Tryon to the west and Charlotte to the east of Albany County, now reduced in size.[29] That county was further segregated into fifteen districts. The area later to become Saratoga County contained two districts. Half-Moon District contained the area south of the Anthony Kill, a steam that meanders eastward from Round Lake to the Hudson River, while the Saratoga District included the area north and west of that steam. By this Act, the freeholders of each district were to elect a Supervisor, two accessors, two Overseers of the Poor, two Constables, a Clerk and a Tax Collector.[30] By 1775, the influx of settlers into Ball's settlement led to the separation of the western half of the Saratoga District into a new district called Ball's Town.[31] The same leadership structure was put in place, but unfortunately the names of the early office-holders have not survived. The Ball's Town District remained unchanged until 1792 when several additional towns, including Milton, Galway and Charlton, were formed and Ballston reverted to the size it is today.

Ball's 400 acres was part of Lot two of the Ninth Division of the Five-Mile Square, beginning "at the Middleline" and extending eastward to the shores of Long Lake. The southern border of this parcel straddles today's Route 50, eastward along Outlet Road, and westward along Charlton road to the Presbyterian Church, which he himself founded. The original church was erected in 1772 on the southwest corner of Route 50 and Charlton Road and was later replaced by a larger building known as the Old Red Meeting House at the same location. Today's imposing white church located farther west was erected in 1803. Because of repeated fires over the years, little remains of the original building. Although Ball was the first settler to claim property along the Middleline, his homestead was located in the eastern section of his property, on the eastern side of Route 50, north of Outlet Road. It was southeast of Ball's homestead along the shores of Long Lake that the first concentration of settlers would make their new homes. Among those joining the McDonalds along the lake were the White, Miller and Kellogg families, all members of Eliphalet Ball's former church in Bedford.[32]

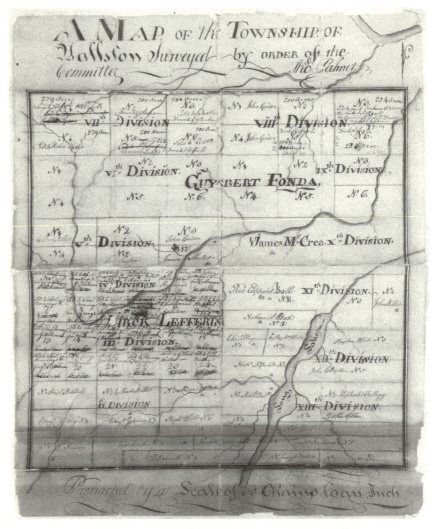

Division of the Five Mile Square Thomas Palmer c. 1772

While the lands adjacent to the lake appear to have been sold directly to settlers, along the Middleline several of the tracts were sold as great lots called Divisions. These Divisions had already been subdivided by Thomas Palmer into six 200 acre lots. They were an ideal size for family farms, both for their affordability and development. As mentioned, several of these Divisions were initially sold to middlemen speculators for resale and Dirck Lefferts was the largest purchaser.[33] Working through Peter Clopper, brother of Cornelius, and his own brother-in-law, he purchased 2,400 acres in 1771 and another 1,600 acres in 1772. Clearly he intended to make money on the sale of the Patent, well beyond his fee for serving as a Trustee.

Other speculators signed up for a piece of the action. Gysbert Fonda bought two of the thirteen divisions totaling 2158 acres. This land was split east and west by the Middleline, but unlike surrounding parcels, these tracts were not immediately settled.[34] Fonda was a successful Albany merchant, and was connected with many downstate business-men. Politically he followed a path similar to that of Isaac Low, with his early support of the patriot cause in opposition to the Stamp Act giving way over time so that by the advent of Independence he was considered a neutral. Faced with deportation in 1778, he finally took the oath of alle-giance to the new country, and avoided the fate in store for Low.[35]

Others responded to the advertisements in the New York newspapers with the intention of settling-in themselves with their extended families. James McCrea bought 1250 acres on the east side of the Middleline, just north of the land given to Reverend Ball and his family. McCrea and his brothers, Samuel and William, were sons of Presbyterian minister James McCrea. The McCrea family were natives of Galloway, Scotland. The three brothers moved north from Lamington, New Jersey, following their brother John McCrea. He graduated from Princeton in 1762 and began his law practice in Albany the following year. He later moved to Northumberland along the Hudson River where we first encountered him as one of the legal representatives of the Proprietors in the negoti-ations with the Indians in 1767.[36] John would later be appointed Colonel of the 13th Regiment of the Albany County Militia. Samuel and William would serve in the 12th Regiment which would be led by their neighbor, James Gordon who settled across the road from them in 1772.

Gordon purchased two separate parcels. Two lots totaling 400 acres were just to the west of the McCrea land across the Middleline. An ad-ditional 600 acres was in the northeasternmost section of the township, again bordering on the all-important Middleline. Gordon's purchase was made with a keen eye for the development of the land. Both of his parcels were crossed by streams. The Mourning Kill, named by the Indians in commemoration of some long forgotten battle, flowed through his homestead lot. The second would become known as Gordon's Creek. Gordon made use of both water sources. It was not long before gristmills and sawmills appeared along these waterways, extending his influence in the community.

Lefferts, McCrea, Fonda and Gordon were the four largest purchasers in the Five- Mile Square, but many others joined them. In a burst of activity during late 1771 and early 1772, twenty-five men purchased 14,370 acres.[37] As noted, the area surrounding Long Lake was completely sold off during this period to settlers who moved north from Bedford to establish their homesteads. The lots purchased to the northwest of the lake by the speculators along Middleline Road were quickly resold to settlers as well. Together, these early sales, which represented almost 90% of the Five-Mile Square, were sold for a total of £5,588, far exceeding the £3,394 in partition expenses incurred by the proprietors. This profit on the set-aside land only sweetened the pot for the proprietors, who were also in the process of subdividing the twenty-five parcels they received during the balloting process.[38]

The work of the surveyors did not end with the division of the Patent among the thirteen original proprietors in February 1771 or even with the partition of the Five-Mile Square. In order to sell the lots assigned to the original proprietors, Charles Webb and Thomas Palmer worked together to divide these parcels further for final disposition among the current owners. For that to be done properly it was required that these owners be identified and their shares confirmed. We have already shown the complexity of such a task. Attempting to trace ownership was an issue that resulted in many court cases, providing a fair livelihood for many lawyers in the years to come. The only known list, almost certainly incomplete, identifies twenty-one individuals and families that supposedly account for 11 3/16 of the thirteen original shares. It was this list that became the basis for the allocation of the proceeds of the sales made by the Trustees in the Five Mile Square, and the second 5,029-acre tract in the Town of Charlton. An attempt has been made in Appendix 1 to trace the path of ownership from the thirteen to the twenty-one families. This summary is included as a tool for those who may be interested in extending this research.

The involvement of the Trustees in the selling, mortgaging, collection and administration of the lots in the Patent would continue for the next thirty years, but the coming dispute with the Crown would focus their attention elsewhere. As wealthy members of the New York aristocratic class, they faced a dilemma as events led inexorably toward war. Benjamin Kissam was a member of the Colonial Assembly at the time of the partitioning of the Patent and joined the First Provincial Assembly that superseded it in 1775. In May of that year both he and Isaac Low, along with Benjamin's brother-in-law John Morin Scott, signed the Association in support of the rights of the colonists. However, Kissam was counted among the conservative faction of the Assembly. In that same month he introduced a motion "that a committee be appointed to prepare and state the terms on which reconciliation may be tendered to Great Britain, consistent with the just liberties and freedom of the subjects in America."[39] Fellow Trustee Cornelius Clopper joined Kissam in the Second Provincial Assembly in December, and both eventually supported American independence.

Isaac Low could not bring himself to join in the final break from Great Britain. As the crisis deepened in 1774, he became chairman of the various committees formed by the Sons of Liberty. They organized resistance to the increasingly provocative actions of the British government made in response to the tea parties in Boston and New York. These committees grew larger as the leaders of the movement tried to balance the views of the radicals who began seeing independence as the only solution, and the more conservative leaders bent on reconciliation.

Low's influence led to his selection, along with John Jay and three others, to represent New York at the first Continental Congress which was held in Philadelphia in September 1774. But he was becoming a reluctant patriot. He was concerned that the more outspoken leaders were pushing the colonies toward an irreversible break with the Crown, something he feared and could not support. When the election was held for the Second Congress, the number of delegates was increased from five to eleven. The additional members were more radical and bent on independence. Isaac Low refused to serve. It was the first step in his journey to becoming a Loyalist.[40]

When independence came, Low left New York for the family home in Raritan Landing, New Jersey, where he was imprisoned for a time before he was released on the recommendation of General Washington. He returned to New York during the British occupation and became head of the Chamber of Commerce. As a Loyalist living in New York, his property was confiscated in 1779 when the New York Assembly passed the first of several acts designed to punish "Traitors." Low was among the twenty thousand Loyalists who returned to England at the conclusion of the war. He died on the Isle of Wight in 1791.[41] His accounts related to the Kayaderosseras were settled about this time by the two remaining Trustees, Lefferts and Clopper. By that time, Benjamin Kissam had also passed on. He had sided with the revolutionary cause, but did not live to see ultimate victory. He died in 1782.

Thereafter administration of the Patent beyond the Five-Mile Square was mainly left to Dirck Lefferts. The account books in later years were maintained by him. He remained based in New York City, but had his own agent to manage his affairs related to the Patent. Beriah Palmer, brother of Thomas, was to become one of the most influential citizens of the growing settlement of Ball's Town. He would share that distinction with James Gordon both later serving as representatives in the Congress of the new nation. Together they would symbolize the common struggles and internal conflicts that the American Revolution would bring to this new settlement.

Once the current owners of the thirteen shares had been established, many of them lost no time in moving to turn their property into cash. Newspaper advertisements appeared frequently in 1772 and 1773 detailing the lots available for sale in each of the allotments. Interested buyers lined up to secure a stake in these newly opened lands, creating more work for Thomas Palmer in drawing up the maps used to document these sales. Known as the A-B maps, they divided up several of the original owners' shares in each allotment into two or more pieces based on the sale agreements. Several of these maps are extant and have been located by the author.[42]

One of the larger purchases was made by Daniel Campbell. Campbell, a native of Ireland, came to Schenectady in 1754. He parlayed his friendship with Sir William Johnson and his business acumen into an extensive and profitable mercantile business. Proof of his success exists today in the Campbell Mansion on State Street in Schenectady. First built in 1762 and modified over the years, the prosperity of its original owner is still evident.[43]

Campbell followed the pattern of many successful traders and invested in land. The Kayaderosseras Patent offered him a great opportunity close to home. In a November 1773 letter, his enthusiasm for his new venture came through clearly.

> I have of late made a very large purchase of land that is well situated to settle on, being some of them within 6-8-10-12-13-14-16-18-20 and the furthest not more than 25 miles from this town and a fine patent of land nearby to water carriage. The whole quantity I have purchased amounts to 24,000 acres. It is free of any quit rent to the King or any other person forever. There are on my lands at present about 8 tenants who must either agree with me for rent or must purchase the land.[44]

In another letter one year later he was still enthusiastic, and outlined his terms of sale, which gives us insight into typical lease arrangements made with new settlers.

> I am exceedingly well pleas'd with my purchase on Kayaderosses. This summer I have settled upwards of sixty families on leases forever on the following terms. They have 4 years free of rent and then to pay £7 per year and all mill places reserved and in case the land be sold I am to receive the 1/6 part of my purchase money. Most of the people are Scotch Lowlanders who are in general both saving and industrious.[45]

The pending Revolution would soon play havoc with these arrangements, as the world of speculators and farmers alike would truly be turned upside down. Much of Campbell's land was located to the west of Middleline Road in the current town of Galway. His tenants, as well as those families that settled along the Middleline, would face many disruptions in the years to come. The inhabitants of these neighboring settlements would often find themselves on opposing sides in the coming conflict.

Within the Five-Mile Square itself, there were two concentrations of settlements in the 1770's. The first was along the shores of Long (Ballston) Lake extending south toward the crossroads at Burnt Hills. These were the lots promoted by Eliphalet Ball. The second concentration included the homesteads on either side of "The Middleline" beginning approximately one mile northwest of Ball's settlement. There, James Gordon would become the most prominent resident, active in both business and government. This experience was to make him a natural leader in the coming conflict.

To understand the impact of the Revolution in general and 1780 British Raid in particular on this settlement we need to take a closer look at the people along the Middleline. What were their roots and their relationships on the eve of war? Where did they come from? What connections brought them here? What motivation did they share in picking up stakes and moving to this new frontier on the edge of the wilderness? What challenges would they face and what bonds would they form here?

CHAPTER 5
People of the Middleline

With a few notable exceptions the people of the Middleline emigrated from Connecticut. For most, their family ties in that colony went back several generations. For some, their heritage can be traced back to the first settlements in the 1630's when their ancestors accompanied the founders of the Colony on their migrations westward from Massachusetts Bay. Thomas Hooker, John Winthrop, Jr., John Davenport and Roger Ludlow are all mentioned in the pages that follow, attesting to the prominent connections of the Middleline Road families. Even those families who migrated first to Long Island, did so under the leadership and influence of the Colony of Connecticut. The primary motivation for the emigration of the first families to Connecticut was religion. Many sought an even purer form of Puritanism than could be found in Massachusetts. A secondary consideration was the quest for land. Even in these early years, the Great Migration of the 1630's was pressuring the settlers of the Bay Colony to look for land further west. These twin concerns would course through the veins of generation after generation of the future settlers along the Middleline.

For many of these families, their move to Ball's Town would be the second relocation in a generation. Men and women considering leaving the homesteads of their extended families in the 1770's had shared that experience with their parents, grandparents, and kinfolk in the 1740's and 1750's. After two or three generations living in the small towns and villages along the rivers and the coastal areas of Connecticut, large extended families could no longer prosper on their ancestors original land grants and subsequent acquisitions. By the early eighteenth century, the younger generations were on the move.[1] Most of the families that became pioneers along the Middleline first moved to the western counties of Connecticut and Massachusetts in a search for land to provide for their families.

Settling on substantial parcels, many of these families raised six to ten children, once again leading to a shortage of land and raised the specter of a decline in the standard of living for the next generation. So just as their older relatives had made the decision to become pioneers — purchasing land, building homes and barns, clearing land for farming, establishing town governments and new churches — the next generation did the same. Drawing on the knowledge they had gained in these frontier settlements, many second generation sons heeded the call for cheaper land in the newly opened Kayaderosseras Patent.[2]

However, we will begin our survey of these families with the man responsible for the exceptions, those settlers that followed a different path to Ball's Town and the Middleline. A man not from Connecticut, a man without a puritan heritage, a man whose initial motivation for emigrating was not land. It is a testament to the influence of this man that others of similar background would settle along the road dominated by families from Connecticut, and that he would become the leader of the community.

∞

Gordon

Lt. Col James Gordon 1739-1810

In 1758 James Gordon crossed the Atlantic from his home in County Antrim, Ireland, sent off by his father with £100 of goods that he hoped to sell upon his arrival in America. Instead of returning on a later vessel as originally planned, he made his way north to Albany, to the home of a distant relative, John Macomb.[3] Macomb was married to Jane Gordon, James' second cousin, and had arrived in New York in 1757, following the British Army's deployment to America during the French and Indian war.[4] McComb was a trader engaged in supplying goods and services to the troops under the command of Generals Abercrombie and Amherst. He sent Gordon north with a boatload of provisions for the army where he had an opportunity to meet and become associated with Sir William Johnson.

After the conclusion of the war, Gordon engaged in supply ventures to the military bases along the Mohawk Valley, westward to Oswego and Fort Niagara. He made two arduous trips to Detroit, while employed by the Albany trading firm of John Askin and Robert Rogers, the leader of Rogers' Rangers. Askin was another relative of Macomb, crossing the Atlantic the same year as Gordon. In 1763 Gordon and Askin set out for Detroit with three boat-loads of supplies, including fifteen kegs of rum hidden among the bales of blankets. They never made it past Niagara, stymied by Pontiac's Rebellion along the frontier.[5] The Askin and Rogers venture soon failed and the partnership was forced to file for bankruptcy.[6]

In 1764 Gordon returned to Ireland to attend to his family's financial affairs, which had not prospered because of lack of attention by his father. Upon returning to New York in 1765, he received consignments from the Schenectady firm of Phyn and Ellice. Alexander Ellice and his four brothers had emigrated from Scotland to Schenectady in 1765 and established a firm engaged in the fur trade, merchandising, and providing supplies to military posts. This proved to be a much more successful and rewarding experience for Gordon, helping him build up both his reputation and his personal estate. After almost losing his life crossing the waters of Oneida Lake, he returned to Schenectady, seeking an opportunity for a new, less dangerous, and more rewarding career. Moving to an area just opening up for settlement seemed to afford him that chance.[7]

James Gordon was busy in the years after he purchased the property along the Middleline in 1771. In addition to building both a grist mill and a saw mill, he returned to Ireland once again in 1773. Apparently his father had died and he went back home to collect his family and bring them to America. He returned with his mother, Martha, his sisters, Sarah and Jane, and Jane's husband, George Scott the next year. Scott purchased fifty acres from Gordon along the creek that would later bear the seller's name. This was part of the larger six-hundred acre lot in the northeast corner of the Five-Mile Square that he apparently purchased as an investment. He subdivided that parcel into eight fifty-acre lots and ironically sold three of them to men who would show sympathy to the British cause in the conflict now looming.[8] Another lot was given to James Gordon, Jr.—presumably his son from a previous relationship.[9]

The next year, 1775, was a landmark year for Gordon. On a personal level his mother died, the first member of Eliphalet Ball's newly organized Presbyterian Church to pass on, and in March he married Mary Ball, the Reverend's daughter. He now had links to the other principal community in the five-mile square. Gordon attended to these family matters while becoming increasingly involved as a leader in the patriot cause. In October he was commissioned by the Provincial Congress as a Lieutenant Colonel in the Albany County Militia.[10] He had become an ardent patriot, leaving little time to develop his commercial activities during the war years. His mills apparently limited their operation to fulfilling the needs of the locals. There is no evidence that he supplied the military with provisions or lumber during the conflict.

∞

Benedict and Barnum

On June 16, 1772 Elisha Benedict purchased a two-hundred-acre lot on the east side of Middleline Road from Gysbert Fonda for £161, twice the amount Fonda had paid the Trustees the year before.[11] With this purchase, Benedict settled up the road from James Gordon and became one of the first of the Connecticut contingent to establish roots along the Middleline. Over the course of the next several years Elisha would be joined by many others making the move north from that Colony. Many of them came from families who traveled similar paths, their journeys going back to the early days of settlement.

Elisha's family history actually begins in Southhold, Long Island where his great-grandfather Thomas Benedict emigrated from England in the 1640's. At that time Long Island was under the influence, if not the strict jurisdiction, of Connecticut. With the English takeover of New Netherlands from the Dutch in 1664, the people on the west end of the

Island became increasingly concerned that the Anglican influence of New York would impact their Puritan religious beliefs. Thomas had been involved in the establishment of the first Presbyterian Church in America in Jamaica on Long Island in 1662. The following year he joined in petitions to the General Court of Connecticut requesting annexation of several Long Island towns to Connecticut. When nothing came of these attempts, he made the decision to move across the Sound to a more secure and comfortable environment, settling in the town of Norwalk. There, in 1665, he purchased a four-acre lot in the center of town, next to the Rev. Thomas Hanford and just across the street from the First Meeting House and the parade ground.[12] Thomas quickly became a man of influence in his new home, holding several town offices including Selectman, Town Clerk and eventually serving as a representative in the General Assembly. He continued his faithful support of the church as well, serving as Deacon for many years. In his 1689 Will he distributed his homestead and household movables to his wife Mary and multiple lots to his sons and grandchildren.[13]

It is in Norwalk that we first see a confluence of families whose names would reappear as first settlers in Ball's Town and along Middleline Road. In a 1687 list of the estates of the inhabitants of Norwalk we find the names of five Benedicts, five Gregories, five Betts and one Barnum family.[14] In a map of the ancient home-lots Thomas Benedict, Jr lived across the street from his father. Thomas Betts, Thomas Barnum, Edward Nash and John Gregory, Sr and Jr. all lived nearby on their four-acre home lots. Clearly, one path to Ball's Town began in Norwalk.

In 1685, Thomas' sons Samuel and James (Elisha's grandfather who had married Sarah Gregory in 1676), joined with their two brothers-in-law, James Beebe and Judah Gregory and four others to found the Town of Danbury, twenty miles north of Norwalk. Their homes were located close together on the east side of the road which was later named Main Street.[15] The Benedict family remained in Danbury for the next several generations and continued to play a leadership role in both the church and the government. Elisha's father Thomas served as Justice of the Peace, District Judge and was a member of the Connecticut Legislature for thirty years, 1737-1766. [16]

Elisha was born in April 1736 in Danbury. By 1758 he was married to Jerusha Starr Barnum, a widow with three children. Several years older than Elisha, she had already experienced tragedy. She had married her first husband, Thomas Barnum, in Danbury in 1748. Their first son, another Thomas, was born in August 1749. In 1755, at the beginning of the French and Indian War, Thomas Sr. was commissioned as a 2nd Lieutenant in the Second Connecticut Regiment under the command of Lieutenant Colonel Nathan Whiting. This regiment fought at the Battle of Lake George on September 8, 1755. Falling into an ambush by the French and their Canadian Indian allies, the British militia suffered severe casualties. Over two hundred fifty were killed. It is likely that Barnum died in this engagement since his recently-written Will was probated on October 1.[17] His son, Thomas Jr., married Achsah Benedict in 1772. They moved to Ball's Town during the winter of 1774, and bought a farm on the Middleline across the road from his mother and stepfather Elisha. There in the spring they built their log house and began clearing the land.[18]

The Thomas Barnum who moved to Ball's Town was the fifth of that name. The first Thomas was born in County Kent, England around 1625. He first appeared in American records when he purchased land in Fairfield in 1673.[19] Five years later he moved on to Norwalk and, in 1685, became one of the first settlers of Danbury, moving in across the street from the Benedict brothers.[20]

The Benedict, Barnum, and Starr families had been intertwined for several generations. Jersuha Starr was the granddaughter of Josiah Starr. As a child, soon after his father died in 1658, Josiah moved from Charlestown, Massachussetts to Long Island. Following the path of the Benedict family, he moved to Danbury, Connecticut in 1693, along with several of his neighbors. There he joined with Samuel and James Benedict as one of the six proprietors who were finally granted a patent for the town in 1702, seventeen years after the first settlement.[21] He became a large landowner in Danbury, owning property in multiple locations in the town, as evidenced by his Will.[22]

With his purchase in 1772, Elisha Benedict and his extended family were among the first settlers on Middleline Road. At thirty-six, he was known as an innkeeper, but apparently had a military background as well. In 1771 he had petitioned the Albany Common Council to be appointed Marshal, and later, in 1774, he was engaged by the New York

Provincial Congress to form military companies in the New Hampshire Grants (Vermont).[23] The next year he was commissioned captain in the 2nd New York Continental Regiment and was present in the campaign against Quebec in 1776.[24]

Apparently Elisha's military service did not impress one of his new neighbors, James Gordon. In the years immediately after his settlement on Middleline Road Gordon became active in the patriot cause, often serving as the spokesman for the local residents in communications with the Albany Committee of Correspondence. In June, 1775 it appears that Benedict had taken it upon himself to promote the cause by bringing an Association agreement to the Ball's Town residents for their signatures. In the early days of the rebellion, signing these Associations was taken as proof of support for the authority of the Continental Congress. Gordon seemed to be much offended by this usurpation of his authority. He felt he had been given that responsibility by the people of his district. Gordon clearly expressed his outrage to the committee stating,

> Mr. Benedict of this place arrived here from Albany and brings an Association with him adopted to this place and some Resolves of the Congress sitting in New York. The people here in general take it much amiss that they should be treated with so much disrespect as to have the public business of this place in a manner committed to a man, neither in whose principles or abilities they choose to place any confidence, when at the same time there was a person appointed for that purpose by their unanimous consent.[25]

While many of the settlers moving to Middleline Road were connected through family relationships and as neighbors in their old hometowns, it seems not everyone were friends.

Apparently Gordon won this argument with the Albany Committee since he was one of five Ball's Town men to form their own committee. Gordon was joined by Andrew Mitchell, Eliphalet Kellogg and Stephen White, who had been recruited by Eliphalet Ball, and made their homesteads along Long Lake. The fifth person, Tyrannus Collins, was Gordon's immediate neighbor. Collins had built his cabin just across the Mourning Kill, near the stream where the Gordon mills were now in production.

∞

Collins and Stow

Guilford, one of the oldest towns in Connecticut, today conducts walking tours that take the visitor past homes once inhabited by the ancestors of several Middleline Road families. Guilford was first settled in 1639, one year after Rev. John Davenport founded the colony of New Haven, just to the west along the Quinnipiac River. In that year the Rev. Henry Whitfield and a group of about forty settlers left England on the *St. John* bound for New Haven, escaping persecution in a country that soon was to be plunged into civil war. While at sea twenty-five heads of families signed a covenant binding themselves together much as the Pilgrims had done aboard the Mayflower nineteen years earlier. Upon arrival, they purchased land from the local Indians and the settlement was established. Three hundred seventy-five years later, in 2014, a contemporary copy of the Guilford Covenant was on display and a large granite slab was erected to celebrate the 375th anniversary of the founding of the town.[26]

John Collins arrived in Guilford from Middletown, Connecticut in 1669, and married Mary Kingsworth that same year. Both had recently lost their spouses. Mary's husband, Henry Kingsworth, had been one of the founders of Guilford. He had built an imposing post and beam salt-box as early as 1645 that became their home. John engaged in the tanning and shoemaking trades that he had learned from his father (also named John) and supplemented his income by teaching at the local grammar school.[27] Like many other early arrivals, Collins acquired property from town land grants as well as private purchases. In 1674, the town gave him eight acres and he purchased five acres near the mill pond from Mathew Bellany. The next year he purchased an additional twenty acres from Nathaniel Chittenden.[28] The Collins family was to reside in Guilford for the next several generations, and built several other 18th century homes that can still be seen today.[29]

While in Middletown, in the 1660's, John would have been aware of a controversy that erupted in the church that involved two families whose descendants would continue to be interrelated one-hundred years later. In 1652 Rev. Samuel Stow, a 1645 graduate of Harvard College, became the minister of the First Congregational Church in Middletown. Samuel had arrived in New England in 1634 on the *Elizabeth* with his father John, his mother and five siblings. He was a leading citizen of Boston, twice elected to the General Court of Massachusetts Bay Colony.[30] Samuel apparently dissatisfied the members of his flock in Middletown. His tenure as minister was short-lived and in 1661 the General Court declared the town "free from Mr. Stow as their engaged minister."[31]

Some years later, in 1668, this vacancy was filled by Rev. Nathaniel Collins at the same time that his cousin John was moving to Guilford. Collins's time in the pulpit proved to be a much more rewarding experience than that of Samuel Stow. He proved to be successful both in the pulpit and in building an estate for his family. He acquired several tracts of land during his tenure. The largest was a 563 acre estate he purchased in 1672 from John Tallcott next to the land of Samuel Stow, the former minister.[32] Noting Collins' death in 1684 at the early age of 42, Cotton Mather lamented "there were more wounds given by his death to the whole colony of Connecticut in our New England than the body of Caesar did receive when he fell wounded in the senate-house."[33]

Both the Collins and Stow families became leading citizens in Middletown in the late 17th and early 18th centuries. But just as John Collins had migrated south to Guilford, members of the Stow family followed. In 1743 Isaac Stow, living in Middletown, married Hepzibah Collins of Guilford and moved there. Hepzibah was the great-granddaughter of the first John Collins who had moved to Guilford seventy years earlier. Both the Stow and Collins families were tradesmen over several generations — tanners, shoemakers, and blacksmiths. Isaac bought a small lot adjacent to the town green and built a home for his new bride. The small piece of land was sufficient for a substantial house with five bays and smokehouse in the attic, as well as a blacksmith shop behind the house where Isaac made horseshoes, hinges and other household hardware.[34] This home, pleasantly restored and maintained, is on the town's walking tour today.

Isaac and Hepzibah Stow brought ten children into the world, but most did not survive childhood. When Isaac Jr. was born in 1756 as the sixth child, only two sisters were there to greet him and only one of those, Olive, would live to adulthood. Isaac himself was the only son that would achieve that milestone and his life was also to be cut short. [35]

A few blocks away Hepzibah's father, John Collins, was equally productive and more fortunate. When Tyrannus was born in 1741 he was the last of twelve children of his parents John and Rachel (Mix). Most of them lived to adulthood, married and raised children of their own.[36] Tyrannus married young and well, and maybe twice. The records conflict on his second marriage. In 1759, at the age of eighteen he married Abigail Peck from the adjacent town of Wallingford.[37] She was the daughter of Samuel Peck and great-granddaughter of William Peck, one of the original proprietors of New Haven.[38] They had three children after which Abigail may have died. Some accounts indicate that he soon remarried to another Abigail, Abigail Bishop, from another family that could trace their roots back to the founding of New Haven.[39] James Bishop had come to the colony as a young man in 1638 while still under the guardianship of his older brother Henry, who served as a farmer for the Rev. Davenport. It is probable that Henry and James would have known Ailing Ball, ancestor of Eliphalet Ball, who managed Davenport's farm during these years.[40] Members of the Bishop family soon drifted eastward. When the General Court issued a patent officially establishing the town of Guilford, John Collins and Stephen Bishop were two of the twelve proprietors.[41]

The Bishop, Peck and Collins families had been established in Guilford for over one hundred years when Tyrannus and Abigail, accompanied by other family members, made a major move. He most likely joined his older brothers, John and Manasseh, in moving north to Berkshire County, Massachusetts around 1765. They became one of the first families to settle in the newly formed Town of Richmond on the New York border. Berkshire had only been set off from the County of Hampshire in 1761. The future towns of Richmond and Lennox were purchased from the Mahican Indians in 1762 for £2,250 and established as towns in 1765 and 1767, the year the Collins family arrived.[42]

In January 1766, their first son, Manasseh was born there. He took the name of his uncle who had no children of his own.[43] Richmond was a remote town in a remote county. In the 1730's a mission church had been established to promote Christianity among the local Indians who became known as the Stockbridge Indians. However, very few whites settled in the area, reticent to locate in a mountainous area subject to incursions by the French and their Indian allies. One could ask why, after all these years of living in a settled community by the sea, they made such a significant decision to pick up and move north to the almost uninhabited mountains.

One of the long accepted catalysts of westward migration throughout American history was the pressure on the younger sons of large families to move away and start a new life on the frontier. Average size farms, of 100-200 acres owned by their parents, could not be divided among several children and still remain viable. In addition, finding suitable adjacent land at a reasonable price was becoming a problem in Connecticut in the 1760's. Land prices were rising as the population increased. In the 1720's land around Guilford was £2.5 an acre, but by the mid 1760's it had risen to £3.8.[44] Connecticut's population had almost doubled during the same period, from 75,000 to 142,000.[45] At the same time, the end of the French and Indian War opened vast new areas for settlement, as we have seen in the pressure to partition the Kayaderosseras Patent. The attraction of these lands motivated young men in Connecticut to move north and west, seeking cheaper and more fertile land in the New Hampshire Grants, Massachusetts, and New York. In a study of migration from the New Haven area, whereas only 3% of men born before 1730 left the colony, 11% of those born in the 1740's did so.[46]

Berkshire County's population grew rapidly after 1763 as the threat of warfare receded. Tyrannus Collins was in that group of pioneers who ventured away from the home that he had known with a wife and a growing family. Together he and Abigail had six children in the next decade. Joined by his brothers and members of his wife's family, the Collins established their own family enclave in Richmond.

While the extended family maintained a presence in Richmond for many years, ten years later we find Tyrannus moving again to the frontier, this time fifty miles northwest to Ball's Town in the Kayaderosseras Patent. We can only speculate on the motives for this second uprooting. He may have found the poor, rocky soil an unsuitable place to provide for his family. He may have been drawn there by the advertisements for the land appearing in newspapers back home in New Haven, Connecticut.

> These lands, cannot but invite many competitors for them, especially as they are intersected by many valuable steams of water, not far distant from, and emptying into the Mohawk or Hudson River, which a part of the premises adjoin, and from whence all sorts of produce and lumber may be transported to New York, with little expense.[47]

Eliphalet Ball, Isaac Low, Dirck Lefferts and the other trustees of the Patent were hard at work marketing the land, not just in New York, but in Connecticut as well. The reference to the prospect for making a living through commerce, rather than simply subsistence farming, may have been very attractive to this thirty-year-old family man from Guilford, whose ancestors were craftsmen, not farmers.

These reasons may have contributed to his decision to relocate, but there may have been another more personal connection. As noted, in 1775 Tryannus was appointed, along with James Gordon to serve on the Ball's Town Committee of Safety. This neighbor of Gordon was soon to become a major in the Albany Militia commanded by him. Given Gordon's influence, it seems likely that the appointment of Tyrannus may have been made based on the support of his neighbor. And there was one more connection that strengthened the bonds between these two men.

Isaac Stow, Tyrannus' nephew, was twenty years old at the beginning of the Revolutionary War and was looking for work. His father, Isaac Sr., had died in 1773 at the age of fifty-five and his mother a year later, only fifty years old. Isaac Jr. had married Phoebe Griswold in 1775 and fathered two children before her death at twenty-seven.[48] Clearly the early deaths of his parents, siblings and now his wife, left this young man with no reason to stay in Guilford. It is not known exactly when Isaac traveled north to Richmond to join his uncle, but it is likely that he soon followed Tyrannus to the land along the Mourning Kill in Ball's Town. James Gordon was in the process of erecting both sawmills and gristmills along the "many valuable streams of water" in the town, and he needed a miller. Tyrannus could provide one. Isaac not only found work, he found love. Before leaving Richmond with his uncle he married Sarah Pierson, daughter of Paul Pierson, another recent arrival to that town.

∞

Pierson

Southampton was another of those Long Island towns with an early affil-iation with Connecticut. Forty families left Lynn, Massachusetts to settle there in 1640, among them their minister, Reverend Abraham Pierson. When Southampton annexed itself to Hartford in 1644, rather than join-ing the more theocratic New Haven Colony, Rev. Pierson moved to the mainland. His cousin Henry remained, establishing the Pierson clan on Long Island for the next several generations.[49] Among his nine children, son Henry was elected as a member of New York's Assembly, rising to become Speaker in the 1690's in the wake of Leisler's Rebellion. He, in turn, sired a large family, among them Josiah Pierson. Josiah outdid both his grandfather and father in that department, being married three times and raising seventeen children. As a farmer raising a large family, he apparently had neither the time nor the ambition to become involved in the civic life of Southampton.[50] His only known involvement in political life was illustrated by what he did not do. At the age of 80, in May 1775, he was the only person identified as refusing to sign an Association pledg-ing support to the actions of the Continental Congress. His allegiance to England remained strong, even if he could not pass that same loyalty on to his sons.[51]

Earlier, three of Josiah's sons had moved north to Berkshire County. In the 1760's Paul, the oldest, joined by younger brothers John and Benjamin, settled in Richmond. Benjamin became active in the affairs of the town serving as a Selectman, and was appointed to draft a peti-tion for a Massachusetts State Constitutional Convention in 1777.[52] Paul served in the Richmond Militia during the Revolutionary War and it was in that town that his daughter Sarah met and married Isaac Stow, recently arrived from Guilford. It is likely that Isaac, his new bride, and his father-in-law's family moved to Ball's Town at the invitation of his uncle, Tyrannus Collins.

Stow built his cabin on the lowlands just north of the Mourning Kill and across the road from Gordon's mills. Isaac Stow could be counted on to maintain the business as best he could while Gordon was away at war.[53]

Paul Pierson had settled up the Middleline from his son-in-law erecting his home along the slope of the highest prominence on the road. He could not have known that this ridge would soon achieve strategic importance in the struggle for independence when it was then referred to as Pierson's Ridge. Years later it became known as Court House Hill. Paul was focused on building his cabin and clearing a small area to begin his farm. We can assume his cabin was similar to others along the Middleline and other frontier abodes. They were usually built as a square, twenty feet long and twenty feet wide. The cabin could be erected quickly with the help of his neighbors to provide shelter for his family. Additions and improvements would soon follow as large stands of pine were harvested and sent to Gordon's sawmills, humming with the business provided by the new arrivals.

Often the next activity would be to grub a small piece of wetland for use as a meadow to grow hay to provide for the cows during the winter. He and his sons would then have begun the painstaking task of clearing the land for planting at the slow pace of about one acre per month. The small trees would be cut first, and then gathered around the base of the larger trees and burned. This would prevent the trees from leafing out, allowing vital sunlight to reach their fields. Wheat and oats would often be the first crop to be sown in these small opening for their own needs as well as providing the family with some surplus for purchasing supplies.[54]

Paul would have acquired a cow or two for milking. In the first years they would not be pastured, but left to roam free in the woods, a cow bell around their necks. The family may have acquired a horse for plowing but the poorest settlers may have had to do without one the first few years. Vegetables would have been planted to feed the family most likely tended to by his wife, Elizabeth, and his daughters, Susannah and Sarah. Necessary farm equipment such as a plough, broad ax, shovels and hay forks were purchased from the credit he received from the sale of his produce and timber. Cash was a rare commodity among the average Middleline Road settler. Many derived what cash they needed by producing and selling potash, a by-product of the land clearing process.[55]

At the end of a long day, Paul could sit in front of his cabin and look across the Middleline to another small opening in the forest where Edward Watrous was hard at work establishing his own homestead.

∞

Watrous

Jacob Waterhouse had no sooner arrived in Wethersfield, Connecticut in 1637 when he was off to war. He was one of eighteen men from that settlement that answered the call to seek revenge on the Pequot tribe for a series of attacks against the first Connecticut settlers. For the men of Wethersfield, the call to arms was personal. John Oldham had led the first contingent of ten families to this location along the Connecticut River in 1635 and established the first settlement in the Colony. In August the next year his mutilated body was found on his ship near Block Island, killed by Indians. This was followed by a larger, more immediate provocation. In April 1637, two hundred Pequot warriors attacked a small group of colonists at work in a meadow outside of Wethersfield. Nine were killed, including a woman and her child. The Wethersfield men joined others from the Connecticut, Plymouth and Massachusetts Bay Colonies under the leadership of Captain John Mason, to destroy the Pequots. This they accomplished by surrounding and burning their palisaded village on the Mystic River killing hundreds of men, women and children.[56]

Jacob returned to Wethersfield and built his cabin on a 2-½ acre lot. There his first three children were born—Rebecca, Isaac and Abraham. Eight years later, in 1645, he moved from this inland village to become one of the original founders of New London under the leadership of John Winthrop Jr., son of the first Governor of the Massachusetts Bay colony, and future governor of Connecticut. Winthrop had founded Saybrook at the mouth of the Connecticut River before the Pequot War and was granted the land known as Pequot Harbor in 1644, where the new colony was planted. Jacob's early association with Winthrop was to prove beneficial for him and his descendants.[57] In 1649 he was chosen to oversee the construction of the weirs (dams) and the next year erected the town grist mill, which still stands. In addition to his six-acre house lot, he received grants for land north of the town, across the Mystic River and along a brook. He would deed these lands to his son Abraham in 1674, the year of his son's marriage.[58]

Jacob died in 1676, either of natural causes, or "riding his horse over a cliff while bringing news to colonists of a victory over the Indians in King Phillip's War" as one unsubstantiated story claims.[59] His son Abraham married Rebecca Clark and later received a fifty-acre allotment in the adjacent town of Lyme. There their son Isaac was born in 1680. Soon thereafter the family moved westward across the Connecticut River to Saybrook, and took up residence on land Rebecca had inherited from her father, John Clark. Although a carpenter by trade, Abraham's inheritances raised his station considerably, allowing him to deed his lands in Lyme to his son Isaac. In 1707 and 1708 Isaac received a total of sixty acres from his father. Later, in 1718, Abraham Waterus deeded to his "well beloved and dutiful son Isaac Waterus of Lyme, yeoman" all his lands in Lyme.[60]

Note that Abraham is no longer "Waterhouse" but "Waterus". Land grants from the town of Lyme indicate that Abraham and his brother Isaac were using that name as early as 1668. The names seem to have been used interchangeably for a couple of generations. In records of Lyme births, marriages and deaths, Abraham's brother Isaac, born in 1641, is listed as Watrous, while Abraham's grandson Andrew, the father of Edward Watrous of Ball's Town is named Waterhouse.[61]

Dutiful son Isaac married Elizabeth Lord in 1700 and together they had one son, Isaac, Jr., before her early death.[62] He remarried and had another ten children, but there is controversy over the name of his second wife. Some genealogies claim she was Elizabeth Bronson, while others dispute that.[63] What is clear is that their son Andrew was born in Lyme in 1717 and married Dinah Westcott of New London in 1743. Together they had five daughters and one son living at the time of his early death in 1759 at the age of forty-two. His only son, Edward Allen Watrous, was six at the time, and Edward's sisters ranged in age from fifteen down to one-year-old. Andrew prepared his will in October, 1758, shortly before he was admitted to the church. His six children were all baptized at the same time, in December of that year.[64]

Dinah was soon remarried to Lieutenant Richard Hayes who became stepfather to Edward and his sisters.[65] Hayes had served in the local militia for the Town of Lyme in 1750 and was commissioned as First Lieutenant of the Third Regiment of Connecticut Troops for the 1758 campaign of the French and Indian War. That he did not participate in the 1759 campaign makes it at least possible that his first wife, Patience Mark, died at that time. Widow and widower began their life together with a blended family of eleven children under the age of nineteen. At age six, Edward was the youngest boy. His step-brothers ranged in age from ten to nineteen.[66]

Edward Allan Watrous came to Ball's Town by 1775 at the age of twenty-two. Soon thereafter he became the second son-in-law of Paul Pierson to live on Middleline Road. He had married Susannah Pierson, "the girl who lived next door", or rather across the road.

∞

Higby

In a time when newly arrived immigrants from England often moved frequently, seeking the ideal location to settle down, one ancestor of another Middleline Road pioneer was known to exhibit a "singularly roaming disposition."[67] Edward Higby was one of the first settlers of New London in 1646, traveling from Cambridge, Massachusetts with his new wife, Jedidah, and father-in-law, Thomas Skidmore. Skidmore had been an associate of John Winthrop, Jr. since they traveled to America together in 1635. They had earlier joined together as part of the group that established the plantation at Saybrook.[68] Higby and Skidmore arrived in New London one year after Jacob Waterhouse, but unlike Jacob, they did not stay long. In 1648 the families moved westward to Stratford and engaged in trading along the coast, and across the Sound with the new settlements on Long Island. By 1658 they had moved to Long Island, first settling in Huntington and soon moving again, westward eight miles to Cold Spring Harbor. One of Edward's sailing ventures almost cost him his life. In 1659 he failed to return from one of his trading voyages and the next year, his family assuming he was lost at sea, probated his will. About this time he reappeared, only to witness the death of his wife of fifteen years in 1662.[69]

Five years on Long Island with five young children was apparently enough for Edward as he parted company with his father-in-law soon after his wife's death. We next find him in Middletown, Connecticut where he married Lydia Smith and started a second family. In 1664 he purchased land from Seaukett, a local Indian sachem, which was confirmed by the General Court the next year. This land was five miles to the west of

Middletown, encompassing the land later named Higby Mountain.[70] This was to become the home of several generations of Higbys, but Edward himself moved on. In 1675 he sold 134 acres to his son John. Two years later Edward exchanged property with Abraham Smith of Jamaica, New York, and moved back to Long Island.[71] This time he resided in the town of Jamaica until his death in 1699. His twenty-year-old son John stayed behind in Middletown to farm the land he received from his father, establishing the Connecticut branch of the family. He and his wife, Rebecca Treadwell, raised several children before his untimely death in 1688 at the age of thirty. His father outlived him by ten years. It must have pained him to include "Rebecca Higby the relic of John Higby" in his Will.[72]

Rebecca's son Edward was four years old when his father died. In 1700, at the age of sixteen, he went to live with his uncle, Samuel Treadwell, in Fairfield. In 1706 he married Rebecca Wheeler of Stratford. They moved back to Middletown when he was appointed administrator of his mother's estate upon her death in 1707.[73] He and his wife raised six children on land in the area known as Newfield. In addition to his farms, Edward became engaged in the mining business. In 1737 he joined a partnership to form the Golden Parlour Mining Company in neighboring Wallingford. This venture was the latest of several attempts to develop the copper mining business in Connecticut, but like earlier attempts, it failed after a few years.[74]

Unlike his parents, Edward lived a long life, dying at the age of ninety-one in 1775. He outlived his wife by four years. After her death he moved north to the adjacent town of Westfield with his son John where they joined the church in 1773. In order to settle his estate, his sons, John and David, found it necessary to seek approval of the Connecticut Assembly to sell land to cover his debts of £14.[75]

By that time, John himself was in his late sixties and his five middle-aged sons were finding it increasingly hard to prosper on the divided family lands. Three generations of large families, rising land values, the increasing attraction of lands on the frontier, and the disruption of the Revolution all combined to cause John's son's to move away from the familiarity of the homesteads and town that had been the home of the Higby clan for a century. Four of the five sons moved away by the 1770's. John Jr. would end up settling on the west side of Middleline Road, but not before passing through other new settlements that had already been a way-station for other families on their travels from Connecticut homelands to Ball's Town. Early histories of Richmond, Massachusetts note that the family of John Higby was living there as early as 1763, as the French and Indian War ended. It is likely that he would have known Tyrannus Collins who arrived a few years later. Interestingly, John's point of origin in the Richmond records is not listed as Middletown, the place of his birth, but Canaan, Connecticut. By the age of thirty, John had already moved twice in his quest for a better life.[76]

Canaan was located in the northwest corner of Connecticut, an area that had remained virtually free of settlers for almost one hundred years after the founding of Hartford, fifty miles to the east. There were several contributing factors to the late opening of the last undeveloped lands in northwest Connecticut in the first half of the 18th century. This entire area had been deeded to the towns of Hartford and Windsor in 1687 but remained unsettled for the next fifty years. With the discovery of high-grade iron ore in the far northwest Town of Salisbury in the early 1700's and the pressure for land from a growing population, the colony decided to act. A deal was made with the older towns to cede back a portion of this land to the colony, which then parceled the land into seven townships.[77] Each township was then divided into shares and sold at public auctions held in various towns in the colony in 1738. Two of those towns, Canaan and Sharon, were to be transitional homesteads for several families that would later move to Middleline Road.

In Canaan and the other western towns the proprietors further divided the land into parcels to be sold to purchasers who agreed to settle on the land in two years, build a house of at least eighteen feet square, and clear and fence at least six acres of land. If these conditions were not met the land would be forfeited.[78] It is not known if John Higby purchased land under these conditions, but he apparently settled in Canaan soon after he married Mindwell Lewis in Middletown in 1755 at the age of twenty-two. Their first four children were born there between 1757 and 1761.[79] His other nine children were born in Richmond, their birth records indicating that he moved to Ball's Town around 1778. Higby built his cabin next to Paul Pierson just over the crest of what would become known as Court House Hill, becoming the latest Richmond resident to settle along the Middleline.

∞

Wilcox

Five miles north of Higby Mountain in Middletown lies a 1747 farmhouse that still stands as a reminder of another old New England Puritan family. Jeremiah Wilcox and his wife, Mary Stow, raised twelve children here in the mid-18th century. Mary Stow was born in 1717, the same year as her cousin Isaac who later moved to Guilford and married Hepzibah Collins. Like their neighbors the Higbys, Jeremiah's family had made their home in Middletown for several generations. In fact, the Wilcox family had been there even longer. Jeremiah's great-grandfather, John Wilcox Jr., was living there by 1654, early enough to be aware of the controversy over the tenure of the first minister, Samuel Stow. At this early date, when Middletown consisted of only a few settlers, it is certain that the Wilcox, Collins, Stowe and Higby families knew each other and interacted on a routine basis, engaging in trade, participating in town affairs, and attending church each Sunday.

John Wilcox's father John was one of the first settlers of Hartford. He had accompanied Rev. Thomas Hooker from Cambridge, Massachusetts in 1636 to establish a new settlement along the banks of the Connecticut River, just north of Wethersfield, which had been established a year earlier. He probably was present in the meeting house in May 1638 when Hooker declared that "The foundation of authority is laid firstly in the free consent of people." This sermon became the driving force in establishing colonial government when the Fundamental Orders of Connecticut were adopted by the General Court in 1639. This document was a departure from the government in Massachusetts Bay since it required no religious test for voting and omitted any reference to the crown.[80]

Wilcox, Sr. was one of the strongest supporters of Hooker and was among a core group of fourteen men closest to the Minister and the church teacher, Samuel Stone. He acquired an extensive amount of property in several different locations around Hartford. His home lot was along a bend in the Little River, now within the bounds of Bushnell Park. He was active in civic affairs, serving as Surveyor of Highways and Selectman. John Wilcox Sr. died in 1651. His Will conveyed his extensive property and mentioned two indentured servants who were to serve out the remainder of their apprenticeship under the supervision of his wife Mary. An inventory of his estate indicated a value of £391, among the largest estates of the original Hartford settlers.[81]

John Jr. married the first two of his four wives in Hartford before his father died, but soon thereafter moved down the river to Middletown. There he was cited in 1653 for failure to occupy the land granted to him. He purchased the home lot as well as meadow and upland from Mathias Treat for £50. As part of the deal, Mathias agreed to "build a substantial barn 40-foot-long and 20 foot wide with a lean-to on one side and both ends." John quickly acquired several additional pieces of land, consistent with the land ownership process in many New England towns. His property was a patchwork of many small lots and larger tracts located throughout the town. By 1656 his list of town lands included at least twelve different parcels. All were small, one to five acres of meadows for grazing, wood lots, swamps, and upland for crops.[82]

John married his second wife, Catharine Stoughton, in 1650 and they had five children before she died in 1660. He then married his third wife, Mary Long Farnsworth, of Dorchester, Massachusetts, and moved there. By 1666 he was back in Middletown and mortgaged his property there to pay her back for £250 he had borrowed from her before they married.[83] Although he was identified in the land and probate records as a pail maker, at the time of his death in 1676 his estate totaled £409 and included: a house, barn, and orchard on his home lot; over 1000 acres in several parcels; 440 foot of boards; 32,000 nails; a crosscut saw and 57 bushels of Indian corn. As an only son and because of his fortunate marriages, John had done well. He had seven children with his four wives, five of them boys. So began the disbursal of property accumulated in the early Wilcox generations.[84]

John's son and grandson, both named Samuel, continued to live in Middletown, but life was not to be kind to them and their families. The first Samuel married Abigail Whitmore in 1683. Samuel Jr. was born a year later and in 1687 Abigail had twins. The girl, Abigail, and her mother died the same month in 1688, leaving Samuel to raise two young sons. He seems to have never remarried, and when he died intestate in 1713 his two sons, Samuel and Frances, shared his estate, but the details are unknown.[85] Samuel married Esther Bushnell, daughter of William Bushnell, a carpenter from Saybrook, in 1707. Together they raised seven children. His life was cut short when he died in 1724 at the age of forty. His wife and his brother, Frances, were his only heirs. In 1732 Esther was granted guardianship of three of her children, including son Jeremiah who was only nine when his father died.[86]

Jeremiah married Mary Stow in 1736 and built his home as a 1-½ story farmhouse. It is not known if the house was enlarged to the full two stories seen today before he died in 1760, or if it was a later addition. Mary was left to raise eight children under sixteen, the youngest of which was Lemuel, only a year old. Jeremiah, like his father, had died young, leaving his large family to make their way in the world as best they could.

For Lemuel, that way would include joining the patriot cause during the Revolutionary War. He was eighteen in 1777 when he joined the 6th Connecticut Line. During that time he was mainly stationed among the continental troops who were bottling up the British around New York City. But in 1781 he marched south with his regiment to participate in the culminating event of the war—the siege of Yorktown and the capture of Lord Cornwallis. His discharge in 1783 was signed off by George Washington himself.[87]

If later accounts concerning the British raid of October 1780 are accurate, Lemuel managed to establish a home near John Higby along the Middleline while serving in the continental army. It may have been that he accompanied Connecticut troops to the area during the Saratoga campaign, and settled here. Or was he tipped off to the prospects of opportunities on the frontier by his cousin, Isaac Stow, who had just arrived in Ball's Town to take up his new job as James Gordon's miller? Or did he already have his eye on Austie, the sixteen-year-old daughter of John Higby?

∞

Filer

It is interesting to note that every family along Middleline Road affected by the 1780 British Raid was related in some way to another family on that road, except one, Jonathan Filer. Filer settled on the next ridge north of the homes of Paul Pierson and John Higby on Pierson's Ridge. The harrowing experience of his family during the raid will be related in a later chapter.

Filer's great-grandfather George Fyler (sic) may have settled first in Westfield along the Connecticut valley. He was a physician in England and continued his occupation as a physician and surgeon after emigrating. At some point he moved to East Hampton, Long Island where the family became ensconced for the next several generations. His son, Samuel, and grandson Thomas, were active in the civic affairs of the town which was located on the remote southern peninsula of Long Island.[88]

It was Thomas' sons, Thomas and Jonathan, responding to the upheaval of the Revolutionary War, who moved away from their hometown and joined the patriot cause. Thomas, the older brother, enlisted first. In November 1776, he joined the 4th New York Regiment. He survived the Battles of Saratoga where the 4th served as part of General Enoch Poor's Brigade under the left wing of the American forces, commanded by Benedict Arnold. One month later, Thomas was killed by a fellow soldier under confused circumstances. Family tradition held that he was killed while duck hunting.[89]

Jonathan's path before he settled on Middleline Road is more difficult to trace. He had married Tryphena Leakes in East Hampton in 1772 and immediately started a family. They had two sons and a daughter by 1777, just the beginning of a family that would grow to include ten children over the next twenty years. In August of that year, a Jonathan Filer served a seven-day enlistment in the Berkshire Militia during the Battle of Bennington.[90] In July 1780 he is listed as a private in the 4th New York Regiment.[91] Presumably, by this time he had established himself and his family along the Middleline. The accounts of the 1780 raid indicate that the Filer household included at least one extended family member, Hannah Leakes, his mother-in-law. The relationships that drew him to this place have so far eluded investigation. His service in the Berkshire Militia may hint at a connection with the Richmond contingent. Hopefully, future researchers will uncover this mystery.

∞

Scott and Kennedy

Five families living along Middleline road were born in Ireland, but were not Irish in any real sense. They were lowland Scots. As previously mentioned, James Gordon had been in the New World the longest, arriving from Killead, County Antrim in Ulster (Northern Ireland) in 1758. In 1773 he was joined by several members of his own family. His mother Martha, sister Jane, and brother-in-law, George Scott, and two of Gordon's unmarried sisters, Martha and Sarah, all made the trip. Gordon persuaded them, along with several of their Ulster neighbors, to join him in the new settlement of Ball's Town. They came across the Atlantic in the *Mary and James*, arriving in New York in the fall of 1773. Jane and George Scott were already middle-aged, bringing with them their three daughters, Mary, Margaret, and Susan.

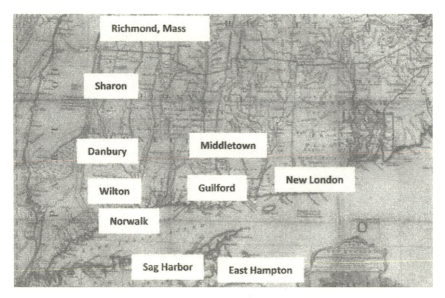

Hometowns of Middleline Road Settlers

In January, their son James was born at the Gordon home. That spring Scott purchased his homestead farm from Gordon, located two miles north on Middleline Road, near the current Ballston-Milton border.

There he engaged in erecting a saw mill, one of several mills Gordon was building in his new community.[92]

By 1780 three brothers, Thomas, John and George Kennedy, had settled north of Scott on the Middleline in what would become the Town of Milton in 1792. They had been born in the adjacent Northern Ireland county of Down and arrived in America sometime in the 1760's. Tracing their journey to Ball's Town has proven to be a challenge, but there are hints. John Kennedy married Hannah Olmstead, granddaughter of Daniel Olmstead, one of the founders of Ridgefield, Connecticut in 1768. The Olmsteads were an early Connecticut family with roots extending back to Hartford at the time of first settlement in the 1640's. Hannah's father, Ezekiel, was born in Ridgefield in 1730, but he moved his family soon after his marriage to Lydia Hoyt in 1750. Their first move was to Richmond, Massachusetts in the 1760's. Here he and his wife raised their growing family, which was to eventually include nine daughters and three sons. In Richmond they joined several of the families that have already been mentioned, including the Higbys. While John Kennedy married into the Olmstead family, his brother, George, married Mindwell Higby, daughter of John Higby. These two Kennedy brothers joined a growing list of Middleline Road residents whose journey can be traced through the small remote town of Richmond nestled in the Berkshire Mountains. However, the third brother, Thomas, married into a different family in a different town.[93]

The Gordons, Scotts and Kennedys were all from ancient clans originating in the western lowlands of Scotland. Migration from this section of Scotland, only twenty miles across the Irish Sea to the counties of Northern Ireland, had been going on for centuries. This migration was accelerated in the early 17th century during the reign of James I when land became available after the English crushed a rebellion of the native Irish. The Scots were welcomed by the English monarchy. They were similar in racial origin to the people of northern England and more importantly, they were Protestant, albeit Presbyterian, not Anglican.

Both of Gordon's grandfathers, John Gordon and John Wallace, had moved to Ireland after the Glorious Revolution in 1688.[94] As a consequence of that upheaval, deposed King James II attempted to regain his throne by rallying his supporters, called Jacobites, in Ireland. He was defeated by King William which led to the consolidation of power by the

Anglican-dominated British monarchy. The Scottish Presbyterians lost their political influence and were subject to the penal laws imposed on both Catholics and dissenters. These laws prevented them from voting or serving in the military and increased restrictions on their industries and commerce. In addition, they were subject to steep increases in rents as their land leases were renewed. This harassment, coupled with periodic crop failures, prompted many Scots-Irish to relocate to America during the 1700's. In several waves, a total of 250,000 emigrated in the decades before the American Revolution. Most arrived in Pennsylvania and from there traveled south on the Great Wagon Road into the mountainous regions of Virginia and North Carolina. But some settled in New England and participated in the migration west. These new arrivals joined sons and daughters from families with deeper roots in America.

∞

Wood

Often the big picture of the growth of the British colonies in America obscures the rich mosaic of people, beliefs and settlement patterns that existed at the local level. One of these assumptions is the uniform spread of people westward, with each new town simply a gradual outmigration from the nearest settlement. We have seen that this was not the case with the Kayaderosseras Patent, nor was it the case in northwest Connecticut. Settlement of both areas was delayed long after prosperous towns developed only a few miles away. This delay was often caused by political and economic considerations, as well as the always present threat of the French and their Indian allies. A second assumption regarding the colony of Connecticut, is that the strong Puritan heritage of its founding leaders continued among the population throughout the colonial period. Both assumptions gloss over the subtleties of the real story which is much more complex. This complexity had implications for the migration patterns of the Middleline Road families. First, let's look at another area with irregular settlement patterns.

On March 1, 1713 a curious notation was made in the Norwalk town records.

"The Town, by a majority vote frees Jonathan Wood, Sr. from paying any rate to ye ministry in Norwalk for ye future after this year's rate is paid, provided ye said Wood attends ye meeting in Ridgefield on ye Sabbath and so long as he continues to do so."[95]

The Town of Norwalk, located on the shore of Long Island Sound, was one of the earliest settlements in Connecticut. The area had been purchased from the local Indians in 1640 and the first group of settlers arrived ten years later.[96] As noted, the early townsmen included several families—Benedicts, Gregories, Betts, and Barnum—whose descendants made their way to Ball's Town. As previously mentioned, in 1685 the Benedict brothers, Samuel and James, were among the eight founders of Danbury. The northern section of Norwalk up to the border with Danbury remained essentially unsettled for the next forty years, leaving the land for the use of the local Indian tribes.

However, even with the absence of a formal settlement, families drifted into these "uninhabited" areas. Much as the McDonald brothers had built their cabin alongside Long Lake in 1763, years before the Kayaderosseras Patent was open for settlement, Jonathan Wood took up residence along the Norwalk River away from any town. Wood was the son of Timothy Wood who had moved to Hempstead, Long Island with his father Edmund.[97] Edmund had arrived in New England in 1635 and passed through Springfield, Wethersfield, and Stamford before settling on Long Island.[98] Hempstead was unlike many of the other settlements on Long Island in that it was not founded by Puritans with connections to Connecticut. Many of the original proprietors had emigrated from Yorkshire, England and were granted a patent by the governor of New Netherlands, Willem Keift, in 1644.

Jonathan never knew his father Timothy who died in 1659 at the age of thirty-seven when his son was only two. At the age of four Jonathan was apprenticed to John Smith by his mother. He became a weaver, married Mary Titus in 1683, and moved to Jamaica, New York. In 1706 he sold his property in Jamaica and purchased land north of Norwalk, in an area known as Pimpewaug, from members of the Betts family for £40.[99] Two years later, in 1708, the town of Ridgefield was established along the New

York border south of Danbury. The church in this new settlement was apparently more convenient for Jonathan and his family. Jonathan chose an ideal location for his farm, a flat fertile land that became known as "Egypt" because it could produce crops that failed everywhere else. His keen eye for good farmland attracted additional settlers who formed the town of Wilton and in 1727 a new parish church was erected.[100]

This church in Wilton was different than the church in Norwalk, and different than most of the churches in Connecticut. The first minister, Reverend Robert Sturgeon, was a Scot who had emigrated from Ireland. The church he led was Presbyterian, not Puritan. The Gordons and the Kennedys would have been comfortable within its walls since the first church in Ball's Town was also Presbyterian. However, the religious link to Ball's Town is stronger than just the similarity of the church denomination. Reverend Sturgeon stayed in Wilton only a few years. In 1731 he moved to Bedford Parish, New York, twenty miles to the west. There he served twelve years at the church later led by the Reverend Eliphalet Ball. The ties between the two towns remained close. When Reverend Ball left Bedford, he was succeeded by Reverend Samuel Mills, well-known to Wiltonians. Thus, we see another town with a close relationship with the "founder of Ballston."[101]

Jonathan Sr. died in 1727 on his original farm at "Egypt", now included in the township of Wilton. His sons had farms there also, but they soon moved a few miles north to Ridgefield where Jonathan, who was one of the proprietors, had purchased additional tracts from the Indians over the years. In Ridgefield, Jonathan Jr. married Elizabeth Munroe in 1715 and together they had twelve children. His oldest son, David, born in 1717, grew up in Ridgefield along with his seven brothers.

Ridgefield was not known as a prosperous community. Twice during the 1720's residents were exempted from paying taxes by the General Assembly, and in 1740 Ridgefield and Litchfield were censured for not submitting the ratable estates of their inhabitants and were ordered to pay £29 to the treasurer of the colony.[102] Apparently, residents struggled to make a respectable living for themselves and their families.

David Wood married Dorothy Rockwell in Ridgefield in 1744 and a new generation began with more mouths to feed. Dorothy was the widow of Josiah Rockwell who had died at the age of thirty in 1740. In

1754 David moved his growing family to Sharon, continuing the Wood family's migration northward along Connecticut's western border with New York. There in 1763 the last of his seven sons, Enoch, was born.

Sharon was another of those western Connecticut townships settled by proprietors who had purchased lots at a public auction in 1738. John Sprague was one of those proprietors who was there when the Wood family arrived. The Sprague and Wood families would become intertwined during their years spent together in Sharon.

∞

Sprague

John Sprague was the great grandson of Francis Sprague, who arrived in Plymouth in 1623 aboard the *Anne*, the earliest immigrant among the families in this study. Throughout his long life Francis proved to be an irritant to the Plymouth Colony leaders. He was an innkeeper and was several times cited in the records for selling liquor and wine without a license.[103] He was finally granted a license to serve wine at his inn in Duxbury in 1646, which was later recalled. Francis' son, John, followed in the footsteps of his father. After being granted permission to keep an inn at Duxbury as his father had done, he was called before the court for "drinking, gaming and uncivil reviling to the dishonor of God and the offence of this government," for which offense he spent two hours in the stocks.[104] John's life was cut short when he was killed at Pawtucket, Rhode Island in 1676 during King Phillip's War.[105]

John's oldest son, also named John, was born in Duxbury in 1656, where he served as a constable and church official. In 1703 he sold his inherited land in Duxbury, Bridgeport, and Dartmouth, Massachusetts and moved to Lebanon in southeastern Connecticut. Lebanon was formed in 1700 by the consolidation of several tracts of land previously purchased from the Mohegan Indians. John Sprague moved with his wife, Lydia, and their four teenage sons—Ephraim, Benjamin, Samuel, and John. There John, Sr. became a large landowner and prominent local official. He served as selectman and representative to the General Court throughout the 1710's. Of his sons, all but John remained in Lebanon and raised large families.[106]

When John, Jr. moved to Sharon in 1739, in the company of several other Lebanon families, he immediately became one of the leading citizens of the town. He was on the committee to select Sharon's first minister, Peter Pratt. When the town government was organized in the same year, John was one of its first Selectmen—even though he apparently could not write his name.[107] As one of the original proprietors, John drew the thirty-seventh home lot in the northern section of the town on the road to Salisbury. Each home lot was approximately eighty acres, a small portion of the 700 acres due to each proprietor. Distribution of the remaining land was granted in the ensuing years. In 1748 he exchanged farms with Cornelius Knickerbacker and moved a few miles north to Lakeville. Two of his sons, Jonathan and Ebenezer, remained behind in Sharon.[108]

By the time David Wood arrived in Sharon in 1754, John Sprague had moved one final time—north to Canaan on the Massachusetts border. In Canaan, John wrote his Will the same year and, upon his death in 1760 at the age of seventy, his estate was valued at £914. This was a considerable sum, partly reflecting the increase in land values during this period.[109] His accumulated wealth could only bode well for his three sons and their families.

John's son, Ebenezer Sprague, had married Elizabeth Thatcher in Lebanon and had three daughters there before moving with his father to Sharon. His wife died in 1744 and in February, 1745 he married Hannah St. John, daughter of Mathew St. John, one of the original proprietors of Ridgefield. The St. John family had just arrived in Sharon, having made that slow, generational trek northward from Norwalk to Wilton to Ridgefield and finally to Sharon, Connecticut. Here they bought a farm in 1745. By that time Mathew was known as captain. He had served in the ranks of the local Wilton militia, rising from ensign in 1727 to captain in 1738.[110]

Ebenezer and his brother, Jonathan, were both married in the same month in 1745 and proceeded to raise large families in Sharon. Ebenezer and Hannah had twelve children over the next twenty-five years. Jonathan and his wife Lydia Barrows raised only seven. Two of Ebenezer's daughters and one of Jonathan's would marry sons of David Wood.

Interrupting these years of child-rearing, both brothers became caught up in the French and Indian War. Ebenezer served during the successful campaign of 1759. That year the British regulars and colonial militia under General Jeffery Amherst captured Fort Ticonderoga and forced the French to retreat to Canada. In 1761 Ebenezer was joined by his brother, Jonathan, and together they served in the 1st Connecticut regiment where they were engaged in repairing and strengthening the captured French forts at Crown Point and Ticonderoga.[111]

In 1769 Stephen Wood married Hannah Sprague, further strengthening the ties between these two families. In 1774 their fathers, David and Ebenezer, jointly purchased two lots north of the Five-Mile Square in an area that would later be known as Milton Hill. These parcels, sub-lots five (595 acres) and nine (200 acres) of the 12th Lot in the 14th allotment of the Kayaderosseras Patent, were purchased from Jacob Walton, Anthony Van Dam and Isaac Low for £511.[112] There is no mention of a road in the deed, but one would soon be cut through these parcels to connect these lots with the Middleline to the south. David Wood, wife Dorothy and five of their sons—Benjamin, Stephen, Elijah, and Nathan—moved north in 1777 and clustered their cabins in a family enclave.[113] Daughter Dolly married Thomas Kennedy in Sharon that same year. They settled in across the cart path from her parents and brothers. Hannah Sprague's parents and her siblings built their cabins south of the Wood family. Her brothers—Ebenezer Jr., John and Elijah—were coming of age and would soon join the 12th Albany County Militia led by Colonel Gordon.

The Wood and Sprague families had become friends and family in Sharon, building a relationship strong enough to make the decision to jointly purchase property in an unknown wilderness. David and Ebenezer, both in their sixties, must have made the decision believing that the prospects for their large families were more favorable in Ball's Town than in Sharon. They were not the only ones. Another family would soon join them. And more marriages would tighten the bonds between the families that settled along the Middleline.

∞

Hollister

Today for five dollars you can cross the Connecticut River between Wethersfield and Glastonbury, Connecticut on the oldest ferry service in the country, in operation since 1655. The original ferry was a small raft pushed across the river using long poles. Today the craft is an open flatboat named the "Hollister III" in honor of one of the oldest families residing in these two towns on opposite sides of the river.[114] Local conjecture says that the original ferry was operated by the first Hollister to settle in the town.[115]

John Hollister arrived in America in 1642 and settled in Wethersfield on the west side of the river, not long before Jacob Waterhouse (Watrous) moved away in 1645. It is likely that they knew each other since John soon became a freeman and served as a representative in the General Court in Hartford for a total of fourteen years.[116] He was active in the real estate market, adding acreage to his holdings on both sides of the river. The east side, originally called Naubuc farms, became the separate town of Glastonbury in 1693. It had been partitioned in 1640 into thirty-four strips of varying widths, all extending three miles eastward from the river into the wilderness. Lot thirty-four was assigned to Matthew Mitchell and by 1649 John came into possession of one quarter of Mitchell's nine-hundred acre lot.[117]

John and his son's fortune followed the trajectory of many first settlers. The original proprietors were in a position to acquire multiple tracts of land, either by direct grants from the town for services rendered, or by buying lots from others, many of whom never settled in the town. In addition, land granted to the town upon founding was often held "in common" for later distribution among the original settlers and their descendants. A third method of increasing their estates was to marry well, often above their station. John profited from all three scenarios. In his early years in Wethersfield, John purchased several home lots on the west side of the River; but his largest acquisitions were on the east side in Glastonbury. In addition to the purchase from Mitchell, he was given fifty acres by the town in 1649 and bought eighty acres more in 1660.[118]

Richard Treat was one of the founders of Wethersfield, arriving with John Oldham in 1636. By the time John Hollister settled in town Richard had already amassed a sizeable estate. So it was Hollister's good fortune to marry Richard's daughter, Joanna, soon after he arrived. They moved across the river and built their homestead on the old Mitchell parcel on the east side, and raised their family there. Their life together was productive, but short. John died in 1665 leaving eight children, most of whom had not yet reached adulthood. As a testament to his prosperity he left an estate valued at £1642, including several tracts of land and a long list of personal property.[119]

His eldest son, John, received the largest share of the bequest, which went immediately to him. His brothers, Thomas and Joseph, had to wait for their inheritance until they reached their majority.[120] John was the recipient of the Mitchell farm. He built his own home there—a building that still stands— that is on the National Register of Historic Places. Although modified over the years, it still exhibits classic late 17th- century features, including a hewn overhang, rear lean-to, and large set-back chimney.[121]

John and Thomas both continued to prosper, following the lead of their father by marrying into well-to-do families. In 1667, John married Sarah Goodrich, daughter of John Goodrich, another first settler. Thomas married Elizabeth Latimer, daughter of John Latimer. Latimer had died in 1662, one of the wealthiest landowners in Wethersfield. Thomas still benefited from his success. He received land from his mother-in-law, Anna Latimer—twenty-eight acres in 1672 and another two hundred twenty-five acres in 1680.[122] John's daughters also married into prominent families. Elizabeth married Samuel Welles, son of Governor Thomas Welles in 1659. Her younger sister, Mary, married John Welles, grandson of the governor.[123]

From this auspicious start, the Hollister family became one of the largest and most important families in Glastonbury. John and Sarah had ten children. Thomas and Elizabeth had eight. However, this idyllic family scene was interrupted by the onset of King Phillip's War in 1675. John's home became one of the garrison houses, fortified to protect the surrounding settlers from the rampages of the Indians. Thomas was engaged in a number of actions, including the "Great Swamp Fight" of December1675 in Rhode Island during which a number of Wethersfield troops were killed or wounded.[124]

John died in 1711. His children remained in Glastonbury for the most part. Son Thomas was employed as a weaver and served as a deacon in the church. Thomas' firstborn son, Josiah, was born in 1696, married Martha Miller in 1718, and they raised their five children there. But in

1742, one hundred years after his great-grandfather had established the family in Wethersfield, Josiah decided it was time to move on. In that year he purchased one full share, the fifty-third home lot, in the newly formed town of Sharon for £650. In 1748, shortly before his death he distributed his Sharon property to his sons, Josiah and Samuel, "for love and good-will."[125] This branch of the large Hollister clan had moved west, if only a few dozen miles. There they would settle as neighbors of David Wood and Ebenezer Sprague.

Samuel married Jemima Phelps the same year he received his inheritance from his father. Jemima was the daughter of Timothy Phelps, one of the founders of the town of Hebron, just east of Glastonbury. They had four boys and four girls, but it was the birth of their last child, Ichabod, that changed Samuel's life. Jemima died ten days after his birth. Ichabod was baptized at her funeral, but died a few days later. Samuel was left with six children to raise, including ten-year-old Josiah.[126] Josiah's two sisters, Jemima and Hannah, both around fifteen years old, managed to keep house until their father remarried to Mary Chamberlin, a widow, in 1766. Samuel died in 1771 at the age of forty-seven and seventeen-year-old Josiah ran the farm for a year before his step-mother remarried to Jonathan Sprague, brother of Ebenezer Sprague. This was another marriage that solidified the relationships among the future settlers of Middleline Road.[127]

We are fortunate that a Journal written by Josiah Hollister has been preserved. It provides a narrative of his personal experiences that can be seen as typical of those that made the transition from established homesteads in Connecticut to carve out new lives along the Middleline. It also provides a detailed picture of the impact of the American Revolution on those that were caught up in it. The first part of his story leading up to his arrival in Ball's Town is briefly summarized here.

After his stepmother's remarriage to Jonathan Sprague, he went to live with his sister and her husband to learn to become a shoemaker and tanner. He had no interest in the trade and in 1775 joined the local militia and participated in the invasion of Canada that was ultimately crippled by General Montgomery's failed attack on Quebec in December 1775. Josiah's company traveled up the Hudson River with stops at Saratoga, Fort Edward and Fort George, Ticonderoga, and Crown Point during that campaign. In 1776 his militia company was called up again to defend New

York City. During this experience, Josiah became very ill and his slow trip back home exposed him to both Tories and Patriots. He was never sure when he and his party sought refuge in a local tavern if he would be welcomed and cared for, or turned away.[128]

In June 1777, back home in Sharon, Connecticut Josiah met and married Mehitable Andrews, daughter of William Andrews. She gave birth to a son, Samuel, and daughter, Ruth, over the next two years. In 1779 he sold his farm in Sharon and traveled to Vermont in search of land. He bought ninety-two acres in Rupert, but sold it when there appeared to be a dispute over the title. He decided to change plans and take up the offer of a friend, Jeremiah Phelps, to move to Ball's Town. Phelps proved to be no friend, cheating him on the land deal in Vermont. However, he was still drawn to Ball's Town by his stepfather's nephew Ebenezer Sprague, Jr. This younger Ebenezer married Mary Chamberlin, the daughter of the Mary who was the second wife of his uncle Jonathan. In the spring of 1780 Josiah bought a ninety-five-acre lot just south of the Sprague family on the Middleline and began working the land. He cleared three acres for rye and another three for wheat. His harvest that first year included fifteen acres of wheat. It was to be his last crop. We will return to his story in a later chapter.[129]

∞

Patchen

Not all of the families living on Middleline Road in 1780 could build on a legacy of prosperous forebears. Some families had struggled for generations, but still managed to make a living by being observant to take advantage of opportunities as they presented themselves. One such family was the Patchens. Joseph Patchen arrived in America on the *Hercules* in March 1635 as the servant of Thomas Besbeech. He settled in Roxbury, Massachusetts where he married Elizabeth Iggleden in 1642.[130] Their two children, Joseph and John, both lived hardscrabble lives. Joseph died insolvent in 1689 and his brother "was living, a poor old man at Stratfield, Connecticut in 1712 when he was provided for in the Will of Deacon Isaac Wheeler, whose servant he has been for thirty years."[131]

Their father, Joseph, fared no better. He moved to Fairfield where he was granted a home lot in 1655, but seemed to struggle as well. After the death of his first wife he married Mary Morehouse. They had a son Jacob born in 1663. He became the grandfather of Jabez Patchen, the Middleline Road pioneer. Mary's father, Thomas, was a founder of Stamford, but soon moved to Fairfield and operated a grist mill there.[132] Mary is mentioned in his will in 1658, but she may have died soon after the birth of Jacob, since he was their only child. In 1669 Joseph Sr. was one of four poor men whose debts were forgiven by Dr. Pell in his will. Upon Joseph's death in 1690 what property he had was turned over to the Edward Adams family, probably in return for his maintenance during his later years.[133]

Joseph's son Jacob continued to improve his family's fortunes by marrying above his station as well. By 1692 he had married Mary Hubbard Grumman, daughter of William Hubbard and granddaughter of George Hubbard, one of the first settlers of Wethersfield. He later moved to Guilford where he served multiple terms as a Deputy of Connecticut General Court.[134] Jacob had been appointed administrator of the estate of Samuel Grumman, Mary's first husband, and married her soon thereafter.

Jacob's son Jacob Jr., born in Fairfield in 1701, moved to Wilton, Connecticut along with his father in the late 1720's, just as that settlement was being developed. Father and son with the same given names makes it difficult to ascertain which person is referred to in the records. Both Patchens were assigned seats in the Wilton Meeting House, probably the father in 1727 and the son in 1733.

Young Jacob married Abigail Cable in about 1725 and together they raised twelve children. They all reached adulthood and married into families that would become familiar to later generations living in Ballston— Betts, Morehouse, Olmstead and Hubbell to name a few. Abigail was a descendant of John Cable who arrived in Massachusetts in 1630 and accompanied William Pynchon in the founding of Springfield in 1636. He soon moved on to Fairfield where his son and grandson, both named John, raised their families.[135]

Jacob was a carpenter, but he seems to have struggled financially with his large family. He purchased some land in Wilton, but was unable to pay for it, and was sued by the seller, John Belden, in 1731. He apparently returned the land to Belden, but repurchased it along with the house in which he was living in 1739.[136] That same year he purchased an interest in a sawmill and was responsible for building the new meeting house in 1747.[137]

Jacob's oldest son, Jabez, was born in 1727 and married Hannah Squire in 1748. Hannah was the great-granddaughter of George Squire, who was another early settler of Fairfield. Squire had moved with other families from Concord, Massachusetts in 1644. His son, Samuel, was an attorney in the 1692 witchcraft trial of Mercy Disbrow in Fairfield. She was sentenced to death, but the decision was reversed. It was considered one of the turning points in the witchcraft hysteria of the time.[138] Records indicate that Jabez and Hannah raised eight children. The first four were baptized together in 1757, probably years after their birth. He was active in the affairs of Wilton, serving on the school committee and a committee to collect minister's rates. He was named an ensign in the Wilton train band (militia) during the French and Indian War.[139]

In the years following the war, the desire to take advantage of the new lands opening up to the north and west affected the residents of Wilton, as it had many others in Connecticut. And just as the connection with the Bedford parish had influenced their neighbor, David Wood, to join Rev. Eliphalet Ball in moving north, other Wilton families soon followed. Jabez had watched as families made the decision to leave their familiar surroundings. Hezekiah Middlebrook and Joseph Bettys soon followed the Wood family to the Five-Mile Square. By 1775, six of the fifteen men who joined Rev. Ball's church in the new settlement of Ball's Town were from Wilton. In 1776, Michael Middlebrook followed his older brother, Hezekiah, to Ball's Town. Jabez chose this time to join the migration. He, Hannah and their four sons, his brother, Jesse, and their cousin, Sarah and her husband, John Birchard, all banded together to make the trek north to the Middleline.[140] There he was able to use his skills as a carpenter to build homes for himself and his family.

∞

Middlebrook

Early settlers of Connecticut came there for a host of reasons, and they often came in groups drawn together by a strong leader. The first to arrive were led across the old Connecticut trail by John Oldham from Watertown, Massachusetts to settle Wethersfield in 1634. Oldham had gotten cross-wise with both the Plymouth and Massachusetts Bay religious leaders. In 1636, the Reverend Thomas Hooker led over a hundred followers from Cambridge to found Hartford and the colony of Connecticut as a result of disagreement over the religious practices of Reverend John Cotton and other Massachusetts Puritan leaders. Hooker and members of his congregation objected to the strict rules limiting voting in that colony to members of the church. Reverend John Davenport established the separate colony of New Haven in 1638 because he and his followers believed that Massachusetts was not strict enough. As we have seen, ancestors of the families living on Middleline Road in 1780 often were in the parties led by these leaders.

Roger Ludlow was also a founder of Connecticut who, after the colonists' victory in the Pequot War, sought to establish settlements along the southwestern coast of Long Island Sound. He had been impressed by both the land and the fine harbors discovered during the campaign against the Pequots. He was not a minister, and his reasons were more economic than religious. Ludlow served as Deputy Governor of Connecticut from 1638 to 1648. In 1639 he purchased land from the local Indians that would later encompass the towns of Bridgeport, Fairfield, and Norwalk.[141]

The small settlement of Fairfield grew slowly but received a boost in population in 1644 when the Reverend John Jones agreed to serve as its first minister. He brought with him a band of sixteen families from Concord, Massachusetts. These migrants were frustrated by their situation in Concord, "finding the lands about the town very barren and the meadows very unuseful."[142] Among those that joined Reverend Jones and George Squire in this move was the family of Joseph Middlebrook. While George settled in the village of Fairfield, Joseph and six other families put down roots a few miles to the east at Pequonnock, later to be named Bridgeport. Those families that settled there were granted 2-½ acre town lots in 1649.[143]

Joseph was married three times. In a clear example of the close family relationships that existed in early America, all three wives were daughters and widows of the men that accompanied him on the journey from Concord. Mary (Bateman) died in 1648. Second wife, Mary (Odell, widow of Benjamin Turney), died around 1659. His third wife was

Hannah (Wheeler, widow of James Bennett).[144] All except Bateman lived on adjoining house lots in Pequonnock. Another not uncommon sign of the times: from these three marriages, only two children survived him.

Joseph died in 1686, but apparently not without some dissention in his family. When his daughter, Phoebe, married Samuel Wilson in 1679, he had given her one-third interest in his lands to be distributed upon his death.[145] But as death approached he confided to a friend, John Sturges, that "he feared Samuel Wilson would ronge his son by reason of riting he had signed and give him and further said that he (Samuel) should have no more of his estate but what he get by that deed of gift." Accordingly, his estate was distributed to his son, Joseph, and daughter Phoebe as he wished. His fears that his son-in-law would wrong his son did not come to pass.[146] The inventory of the estate indicated that Joseph had become a successful farmer in Fairfield. His lands were valued at close to £500 and were estimated at 858 acres, most of which was held "in common", not yet partitioned and distributed. Worthy of note, his old friend George Squire conducted the inventory.[147] George's granddaughter, Martha, would marry Joseph's grandson, Jonathan, twenty-five years later.

Joseph Jr. had three sons, John, Joseph and Jonathan and he began to pass his inheritance on to them. In 1706 he gave them each one-third share of his undivided lands. In 1709 he was in his early sixties and not well. His older sons had married but his youngest son, Jonathan, was still a bachelor and in that year Joseph deeded Jonathan his house, home lot, and several additional parcels of land. In exchange, Jonathan agreed to take care of his father and step-mother. They died soon thereafter and he then married Martha Squire.[148]

Jonathan followed in the footsteps of his father and grandfathers as a yeoman farmer, adding to the property he had inherited. They had six children, including four boys to support. Their oldest, Michael, was born in 1712. For the most part the Middlebrooks stayed in Fairfield and surrounding towns and, with Michael's generation, were represented there by almost twenty families. The first person to move away was his cousin David. He became one of the early settlers of North Carolina when he came of age in the 1720's. Michael's brother, Ebenezer, had his own faraway experience when he served in the expedition against Louisbourg, Nova Scotia, during King George's War in 1744. Michael himself stayed in

Fairfield in the years after he married Abiah Summers in the late 1730's. The first-born of their nine children was Hezekiah who arrived in 1740.[149]

The year 1754 proved to be a turning point for Michael. In that year his father died leaving a considerable estate to him and his three brothers. However, his brother, Ebenezer, died about the same time at the age of twenty-four, leaving a five-year-old daughter, Sarah. These events may have influenced Michael to make a decision to seek a fresh start.

The economic climate may also have had an impact. The early 1750's was a period of rampant inflation in Connecticut. In 1756 the currency was devalued which significantly reduced the value of real estate. If Michael had been able to sell his property in Fairfield at a high price in 1754, he was in a position to capitalize on the revaluation two years later.[150] Various accounts indicate that he had relocated to Wilton by 1756, purchasing the home of Nathan Betts, who had also recently died. Betts' home had previously been used as a tavern, indicating it had a fair number of bedrooms, something Michael and Abiah certainly needed.[151]

Soon after settling in Wilton, his son Hezekiah was off to war. He joined Isaac Isaac's Company of the 4th Connecticut Regiment in 1758 and participated in General Abercrombie's disastrous attack on Fort Ticonderoga in which six members of his company were killed. He re-enlisted in 1759 when the fort was taken by General Amherst, as the tide finally turned against the French.[152] In both years, Hezekiah would have been in Albany and traveled up the Hudson River to Saratoga (Schuylerville), Fort Edward, and Lake George in preparation for the assault on Ticonderoga. He probably hadn't heard of the Kayaderosseras Patent which was still the land of the Mohawks and uninhabited by the English. Ball's Town and Middleline Road did not exist in 1759. But little more than a decade later, Hezekiah would return to the area as a leader of a contingent of Wilton men, several of whom had served with him in the war.[153] They would seek to take advantage of the lands now available as a result of their efforts to rid the area of the French, and to open the now peaceful lands to settlement.

∞

Betts

A generation before John Collins settled in Guilford in 1669 we see the arrival there of Thomas Betts. Although not a signer of the 1639 Guilford Covenant and not an original settler, he arrived soon thereafter. He is named among those who shared in the first distribution of land in 1640, took his oath of allegiance in 1645, and was made a freeman in 1649.[154] In 1657 he sold his land there and moved to the town of Milford, to the west of New Haven. Three years later he moved again, this time farther west to Norwalk, and purchased the home-lot of Nathaniel Eli and Ralph Keeler, lot number thirteen. By the time of his arrival in Norwalk, Thomas and his first wife had six children ranging in age from sixteen-year-old Thomas, Jr to newborn Samuel. Two more children, James and Sarah, would be born in his new town. In 1671 his taxable estate was valued at £146, and in the census of the following year his family of ten was the largest in town.[155]

Since this is the last family sketch in our narrative, it may be useful to pause here and view the home lots of the town of Norwalk as they existed in 1660. We have already seen that the ancestors of many Ballston families could be found in Norwalk one hundred twenty years before the British raid of 1780 along the Middleline. However, in the 21st century it is hard to imagine how small their world was, and how tight and interlocking the connections were between the families. A quick look at the map of the Ancient Home-Lots of Norwalk focusing on the Betts family can serve to illustrate these associations.

The town was laid out in four blocks with an offset crossroads in the center. Arriving from the northeast along the Fairfield Path, you would first notice the home of Thomas Barnum (lot 23). He would later move on to found Danbury with the sons of Thomas Benedict (lot 30) and John Gregory (lot 1). Thomas' son John would marry John Gregory's daughter Phoebe in 1670 and son James would marry Sarah Gregory in 1676.[156]

In the next home on the right beyond Barnum lived Thomas Betts and his large family (lot 13). Betts would live out the remainder of his life here. In his 1688 Will, he distributed his estate to his eight children. By this time six of them were married to the children of local settlers: Oldest daughter Mary married John Raymond, son of Richard Raymond (lot 7) in 1664; oldest son Thomas married Sarah Marvin, daughter of Matthew Marvin, Jr (lot 31) in 1680; and Thomas would settle into lot 33, with only the homestead of Daniel Kellogg (lot 34) separating him from his in-laws. Kellogg's daughter Sarah marred Betts' second son John. Later, in 1692, third son Daniel married Deborah Taylor, daughter of Thomas Taylor and fourth son Samuel married Judith Reynolds, daughter of John Reynolds. Fifth son James married Hannah Bouton, daughter of John Bouton (lot 28) in 1704. Youngest daughter Sarah married Joseph St. John, son of Mark St. John (lot 3) in 1696.[157] These surnames would appear again and again in future marriages within the Betts family, the origin of which can be traced back to the homesteads within four blocks of early Norwalk.

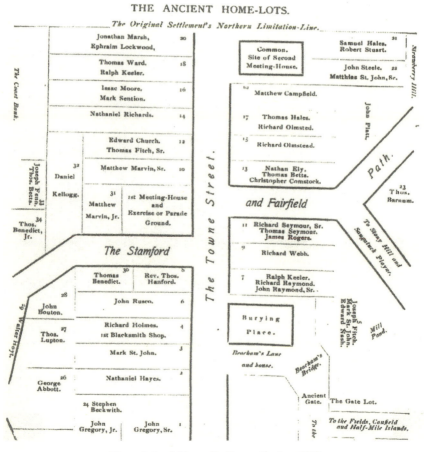

Home Lots of Norwalk, Connecticut ca 1660

Although beyond the scope of this study, other family names with home-lots in Norwalk that appear later in the early history of Ballston and surrounding towns include Gregory, Kellogg, Keeler, and Nash.

As we have seen, other Connecticut towns appearing in these sketches exhibit similar connections between families that would carry on throughout many years. The initially small number of families with large numbers of children; the tendency—especially in New England—to gather together in small villages with home-lots; and the multiple economic activities engaged in by these families: all contributed to the development of close relationships among these early settlers. It is therefore not a surprise that inter-marriages between families over several generations would become the norm.

Thomas Betts, Jr. became a leading citizen of Norwalk at the turn of the 18th century. He represented his hometown in the Colony's Assembly in 1692-94 and again in 1704-07. He was an active member of the church, serving on several committees over the years.[158] In 1709 the town granted to Thomas and John Betts, John Gregory, Jr., and Joseph Birchard the right to "damn up the crick lying before ye said Gregory's for the purpose of erecting a grist mill upon the damn that they shall so erect."[159] It is likely that Tom and John were sons of Thomas, Jr., since they would have been twenty-seven and twenty-five at the time. Thomas seems to have parlayed the bequest left him by his father into a sizeable estate by his death in 1717 when his legacy was valued at £661.[160]

John Betts had married Hannah Burwell in 1708, the year before the joint venture to build the grist mill. Hannah was the only daughter of John Burwell, and disputes over her inheritance would continue for more than 150 years after his death in 1690. John Burwell had arrived in America in 1685, leaving behind a large estate in England that never benefited Betts and his wife. In 1745 shortly before his death, John attempted to collect rents due Hannah since her father's death. Nothing came of the attempt and descendants were still attempting to settle the matter in the 1830s.[161] John remained in Norwalk while his cousins, the sons of his uncles Daniel, Samuel, and James moved northward a few miles to Wilton in the 1720's, establishing the larger branch of the Betts family there. Four of them were assigned seats in the meeting house when the church was first established in 1727.[162]

John and Hannah had a large family of their own, a total of nine children, including son Joseph, born in 1717. Most of their offspring remained in the Norwalk area, but some moved northward to Ridgefield. When his father John died in 1745, Joseph shared executor responsibility with his older brothers, John and Burwell. Remaining in Norwalk gave both older brothers the opportunity to strengthen the bonds among families. John had married Sarah Gregory in 1736 and Burwell married Thankful Gregory four years later.

In 1749 Joseph married Abigail Whitney of Westfield, the town to the east of Norwalk. They began to raise their family in Norwalk, but at some point Joseph relocated to Wilton. In 1749 he was a donor to the Episcopal Church there, and by 1762 he sold land on Chestnut Hill in that town. Unreliable birth records for his children indicate they moved sometime after his son Jeremiah was born in Norwalk in 1756, and the birth of his daughter Abigail in Wilton in 1762.[163]

In 1770, after twenty years of marriage, Joseph sold his home farm, barns, and orchard of 102 acres to Mathew Gregory, Jr for £260 and moved his family north to Ball's Town.[164] His first purchase was made there in January 1772. He bought two lots in the Five-Mile Square on either side of Long Lake, totaling 298 acres for £119.[165] It was here that he established his home and opened his tavern which can be seen today along Route 50 north of Burnt Hills. In November 1773, "Joseph Bettes of Ballston, carpenter" purchased two parcels in the Fifth Allotment south of his tavern totaling 284 acres from Cornelius Tiebout for £150.[166] His total purchase of 582 acres for £269 demonstrates the economic attraction of the new lands that were available for sale in the patent. He sold his land in Wilton for £2.5 per acre. In Ballston he was able to purchase a much larger estate for less than £.5 per acre.

Joseph brought his large family with him, including his oldest son Joseph, Jr. who was just growing into adulthood. Accounts written later, and most probably colored by his exploits during the Revolutionary War, describe him as a troublesome youth.

> His character at this early period, as described by his playmates now living, was notoriously bad. He was a tyrant as soon as he was able to exercise the power of tyranny.

He was willful, headstrong, disobedient to parental authority, overbearing, hasty and ill-tempered and as great
a scoundrel as ever breathed.[167]

An extreme characterization, but one born of the emotions that were
about to divide the pioneers who were just beginning to settle in Ball's
Town and surrounding towns. The families along Middleline Road were
primarily of one mind in the looming struggle, but they were surrounded
by many neighbors who did not necessarily agree with them.

CHAPTER 6
Rebels and Loyalists

The Battle of Lake George, fought on September 8, 1755, was the opening engagement of the French and Indian War in New York. The British troops were led by William Johnson accompanied by 250 Mohawk Indians under the leadership of Theyanoguin (King Hendrick). The battle began when the British colonial forces were ambushed while marching south from Lake George to engage the French under Baron Jean-Armand de Dieskau, a German officer in the service of the French. During this phase of the battle, known as the Bloody Morning Scout, the lead regiment under Colonel Ephraim Williams bore the brunt of the assault. Both he and Hendrick were killed. However, the colonial provincials recovered and were able to beat a slow retreat to the British breastworks at the lake where they held off the French attacks. The British victory was secured when a contingent of New York and New Hampshire men fell upon 300 French Canadians and Indians near the site of the morning ambush, forever known as the Battle of Bloody Pond.[1]

The day had indeed been a bloody one. The British forces lost 400 men killed, wounded or missing, the French 300. The British troops were not from England, but consisted of 2,500 provincials, mainly from the New England colonies of Massachusetts, Connecticut, and Rhode Island. And the French soldiers were mostly not from France. The 200 French regulars were supported by 1,300 Canadians and Indians. The Old French War, as it came to be called by later generations, was a colonial war, affecting the lives of families, friends and neighbors. For many this war would change everything. Year after year the colonies would support this world war with their sons. Each year the provincial assemblies, pressured by the British commanders, would authorize regiments and establish targets for their colonies. Connecticut alone enlisted 22,858 men before the war was over in 1763. This represented about 16,000 individuals, many signing up in more than one year.[2] Some had previously served in local militia units, but for many, this was their first military experience. And for most it was their first time away from home, seeing the larger world beyond their town and forming lifelong relationships with their fellow soldiers.[3]

In 1780 another battle would be fought at Bloody Pond toward the end of the American Revolution. It too would involve Provincials from Canada, Americans and Indians. But the dispute would not be between the French and British. The opposing sides would then be called Rebels and Loyalists. During the twenty-five-year interim many families from different backgrounds, cultures and political philosophies moved into the hinterlands north of Albany. Some of them were New Englanders, returning to the lands they had first seen as they served and suffered during the French War. Others came from the old country – Scotland, Ireland and England – often traveling in groups to form small communities in the wilderness. This wilderness now offered opportunity, available now that the century-old conflict with the French and their Indian allies had ended. The partitioning of the Kayaderosseras Patent by 1770 resulted in the formation of several of these communities. The Five-Mile Square, with its settlement along Middleline Road, was one of them. But there were many others, each unique unto itself. The heritage of the inhabitants and their relationships ultimately led them to take sides in the civil war that played out in their own neighborhood, part of the larger conflict of the American Revolution.

One cohort of settlers were those British regulars who had served in the regiments that were sent to the colonies in the years after the outbreak of the war with France in 1755. These regiments reinforced the provincial troops that during the first year of the war had been left to fight by themselves at Lake George. Together the provincials and the regulars played a significant role in the momentous battles along the Lake George—Lake Champlain corridor in 1758 and 1759.

The 60th Foot was one of those regiments. With the defeat of General Braddock near Fort Duquesne, the site of modern day Pittsburg, the British Parliament was quick to authorize ten new regiments to serve in

North America. Unlike the other nine, the 60th was trained to fight in the frontier style of warfare, while maintaining the discipline of the British regulars. Comprised of four battalions, elements of this regiment saw action in all the major battles of the conflict. In 1758 and 1759 the 2nd and 3rd Battalions participated in the capture of Louisburg and Quebec. Those same years the 1st and 2nd Battalions were actively involved in the campaigns to capture Fort Carillon. These units were devastated in General Abercrombie's failed assault on the fort in July 1758, losing fifty men killed and over 200 wounded. The next year the fort was abandoned, taken over by the British, and renamed Fort Ticonderoga.[4]

The officers of the 60th Foot were Protestants recruited mostly from England and Scotland, as well as Germany, while the soldiers were raised in America. These officers gained experience in the battles against the French that served them well in the revolutionary conflict twenty years later. Among the officers was Lieutenant Colonel Frederick Haldimand, a Swiss-born soldier who had previously served in the Prussian Army. Later, in 1778, he was appointed as the Governor-General of the Province of Quebec. From this position he coordinated Loyalist raids into New York and Vermont in the years after the Battle of Saratoga.

Several officers of lesser rank would settle in the colonies at the conclusion of the war, and would later have to choose sides in America's war for independence. Lieutenant Arthur St. Clair became one of the largest landowners in western Pennsylvania and later joined the rebellion. He was commander of Fort Ticonderoga which he abandoned to General Burgoyne in 1777 during the Saratoga campaign when he awoke to see the British guns staring down at him from Mount Defiance.

Other officers and soldiers of the 60th took advantage of the generous terms of their enlistment. Recruited to serve for three years, and only in North America, they were promised grants of land ranging from fifty acres for privates, to 2,000 for lieutenants and ensigns. Captains were to receive 5,000 acres.[5] As regiments were disbanded at the end of the war, many officers remained in America. With their land grants and half-pay status they were able to do very well for themselves, garnering considerable estates. Several of these officers settled in Albany County, New York, an area encompassing the present-day counties of Albany, Saratoga, Montgomery, and Washington.

Daniel McAlpin was one of those officers. A career military man, he served as a lieutenant in the 2nd Battalion of the 60th Foot. McAlpin had led his men up a wooded cliff and routed the French defenders during the assault on Quebec in 1759. After the war he stayed in America and served under Sir William Johnson during Pontiac's Rebellion. Retiring as a captain, he had received land grants along the Connecticut River under a deed from New York. This was not a wise acquisition due to the continuing dispute between New Hampshire and New York over the "Hampshire Grants", which was to grow more violent in the 1770s.[6]

Unable to settle on this 6,000 acre grant, in 1774 he purchased a 1,000 acre parcel on the west side of Saratoga Lake from Beriah Palmer, who was acting as agent for the proprietors of the Kayaderosseras Patent. There McAlpin built his first temporary home in 1775 and a larger, more permanent residence a year later. McAlpin apparently had the resources to quickly turn this land into a profitable farm. By 1777 his friend James Campbell, another retired soldier from the 60th Foot, who had set down roots along the Battenkill in Charlotte (Washington) County, documented his success. In the year when the Burgoyne campaign would change everything for McAlpin, he had 170 acres under cultivation, supported by a well-stocked farm, with "many hundreds of bushels of wheat in the barn and a large quantity of farm utensils." His wife Mary and three children also were fortunate to be surrounded by furniture worth £125.[7] The McAlpin family would soon lose it all.

John Munro was another Scotsman who had come to America to serve in the French War. He was a sergeant in the 48th Regiment of Foot which served longer than any other British regiment in that war. In January 1755 the regiment of 500 men embarked from Ireland to join in General Braddock's disastrous campaign against Fort Duquesne. From there the regiment participated in the successful expeditions against Louisburg in 1758 and Quebec in 1759. After the conquest of Canada was completed with the capture of Montreal in 1760, the 48th went to the Caribbean where they were part of the British forces that captured Fort Royal and Havana in 1762.[8]

Munro was another beneficiary of the largess bestowed on soldiers who decided to remain in America at the termination of the war. Of modest means in Scotland, he was unable to purchase an officer's commission in 1755. By 1765 he was in possession of over 11,000 acres in the territory east of Albany, in Shaftsbury in what was then known as the Hampshire Grants. In 1760 he married his second wife, Mary Brouwer, daughter of Cornelius Brouwer of Schenectady. The Brouwers were an old Dutch family and were moderately successful agrarian businessmen.

John Munro 1728-1800

In his 1765 Will Cornelius gave his daughter £120 and forgave John a debt of £80, indicating a healthy relationship between parents, daughter and son-in-law. That family relationship would not survive the upcoming struggle.[9]

In Cornelius' Will, Munro is described as an Albany merchant. He prospered in business and established relationships with the Albany elite, serving as an Elder of the Presbyterian Church there. His connections also resulted in his appointment as a Justice of the Peace for Albany County, an influential position that he administered from his growing estate in Shaftsbury, where he operated sawmills, gristmills, a pot ashery and nail factory.[10]

Munro's term as Justice of the Peace was anything but peaceful. Ethan Allen saw to that. Allen was the leader of the Green Mountain Boys that had been formed in neighboring Bennington in 1770. They were a paramilitary force of New Hampshire grantees whose purpose was to resist and, if possible, evict settlers holding New York titles to land in the Hampshire Grants which later became the state of Vermont.[11] In many ways they were a vigilante group and John Munro saw it as his responsibility to bring them to justice. In March 1772 he led a dozen men to arrest Remember Baker, Allen's cousin and a fellow leader of the Green Mountain Boys. Munro's group captured Baker, but before they could take him back to Albany, Baker's fellow "Boys" rescued him. Later, Munro tried to capture another of their leaders, Seth Warner, who fought back and sent Munro packing. Warner would later become a general on the American side. Munro, true to his British military roots, remained loyal to the King.[12]

∞

New York was different from its neighbors to the east in New England. We have highlighted the patrician roots of its leadership throughout the 18th century in the founding of the Kayaderosseras Patent. Its legacy of large estates granted to the powerful created an almost feudal system of landlords and tenant farmers. In many ways the settlement of the Patent was a break from this tradition. Its more transparent process of partitioning into allotments and individual lots made it possible to benefit members of the "middling class". However, vestiges of the old system remained. Many of these farmers worked the land on leases obtained from speculators such as Gysbert Fonda and Daniel Campbell, not outright purchase. But the promise of eventual ownership was there and this new system was certainly more egalitarian than the old.

On the eve of the Revolution, the old ways were still the norm in the territories surrounding the Kayaderosseras Patent. Patricians still controlled the land to the east and west. But this did not mean that they were politically of the same mind. Their backgrounds, relationships and allegiances would take them in different directions in the upcoming struggle.

To the west, Sir William Johnson remained supportive of the Crown and its colonial leaders. His long years of service as Indian Commissioner and military officer assured his loyalty. He had populated his estate with tenants of the same persuasion. In the years before his death in 1774, he successfully attracted several hundred Scottish Highlanders to his lands with the lure of hundred-acre lots which they settled rent-free until their farms were established. Surely these newly arrived immigrants would be beholden to Sir William. This loyalty was transferred to his son John as the dispute escalated into war.[13]

To the east, Phillip Schuyler had built his country home along the Hudson River in the Saratoga Patent during the 1760's near present-day Schuylerville. He was the fourth generation of this Dutch family to live in America. They were among the wealthiest families in Albany, becoming rich off the fur trade, their real estate investments, and their fortuitous marriages into other well-known Dutch dynasties. His father had married Cornelia Van Cortlandt and in 1755 Phillip married Catherine Van Rensselaer.[14] The Schuyler family had been associated with the Saratoga Patent since it was granted in 1685. By 1710 they had erected a mill on the south side of Fish Creek and a small community had grown up around it. By 1745 thirty families were living there, only to be killed, captured or driven off by the French during King George's War.[15]

The land lay dormant for the next fifteen years until Phillip decided to restore the saw and grist mills and build his mansion on 1,900 acres he had inherited. He was able to attract both Dutch and Scottish tenants with favorable terms, much as William Johnson had done.[16] Politically however, he differed from Johnson in several respects. His Dutch background and extensive business connections in Albany wedded him to the emerging rebel movement to throw off the restraints that were being imposed by the royal authorities. As a member of the New York Assembly, he increasingly aligned with the Whigs, as the advocates of independence came to be known. His tenants followed his lead, but only to a certain extent. Schuyler could not count on the unwavering loyalty that the Johnsons enjoyed, born of the ethnic bonds of the Scottish and Irish clans. So when Daniel McAlpin moved into his neighborhood it was inevitable that conflicts would arise.

To the north two brothers were busy accumulating land grants in the years after the French War. On the surface their family history seems similar to the several sketches developed in the last chapter. They were relative newcomers to New York. Edward Jessup, the immigrant ancestor of Edward and Ebenezer Jessup was living in Stamford, Connecticut as early as 1640. After a short detour to Long Island the family returned to southwestern Connecticut and remained there for the next 100 years. In 1744, Joseph Jessup emigrated with his young sons across the border to Dutchess County, New York, and purchased 911 acres of land in the Nine-Partners Patent. Soon after, Edward and Ebenezer married the Dibble sisters back in Stamford. In 1760, Joseph gifted each son land sufficient to start a farm.[17]

However, the brothers were more ambitious than to remain yeoman farmers. In 1764 they sold their land and moved north to Albany where they made business connections with the influential people of that town.

Their names soon appeared alongside the Albany elite in land grants from Governor Moore. In 1767 they were among those named as proprietors for two large tracts totaling 11,600 acres located along the upper Hudson River north of the Kayaderosseras Patent. There at the confluence of the Sacandaga and Hudson Rivers they built their spacious log homes, erected saw and grist mills, and established a ferry service. The settlement became known as Jessup's Landing. This was only the beginning. In 1774 they were among forty recipients of 40,000 acres north of Hudson encompassing most of today's Warren County, New York. They also played a leading role in the largest patent ever granted by the colonial authorities, the Totten and Crossfield Purchase, which secured most of the Adirondacks for the colony.[18]

It is hard to imagine how these brothers had risen so far so fast, until you see the names of their associates in these deals. Sir William Johnson was part of the 1767 grants and he negotiated the purchase of the larger tract from the Mohawks in 1772. The Jessup brothers had cultivated a close relationship with Sir William. In 1774 Edward was among the dozen gentlemen present at the Iroquois Ceremony of Condolence that was performed after his death. Their close association with Johnson and the royal governors predicted their allegiance to the King as war approached.[19]

The settlers of Middleline Road had no such lofty connections. Their connections were to their Yankee roots, family ties and their relationship with James Gordon who would soon become an outspoken advocate for the rebel cause.

The opening battle of the conflict at Lexington and Concord was indeed "the shot heard round the world". But, in reality, the insurgency had begun almost a year earlier in New England as a result of the onerous response of the British government to the Boston Tea Party in December 1773. Under these laws, known in the colonies as the Intolerable Acts, the Port of Boston was closed, the government of Massachusetts came under direct control of the Crown, soldiers could be quartered in private buildings, and accused government officials could be sent back to England for trial. Parliament passed these laws in March 1774 and General Gage arrived in Boston in May, bringing with him a contingent of British regulars, to enforce them. During the next several months, the outrage of New Englanders spread throughout the thirteen colonies. Average Americans, fearful of the loss of their rights as British subjects, came around to the necessity of separating from the mother country, often in advance of their more conservative patriot leaders.[20]

Many New Yorkers joined their New England brethren on the path to independence. However, for the colony as a whole, it was not going to be an easy path. Many in the colony, from New York City northward along the Hudson and westward along the Mohawk, were not so sure they wanted to sign on to with the rebels. They were uncertain of the outcome of the struggle and unsure of their own allegiance. Many wanted the conflict to just go away, so they could go on with their normal lives.

The uncertainly that New York would fully support the revolution was based on the complexity of its society. Founded as a Dutch colony, the old ways still influenced the politics of New York. Old Dutch families in Albany were not always loyal to the British authorities, often engaging in trade with the French Canadians, even in time of war. Struggles for influence over the Iroquois, their trade and their lands, created schisms between the Albany Dutch and William Johnson, whom they considered an upstart from Ireland. The large patroonships, such as Rennesselaerswyck, created their own schisms between land owners and tenants. As settlers moved into New York from Massachusetts and Connecticut, relationships were not always cordial between the "Yorkers" and the "Yankees". New York had a large contingent of black slaves, always a potential source of unrest. New immigrants from Ireland and Scotland and British soldiers who remained in America after the French War added to the ethnic mix. Relationships between these different groups would impact how the revolution would unfold—in the state, in Albany County and at the local level in new settlements like Ball's Town.

In July 1774, Lt. Governor Colden, in a letter to Lord North, noted the creation of the Committee of Fifty-One, formed in New York City in response to the Intolerable Acts. He seem pleased that many on the committee were "most considerable merchants, and men of cool tempers, who would endeavor to avoid all extravagant and dangerous measures." He further reassured North that "the present political zeal and phrenzy is almost entirely confined to the City of New-York, the people in the counties are no ways disposed to become active, or to hear any part of what is proposed by the citizens."[21] Colden underestimated the forces being unleashed in New York by the British occupation of Boston.

In August, in Tryon County west of Albany, the Palatine Committee forcefully sided with the growing insurgency. In their resolutions they condemned the occupation and resolved "that we will unite and join with the different districts of this county, in giving whatever relief is in our power to the poor distressed inhabitants of Boston."[22] Events on the continental stage were forcing individuals and families to consider how they would respond to the coming conflict. In New York these decisions may have come slower and were complicated by ethnic, religious, racial and economic fault lines. But by mid-1774, many of the farmers of Tryon County, the home of the powerful pro-British Johnson family, were poised to rise in rebellion.

In September 1774, the First Continental Congress met in Philadelphia to address the growing crisis. The response of the Congress was to impose a boycott on British goods which was to reduce imports by 97 percent during 1775.[23] This was accomplished through the approval of a fourteen-point Association, in which the representatives outlined the specific items that could not be imported, including all "Good Wares and Merchandises" as well as East India tea, molasses and wines. The Association also included a provision that the colonies would "neither import nor purchase any Slave imported after the first day of December next, after which time we will wholly discontinue the slave trade."[24] Agreeing to these provisions would have a major economic impact on the colonies as well as the mother country.

More important than this prohibited list, was the means established to enforce the non-importation provisions. The Association included a provision (article eleven) "That a Committee be chose in every County, City and Town...whose business it shall be attentively to observe all persons touching this Association." and that the names of anyone found violating its provisions shall be published "to the end that all such foes to the rights of British America may be publickly known and universally contemned(sic) as the enemies of American Liberty."[25] This legitimized and expanded the role of the local committees that had been a part of the colonial political landscape since the Stamp Act uprising in 1765. In effect, by providing a direct link between the Continental Congress and local authorities, this legislation was a major step in creating the mechanisms to enforce the later decision to declare independence.[26]

Local officials throughout the colonies immediately proceeded to establish these committees. On November 7th, Isaac Low, returning to New York City after the adjournment of the Continental Congress, called for the election of eight members in each Ward of the city to enforce the provisions of the Association. The Committee of Sixty began its work on November 22.[27] This committee was similar to its predecessor, the Committee of Fifty-One, in that it was controlled by the more moderate, established leaders of the city, even though many radicals were included in its membership.[28] Isaac Low, a Trustee of the Kayaderosseras Patent, served as chairman of both of these committees.[29]

∞

On January 24, 1775 the Albany Committee of Correspondence held its first official meeting at the inn of Richard Cartwright in Albany. Unbeknownst to the men of the committee, Cartwright was a Loyalist who was in the business of passing secret messages for the British authorities. His son Richard later journeyed to Niagara and became the secretary to John Butler who later formed Butler's Rangers.[30] The committee soon relocated to the Town Hall, a building they would share with the suspected traitors that they would imprison in the basement.[31]

The records of this Committee and its successor, the Commission for Detecting and Defeating Conspiracies, provide a window into the activities of the Patriots and Loyalists of Ballston and surrounding towns. The first mention of Ballston is in May, 1775 when Elisha Benedict "made application to this board for the privilege of raising a company to be ready to take the field when called upon by the province."[32] As we have seen in the last chapter, Benedict and James Gordon did not get along so well. Apparently Benedict's prior military experience had not impressed Gordon. However, Gordon himself could be a difficult person to deal with. After being chastised by the committee for acting informally and not properly organizing a local Committee and attending meetings in Albany, he pushed back.

> I must again plead our poverty it being clear to me that if it pleased God to blast our crops this year the same as last it would ruin above one half of the people of this place, this makes it more incumbent upon them to give due attention to their farms, for you can't conceive how inconvenient it is for anyone here to leave their business but for one day.[33]

This gives an indication of how precarious life was for these newly-arriving pioneers, struggling to establish their homesteads on land still more woodland wilderness than settled farmland. But Gordon's letter also gives us an insight into his character. An ambitious man and an ardent patriot, he was nonetheless willing to come to the defense of his fellow pioneers. As a leader in the new community he displayed an obligation to protect their interests. However, the Ballston community would comply with the rules established by the Continental Congress and the Albany Committee. Later that month Beriah Palmer notified the Committee that the local leadership was in place. Tyrannus Collins, Eliphalet Kellog, Stephen White, and Andrew Mitchell joined Gordon on the Ballston committee.[34]

The next step was to organize the military response to the British. Both the Continental Congress and the New York Provincial Assembly had recommended the formation of militia companies, but it fell to the Committees of Correspondence to work out the details, since they were best positioned to understand the geographic distribution of the units. They also were knowledgeable of the leadership capabilities of the local men. In August 1775 the committee tentatively proposed the formation of thirteen companies in Albany County. The 10th Militia was to include the towns of "Half Moon, Newtown, Niscajonie, Clifton Park, Ball's Town and the southern part of Cayaderossras."[35] The next month elections were held and the field officers were named. For the "Half Moon and Ball's Town District" (now designated as the 12th Albany County Militia) Jacobus Van Schoonhoven was appointed colonel and James Gordon became the lieutenant colonel.[36] Van Schoonhoven was a well-connected merchant from one of the early Dutch families of Albany.

The work of discerning friend from foe began. The Committee and the militia became the two organizations responsible to ferret out the disaffected. The militia, the military arm, would be the boots on the ground, while the Committee would pass judgment on those brought before them. The first tool used to determine allegiances was the Association supporting the actions of the Continental Congress in response to the Intolerable Acts. As the conflict evolved into full-scale rebellion, local committees circulated Association documents among the people in their district which all residents were encouraged to sign. They were designed as a litmus test to prove loyalty to the Continental Congress, and after 1776, to the United States. Each local committee was instructed to return their list to the Albany committee, along with the names of those who refused to sign.

Often those that refused were brought before the Albany committee to be examined. If there was additional evidence that they were "disaffected" (loyal to the King), they faced the possibility of being sent downstairs to the gaol, or worse. Some of the disaffected were sent to prison ships on the Hudson at Esopus (Kingston), or to the underground copper mines in Simsbury, Connecticut. For many their appearance would end with their release, often with written assurances of their loyalty and good behavior reinforced by bonds put up on their behalf.

The first prominent suspected Tories to come under the scrutiny of the Committee were Guy Johnson and his brother-in-law Sir John Johnson, son of Sir William Johnson. Guy Johnson had succeeded Sir William as Indian Department Superintendent in July 1774. His activities in recruiting the Iroquois to join the British side in the deepening dispute had drawn the ire of the local rebels in Tryon County. In May 1775 he fled to Montreal and later that year sailed back to England to seek restoration of his position as Indian Superintendent. In this journey he was accompanied by Daniel Claus, son-in-law of William Johnson, and the Mohawk Joseph Brant, brother of Molly Brant, consort of Sir William. A family excursion, to be sure.[37]

Meanwhile John Johnson and Loyalist Tryon County Sherriff Alexander White, along with several hundred local residents, many of them tenants of the Johnsons, had taken up defensive positions at Johnson Hall. In July 1775, Johnson agreed to "take no further active part in the dispute between Great Britain and the American colonies", but his "subversive" activities continued.[38] General Schuyler, fresh from his appointment as one of four major generals of the Continental Army, marched west along the Mohawk with 3000 troops and confronted him along the road to Johnson Hall in January 1776. Johnson once again demurred and agreed to give up his arms and military stores. This agreement was also ignored and Schuyler ordered his arrest. In May 1776 Colonel Dayton and the newly formed 3rd New Jersey Regiment was dispatched to Johnstown to arrest him, but Johnson fled to Canada, bringing with him a considerable cadre of supporters.[39] Johnson and his followers formed the core of the King's Royal Regiment of New York, which would make its presence known to area settlers along the frontier throughout the war years.

By July 1776, the die had been cast for independence. As word spread that the Continental Congress had taken the fateful, final step toward separation, Loyalists groups who still harbored the hope of reconciliation took their own steps northward to the security of the British lines in Canada. By that time, the last of the American troops had been forced out of Canada after their year-long effort to secure a fourteenth colony for the new nation.

The British, under Governor Guy Carleton, advanced to Crown Point and Loyalists began joining him there in the fall of 1776 after the rebels were forced to abandon Lake Champlain as a result of the defeat of Benedict Arnold's naval force at Valcour Island in October. One of the largest contingents was led by the Jessup brothers. As their Tory sympathies had become known, Ebenezer and Edward had seen their enclave on the upper Hudson disintegrate. Their mills and ferries were no longer operating, having been burned by marauding rebels. They carefully planned their move, assembling the provisions necessary to support the ninety men they brought into Carleton's camp at Crown Point in October. There they initially were assigned to Johnson's King's Royal Regiment, but lobbied for an independent command, which they received during Burgoyne's campaign the next year.[40]

Other supporters of the King were not as fortunate in these first years of the revolution. For them the final escape to Canada came only after a

long running battle of wits with the Albany Committee and its supporting militia. John Munro the strong advocate for the New York authorities
in the struggle over land titles in the Hampshire Grants, soon came under
suspicion as well. He was turned in by his brother Daniel, who tipped off
the committee that John had accepted a captain's commission in the Royal
Highland Emigrants under the command of Colonel Allan Maclean. On
August 22, 1775 the Albany Committee authorized the Cambridge district to seek out both Daniel and John, to get at the truth of the matter.
Upon confronting them Daniel admitted he had made up the story as a
result of a grudge he held against his brother. Nonetheless, the militia
searched through John's papers, found nothing incriminating and left.
In his report to the Albany Committee, Daniel Bratt, a member of the
Hoosick Committee, praised Munro who appeared to be a very willing
defendant, stating that "during the whole transaction, Mr. Munro's behavior was very manly and we cannot think he is in the least guilty."[41]

They were wrong. John had gone to New York to meet with Col.
Maclean. This British officer had been given authority to raise Loyalists in
America. Munro was one of the recruiters for Maclean's regiment, known
as the Royal Highland Emigrants. Munro had met Maclean in New York
City and guided him through the Mohawk Valley west of Albany towards
Canada. He then returned home, recruiting partisans in his Bennington
neighborhood to join in the Tory resistance movement.[42] Maclean went
on to assist in the defense of Canada. After recruiting a number of men
in Montreal, he arrived in Quebec City in November 1775 with a relief
force on the day before Benedict Arnold crossed the St. Lawrence to lay
siege to the city.[43]

On April 30, 1776, Munro was brought before the Committee again.
They released him on his promise to stand down from his activities. He
could "live quietly and unmolested as long as he continued to observe the
terms of his parole."[44] Munro, being committed to the cause of the King,
was not about to follow those strictures. Three weeks later he was among
those named to be taken prisoner during the general Tory roundup related to the confrontation with John Johnson.

Captain Daniel McAlpin was on the same list and both were arrested
a week later.[45] Initially held in the basement cells of the Albany Town Hall,
they were soon moved to better accommodations in the fort up the hill.

Apparently their status as well-known, and previously well-respected, members of the community still counted for something.[46] In July the committee decided to remove them to Connecticut but at the last minute McAlpin received a reprieve from General Schuyler due to his age and ill health and was allowed to return to his home with the usual admonition to behave himself. Like Munro he ignored it and went on recruiting from his Saratoga Lake home. By the spring of 1777 the Committee had had enough. On April 2nd, the Saratoga Militia was instructed to bring him in once again. This time he had no choice but to escape north to Canada with his recruits, leaving his family behind.[47]

McAlpin's decision to seek refuge with the British was increasingly common among Loyalists in 1777. The authorities of the new American government were coming down hard on them—the joint efforts of the local committees and the militia were beginning to have their effects. And as the year wore on, the possibility of joining Burgoyne's campaign, whose success they thought inevitable, further increased the northward migration. However, these decisions were made at great personal sacrifice. Their families and their livelihoods were left exposed to their enemies. In the McAlpin's case all was lost. Under orders from the Committee, Lt. Col. James Gordon along with 150 men from the Ballston militia, seized everything they had.[48] Mary McAlpin refused to cooperate. She and her three children were brought to Albany and paraded around in a cart, "in a very scandalous manner, so much that the Americans themselves cried out about it."[49]

Meanwhile Munro was imprisoned and removed to Connecticut under the custody of Governor Jonathan Trumbull. However, to the surprise of the Committee, he turned up in Albany in February 1777 where Munro produced a parole issued by Trumbull on December 23, 1776, allowing him to return to his family in Cambridge, New York, until March, 1777.[50] The Committee would have none of that. Being labeled a "dangerous enemy to the cause of America" he was held in confinement in the Albany fort.[51] Some accounts state that he escaped to join Burgoyne while others indicate that he may have been among a group that was released to join the enemy.[52] In any case, his family suffered as had the McAlpins. The Vermont Council of Safely seized all property, leaving only two cows to sustain Mary and her eight children. She was even turned away by her own family, who refused to help her. In a letter to John in Canada she tells of her plight. While the children were well, she was not, and under much stress.

> I must leave my house in a very short time and God knows where I shall get a place to put my head in, for my own relations are my greatest enemies, They have distressed me beyond expression. I have scarcely a mouthful of bread for myself or children.[53]

The tug of war between the rebels and the Loyalists was felt on a daily basis. By 1777 this struggle for survival and revenge was beginning to affect everyone on the northern frontier. Burgoyne's invasion had laid waste to the land and scattered the inhabitants in its wake. The uncertainty of determining who remained loyal to the Crown and who supported the new nation was complicated by the strategy of Burgoyne to offer protection to those locals who would come into his camp. In August many came and brought their livestock to support British and Hessian troops assembled around Fort Edward. Some were Tories, some were neutrals—it was hard to tell.[54] After Burgoyne's surrender a certain amount of lawlessness prevailed, as vigilantes roamed the countryside seeking revenge against those perceived Tories that remained. The Committee attempted to restore order, reminding the local districts to reign in their citizens.

> Resolved. That the inflicting of any Corporal punishment or the depriving of any of the Subjects of this State of their property without proper authority is an infringement of the Privileges of the People contrary to sound Policy and in direct violation of all Law and Justice. This committee will do the utmost of their endeavor to suppress every such Riotous and illegal proceedings, and will exert themselves in causing such Riotous Persons to be brought to Justice.[55]

In spite of these attempts to restore law and order, for many there would be no peace in the years to follow.

∞

Located twenty miles to the west of the battle zone along the Hudson River, the town of Ballston escaped the invasion of Burgoyne's army in 1777. However, that did not mean its citizens were unaffected by the events of that year. Until the Revolution began to command their attention, the new families of Ballston and Middleline Road were fully engaged in the everyday activities of all pioneers—building their small log cabins, clearing the fields to plant crops, and bartering timber and potash for the necessities they could not make themselves.

It had been five years since James Gordon purchased his 1,000 acres and began erecting his mills along the Mourning Kill. On the same day—April 21, 1772— William Fraser had purchased 202 acres from Dirck Lefferts for £90. His lot was located in the southwest corner of the Five-Mile Square in an area known as Scotch Bush, about two miles from Gordon's mills. William and his brother Thomas had emigrated with their parents from Inverness, Scotland, in 1767. They settled as tenant farmers on 100 acres leased from William Johnson in the Kingsborough Patent, a few miles east of Johnson Hall. The Fraser's Kayaderosseras Patent purchase indicated that they were enterprising farmers eager to take advantage of the opportunity to improve their circumstances and leave the life of a tenant farmer behind.

However, they maintained their allegiance to the Johnson family and Thomas may have been among those with John Johnson when he fled to Canada in 1776. Both William and Thomas became members of Daniel McAlpin's Loyalists and in 1777 were increasingly active in recruiting men for the King's service. William's activities brought him to the attention of the Albany Committee and the local militia. Lt. Colonel Gordon had infiltrated Fraser's band and was aware of their plans to join Burgoyne. In May, after skulking in the woods for some time, they made a dash north to meet up with the British troops assembling along Lake Champlain. They didn't get very far, before being caught on the upper Hudson River near the settlement of the Jessup brothers. The Frasers and their forty men were brought back to Albany by Gordon's captain, Tyrannus Collins, and other militiamen.[56] William and Thomas were sentenced to a year in the Albany jail, but their followers were fined $15 and released. At their court-martial they were convicted of withholding their service from the state and professing loyalty to the King, but exonerated of the more serious charge of "wickedly, traitorously and treasonably... attempting to go privately to the enemy."[57]

The story does not end there, however. The Albany jail was not a very secure place. Family members often came and went, bringing food to the prisoners. In July the wife of Thomas made her usual visit with an unusual gift—a file and rope she had baked into a cake. With these items the brothers and their cellmates escaped and were able to meet up with Burgoyne at Fort Edward.[58]

The Burgoyne campaign had drawn out many locals willing to join and fight alongside the invaders. His army of over 8,000 British, Hessians, Indians and Canadians included only eighty-three Loyalists at the start of the campaign. As groups filtered in over the summer those numbers grew to over 800 at their peak.[59] Jessup's and McAlpin's units made up many of this number and a significant portion were recruited from the local area—today's Washington, Saratoga and Montgomery counties. Jessup's men were among the British force that placed cannon on Mount Defiance, forcing the surrender of Fort Ticonderoga in early July. Hugh Munro of Jessup's Corps commanded a bateaux company which included men from McAlpin's Corps. Both Loyalist units saw limited action during the two battles at Saratoga where they were assigned to General Simon Fraser's advanced corps.[60]

On the rebel side, the extent of the participation of the Ballston men of 12th Albany County Militia in the Saratoga campaign is unclear. On August 1, 1777, Governor Clinton ordered that 1000 men be recruited from the Albany County Militia to join in the defense against Burgoyne. To insure a full and speedy response to this draft, the troops that were raised would be "entitled to continental pay and rations, and a bounty from the fines to be levied upon exempts refusing service."[61] On August 20th, this detachment was organized into two brigades, under the command of Colonel Abraham Wemple of the 2nd Regiment and Colonel William Whiting, who led the 17th Regiment. These men were assigned to the Brigade of General John Glover, which was held in reserve during the first battle at Freeman's Farm on September 19.

On September 18th Governor Clinton ordered General Ten Broeck, the overall commander of the Albany County Militia, to join Gates' army with the remainder of his brigade.[62] It is probable that some soldiers of

James Gordon's 12th militia participated in the second battle on October 7, assigned to the left wing of the army that attacked the Balcarres and Breyman redoubts, the actions in which Benedict Arnold gained much notoriety for the American cause.[63] A recently discovered letter refutes the long held assumption that Arnold led the attack without orders. Rather, the letter, written by an adjutant at Arnold's headquarters, claims that Arnold asked Gates to "let me have men and we will have some fun with them before sunset."[64] Apparently the Albany County Militia were engaged in this late afternoon attack. General James Wilkinson, at Gates' direction, personally ordered Ten Broeck to move his 3000 man brigade forward to join the fight.[65] His troops arrived on the field shortly after British General Fraser fell mortally wounded, and participated in the rout of the British.[66] In the enumeration of the American forces taken in the days preceding Burgoyne's surrender a total of 987 Albany militia rank and file were present and fit for duty. Unfortunately, no breakdown by regiment exists.[67]

Pension records confirm that some of Gordon's neighbors along Middleline Road were involved in the Saratoga campaign and the subsequent siege and surrender of Burgoyne on October 19. Thomas Barnum, who lived just north of Gordon, was part of a contingent that removed military stores from Fort George to Fort Edward in July. After assisting in the efforts to destroy the road and bridges in front of Burgoyne's advance, he returned home to harvest his crops, as did many of the local militia units during the month of August. However, he did return to active duty in time for the first battle, where he was in the reserve corps that was not called into action. It appears that he was present throughout the second battle continuing until Burgoyne's surrender. It is probable that Barnum's experience was shared by other members of the militia living along Middleline Road.[68]

With Burgoyne's surrender most of the Loyalist units were allowed to travel to Canada where they maintained their allegiance to the British cause. The Convention of Saratoga between Gates and Burgoyne exempted the Loyalists from being surrendered along with the British and German troops. Fearful that Loyalists held as prisoners would be subject to worse treatment than their British and Germany comrades, Article Nine spared them that fate.

All Canadians and persons belonging to the Canadian establishment consisting of sailors, bateaux men, artificers, drivers, independent companies and many other followers of the army who come under no particular description are to be permitted to return there. They are to be conducted immediately by the shortest route to the first British post on Lake George, are to be supplied with provisions in the same manner as the other troops, and are to be bound by the same conditions of not serving during the present contest in North America.[69]

Circumstances allowed them not to adhere to this last provision. The Convention, which allowed Burgoyne's army to return to England, was not accepted by the Continental Congress, and the British troops were held as prisoners of war until the end of the conflict. The Loyalists were freed from their obligations not to take up arms against the Americans. Safely back in Canada, these companies would be heard from again in the remaining years of the revolution, as the conflict became a small scale, but increasingly bitter, civil war.

∞

Not all Loyalists returned to Canada after Burgoyne's capitulation. Some were willing to accept defeat, take the oath to support the new nation, and return quietly to their farms. They may still have harbored animus for the rebels and may have on occasion found opportunity to support the self-styled "Cowboy" Tories lurking in the countryside. But for the sake of their families and their prospects they remained at home. In Ballston, an example of this cohort was noted in the minutes of the Committee on Conspiracies, dated April 15, 1778.

Col. Gordon and Capt. Collins appeared before this board and represented that Robert Russell, Roger Hyatt, John Smyth, Archibald Mc Nue-McNight, James Robison, John Fairman, George Gardiner, Jonathan Tuttle, Stutley Scranton, Henry Bolton and George Bolton, persons now residing in Ballston, after having taken up arms against the United States with Gen. Burgoyne, and from appearances they judge that the above persons will return to their duty. Thereupon resolve that Col Gordon and Cap Collins be requested to cause the said offenders to appear before them to enter into bail for their future good conduct."[70]

Most of these men returned to their quiet lives since nothing more is heard of them in the Committee records, although there is evidence that at least one of them may have turned once again. Stutley Scranton was brought before the Committee again in August, found guilty of going over to the enemy and fined £100.[71]

On the same day as Gordon presented the above list to the board, "Nicholas Hagerman of Ball's Town" was charged with deserting and planning to go to the enemy. With no proof, he was released on bail put up by his father Christopher Hagerman.[72] Christopher was a veteran of the French and Indian War who had been granted 2,000 acres in Albany County for his service.[73] Nicholas' father (or brother) Christopher was on the tax rolls in 1779, with an assessed value of £155.[74] Nicholas was born in 1761 and served in the 1st Regiment of the New York Continental Line and the 12th Albany County Militia, Gordon's unit. In spite of his release by the Board, he apparently went over to the British side in 1778. He was also among a group of Loyalists who boarded a vessel in New York City to go to Canada in 1783.[75] He settled and married there in 1780. He was apparently a lawyer as was his son Christopher who served several years in the Legislative Assembly of Upper Canada. Nicholas died in 1819 and is buried in the United Empire Loyalist Cemetery in Adolphustown, Ontario, Canada. Hagerman's time in Ballston was brief and he was able to find success in his new home in Canada.

Others may have considered supporting the King but wavered and eventually either remained neutral or turned to the rebel cause. In most cases they were able to go on with their normal lives while under the watchful eyes of the local committee. Gilbert Miller was one of those men who walked a fine line. He and his brother Elisha, a physician, had been early arrivals in Ballston, one of the families from Bedford enticed to the new township by Rev. Eliphalet Ball. Gilbert purchased 403 acres from Dirck Lefferts in March 1772 and soon thereafter acquired additional lots in the third division of the Five-Mile Square, west of Middleline Road. His land holdings of more than 1,000 acres equaled that of James Gordon. His 1779 tax assessment of £778 actually exceeded Gordon's and was among the highest in the town.[76]

However, unlike Gordon, Miller was a reluctant patriot at best. In April 1776 he was given a reprimand by the Albany Committee and encouraged to "behave better in the future."[77] Almost four years later he was arrested and released on £100 bail put up by his neighbor, Joseph Bettys, Sr.[78] Apparently he later returned to the good graces of the local authorities because in 1787 he was the tax collector for the Town of Ballston. The tax assessment that year indicated that his real property was valued at £52, again one of the highest in the town.[79] His economic situation had not been adversely affected by his flirtation with the Loyalists. It is interesting that the supervisor in 1787 was James Gordon an example of former adversaries serving together in post-war America.

Another interesting case involved Edward Finn. He was brought before the Board in April, 1779 under suspicion of being involved in robberies in the area. He was confined but released on bail provided by Dr. George Smyth, who had provided surety for a number of men suspected of Tory tendencies. In February 1780, Finn petitioned the board to be allowed to go to Ballston to work as a schoolmaster. The board agreed with the restriction that he should not leave the town without the approval of James Gordon. Smyth himself was a ringleader of the local Tory spy network and would later flee to Canada.[80]

Men of much higher local visibility than Scranton, Hagerman, Miller or Finn were also making their decisions, or trying to avoid making them, as the Revolution unfolded. Prominent landowners of the Kayaderosseras Patent were among those whose choices would have a major impact on their future. As we have seen, Isaac Low became a Loyalist and his property was confiscated, including his lands in the Patent. Another trustee, Dirck Lefferts, sided with the Americans and continued to manage the sales of the Patent lands with Beriah Palmer as his local agent. They had both been fortunate to choose the winning side in the conflict.

Several successful businessmen turned land speculators in the Patent

wavered in their allegiance, hoping that the outcome would be determined before they were forced to choose sides. As the conflict continued
year after year, waiting became increasingly hard to do. Daniel Campbell,
that enthusiastic investor in the Kayaderosseras lands, walked a fine line
with the authorities. He was detained in May 1777 by the Schenectady
Committee of Correspondence along with several other local businessmen, including James Ellice, Gysbert Fonda, John Glen and Robert
Clench, all previously mentioned in this narrative. Apparently Campbell
was involved in trading with the British or their local supporters. Under
threat of being sent down to the prison ships at Kingston, they all agreed
to sign the Oath, which stated in part

> I do most solemnly swear in the presence of Almighty
> God that I will not by words or deeds give any Concel
> advice Derections aid or Comfort to any of the Enemies
> of the United States of America.[81]

For Campbell the allure of profits proved too much to forsake and he
continued selling goods to both sides during the conflict. In May 1778 he
and James Ellice were fined £500 each. In July they were ordered held to
be removed to enemy lines, but then in August they agreed to take another Oath of Allegiance. The board referred this request to New York's
Supreme Court and they were eventually allowed to take the oath in
May 1779 as a result of an act of the legislature. With this resolution they
were able to resume their business enterprises, this time selling only to
the Americans, not the British.[82]

∞

The war took a different turn in New York after 1777. Gone were the
large invading British armies and the mass assemblage of Continental and
militia troops to oppose them. The war had reached a stalemate in the
north with General Henry Clinton secure in New York City and the troops
of George Washington ringing the city. Further north the war became
local and low-key. The Committees and local militia continued to play
cat-and-mouse with the Loyalists still in their midst. The longer the war

continued, the more personal the conflict became. Each year both sides acted under the assumption that another large-scale invasion would come. The British in Canada feared that the Rebels new ally, France, would appear beneath the cliffs of Quebec to take back their old province. Frederick Haldimand, returning to Canada where he had served in the 60th Foot during the French War, became the new Governor of Quebec Province in 1778. He took what steps he could to keep the Americans to the south weak and off balance, to prevent a repetition of the 1775 invasion of Canada.

In fact, northern New York had much more to fear from the British and Loyalists in Canada. Incursions from the north occurred every year after 1777, as we will see in the next chapter. The British controlled Lake Champlain and the Niagara frontier and could rely on their Loyalist and Indian allies to take the fight to the Americans, often seeking revenge from those who had evicted them from their homeland. In addition, the new nation was not very effective in providing resources to control their northern border. General Gates' army essentially disappeared after the battles at Saratoga. The militia units dispersed to their homes and the brigades of the Continental Army were recalled to defend Philadelphia. Another simmering dispute further weakened the American defense of the northern frontier. Ethan Allen and other leaders of the nascent state of Vermont entered into negotiations with Haldimand, who wanted to attach this area to Canada. This effectively took the Hampshire Grants out of the war.[83]

Haldimand proved to be an effective leader of the British in Canada by playing the hand he was dealt. He was reluctant at first to actively engage the Loyalists for incursions into New York, preferring to keep the forces of Sir John Johnson, the Jessup brothers and others on garrison duty at posts along the Richelieu River. These units were under-strength and he was willing to allow Loyalist recruiters to return to their old neighborhoods and bring in additional men. In addition, Haldimand needed intelligence on the activities of the rebels and for that he established a spy network to act as his eyes and ears on the pathways between the two centers of British control, Quebec and occupied New York City. Two Loyalists were given the assignment to put this plan into action. Dr. George Smyth of Albany, who had become an "agent in place" for the British cause in Albany, and Justus Sherwood, a former Green Mountain Boy now turned

Loyalist, teamed up in 1781 to run this operation for Haldimand. They established their headquarters at the Loyal Blockhouse, a remote and secure location on Grand Isle in Lake Champlain. From there they had no shortage of volunteers to skulk southward to do what they could to keep the rebels off balance. Many of these men were anxious to return to their old neighborhoods and settle old scores.[84]

Joe Bettys[85] grew into adulthood listening to the conversations of the people who would frequent his father's tavern along the Middleline. He would certainly have known the influential people of the new settlement, including James Gordon, Tyrannus Collins and John Ball, the oldest surviving son of Rev. Eliphalet Ball. Patriots all, the discussions at the tavern in 1775 would have been all about the growing conflict and what their response should be. Gordon and Collins had already taken up the challenge, joining both the local Committee of Correspondence and the Albany County Militia.

Twenty-year-old John Ball was anxious to become involved and in March 1776 he was appointed a second lieutenant under Captain Samuel Van Veghten in the regiment of Colonel Cornelius Wynkoop. The well-connected Ball knew his friend Joe Bettys to be "bold, athletic and intelligent to an uncommon degree" and was able to obtain a position for him as a sergeant in his company. Ball also knew that Bettys had an "irritable and determined spirit", aware of his willingness to settle arguments with his fists. This volatility soon got him in trouble when he got into a fight with an officer. Reduced in rank, in the summer of 1776 John Ball was able to use his influence to get Bettys transferred to the command of General Benedict Arnold, whose troops were busily engaged in building the vessels at Skenesborough to take on the British on Lake Champlain.[86] Wynkoop seems to have noticed something in Bettys that disturbed him. In a letter to General Horatio Gates he mentioned his concern: "I also send you one sailor (Bettys) out of my regiment down. I would be glad you would order him down immediately or I am afraid he will run off and leave you."[87] Bettys was assigned as first mate on the Gondola *Philadelphia* about two weeks after the vessel arrived at Mount Independence across from Fort Ticonderoga for rigging and arming on August 1, 1775.[88]

The high point of Bettys' American service came at the Battle of Valcour Island in October 1776 where his courage was on display. Serving on the *Philadelphia*, he fought desperately until forced to abandon the ship. The survivors transferred to the heavily damaged *Washington*, the flagship of General David Waterbury, which was forced to surrender the next day. Bettys was among eighteen members of the *Philadelphia* who were captured but paroled by Governor Guy Carleton after they agreed not to take up arms again against the King.[89] Although praised by Waterbury, Bettys switched sides and traveled to Canada where the British offered him an ensign's commission in the Loyalist forces.[90]

His skills, daring, and local knowledge of both people and geography soon were put to use. In September 1777 he arrived in Burgoyne's camp with six other men just before the first Battle at Freeman's Farm, and was sent into the American lines to gather intelligence. He next went on a recruiting trip below Albany and returned with fourteen men. Bettys then traveled south as far as Catskill to confirm whether General Henry Clinton was on his way up the Hudson to relieve Burgoyne's beleaguered army. This mission was ordered by General Fraser who was killed during the second battle on October 7. Bettys returned on October 16 and was immediately sent by General Burgoyne to carry the message of the dire situation of the British army to Henry Clinton in New York.[91]

In January of 1779 he was captured in the Hudson Valley and sentenced to death, only to be released by General Washington on July 4, 1779, as part of a general pardon. Several sources attribute his release to the requests of his parents and local patriots.[92] In Bettys' own account, he was held in irons at Fishkill until he escaped on August 16 and went home to Ballston to recover from his ordeal.[93] He returned to Canada and in 1780 participated in several incursions, including an attack on Skenesborough in March and Sir John Johnson's raid on Johnstown in May. He also successfully recruited additional men to the Loyalist cause, guiding them back to Canada. His possible involvement in the 1780 raid on Ballston will be described in a later chapter.

In 1781 he teamed up with another "notorious Tory", John Walden Meyers, to capture several Ballston residents and carry them back to Canada. In early June, Meyers entered the center of the little village in the vicinity of Bettys' father's tavern, released twelve prisoners from the town jail and proceeded up the east side of Long (Ballston) Lake where he captured John Fulmer, Epenetus White, David Ramsey and Christian and Henry Banta. Bettys proceeded west of the Middleline where he took Samuel Nash, Joseph Chard, Uri and Ephraim Tracey and Samuel Patchen, son of Jabez who had been captured in the larger British raid the year before.[94] While the others took the Oath of Loyalty to the king and were released, Patchen was held prisoner in Canada until he escaped with several others in 1782. Leaving his companions, he constructed a raft to navigate Lake Champlain, only to be captured by a British ship, which took him to Quebec where he was exchanged and sent to Boston.[95]

In the most ambitious Tory action of 1781, Joe Bettys' string of successful raids came to an end, thanks to his own dalliance. Governor Haldimand was becoming increasingly frustrated with the course of the war. The Rebels were winning the civil war in northern New York. The Committee on Conspiracies had become increasingly effective in ferreting out Loyalists among the population. General Philip Schuyler was especially adept at disseminating misinformation and infiltrating Tory units with double agents. Haldimand, with the support of Dr. Smyth and Sherwood, devised a bold plan to kidnap prominent rebel leaders, including General Schuyler himself. Several teams were in place on July 31, 1781 for the coordinated attacks. Bettys' target was Samuel Stringer of Ballston, a physician in Albany and a leading member of the Committee on Conspiracies.[96]

John Meyers had about a dozen men in place for an assault on Schuyler at his Albany home. When they arrived the area was swarming with militia patrols. The authorities had been tipped off by Jellis Legrange. Legrange, a nominal Loyalist, was incensed that his daughter had run off with Joe Bettys on the eve of the raids and had alerted the Committee that he was in the area. The militia was on high alert. Several days later when the situation had calmed, Meyers' attempt to capture Schuyler was thwarted when Schulyer himself sounded the alarm. None of the planned kidnappings were successful. Haldimand was furious with Bettys, who had brought his new love back to Canada with him, leaving his wife Abigail and his children back in Ballston. It is a testament to his skills as a spy that the governor allowed him to remain in the British service.[97]

The next year Bettys' luck ran out. Spotted crossing a field near the present town of Jonesville, southeast of Ballston, he was tracked to the house of a local Tory and he was captured by three local men. He was carrying dispatches which proved his guilt and he was marched under guard to Albany where he was convicted and hanged on April 1, 1782. Some forty years later, John Ball compared the capture of Bettys to that of Major André, the accomplice of Benedict Arnold.

> The conduct of the captors of André was noble, but that of the captors of Bettys was both noble and heroic. Andre was a gentleman and without means of defense. Bettys was fully armed and known to be a desperado. The capture of the former was by accident, of the latter by enterprise and design. That of the former was without danger; of the latter, at the imminent peril of life. None have claims to celebrity superior to those of Fulmer, Cory and Perkins. [98]

Ball, Bettys' old friend and early advocate, raised his glass to toast the captors of this notorious Tory of Ballston. The rekindled passions of these old men toasting the local heroes of a conflict long past is a testament to the effect the war had on those that lived through it.

CHAPTER 7
War on the Frontier

Personal animosities had certainly grown and festered over the five years since the outbreak of hostilities in 1775. The longer the conflict went on, the more impassioned were the participants in seeking victory on their own terms. British Regulars, Loyalists and their Indian allies squared off against Continental, state and militia forces in escalating raids throughout the borderlands of New York. These raids sought revenge for an ever-increasing list of atrocities committed by both sides.

The back story of these raids was the continuing fear by the British that the Americans would attempt another invasion of Canada after the surrender of Burgoyne. General Washington certainly stoked this fear, if for no other reason than to forestall the British from launching another invasion themselves. In February 1778 he sent the Marquis de Lafayette to Albany to investigate the feasibility of another invasion of Canada. Later that year the Continental Congress developed a multi-pronged strategy that included the utilization of the fleet of their new ally, the French, to capture Quebec, supported by an American army following the Lake Champlain invasion route.[1]

The resources to operationalize such a plan were not there and the plan may have been more bluff than real, but it drew the attention of the new governor of Canada, Frederic Haldimand. In planning forays along the borderland, he was able to rely on a growing cadre of Loyalists and Indian allies assembled in Canada and on the Niagara frontier. Sir John Johnson, the Tory commander of the King's Royal Regiment, was joined by two other men who proved to be great assets to the British cause and a great scourge to the American settlers along the New York frontier.

Joseph Brant (Mohawk name Thayendanegea) was a protégé of Sir William Johnson. Born in 1742, he was the younger brother of Molly Brant, the consort of Johnson. He participated in the unsuccessful 1758 campaign against Fort Carillon (Ticonderoga) and the next year accompanied Johnson on the expedition against Niagara. Recognizing the intelligence of the boy, Johnson ensured that Brant received an education, and even considered sending him to King's College in New York.[2] When Guy Johnson was forced out of New York in 1775, Brant accompanied him to England to appeal for support for the Loyalist cause. Upon returning to America he raised a force of 300 Indian warriors and participated in St. Leger's campaign, including the siege of Fort Stanwix and the Battle of Oriskany.

Oriskany proved to be a turning point in the war on the frontier. The ambush and defeat of General Nicholas Herkimers's regiment on their way to relieve the besieged American forces at Fort Stanwix came at a cost to all involved. The Tryon County Militia was devastated, both physically and emotionally. This defeat would impact their response to subsequent incursions in the Mohawk and Schoharie valleys for the remainder of the war. For the British, the victory was short-lived. Their Iroquois allies had sustained substantial losses: thirty-three killed and twenty-nine wounded.[3] Fearing greater losses in front of Fort Stanwix, they abandoned St. Leger, who was forced to lift the siege and retreat to Canada.

This campaign had the effect of splitting the Iroquois into British and American factions. Up until that point the tribal leaders, known as sachems, had attempted to remain neutral, not sure what to make of the conflict between their English friends. This was a natural inclination. The Iroquois had a long history of attempting to enhance their influence by playing off the English and the French.

Although the Iroquois are often referred to as the Six Nations, the tribes were not at all equal in size. Reduced by their proximity to the English settlements and the defection of some of their members to Canada, the Mohawks could muster only about 400 men, women and children at the beginning of the Revolutionary War. The westernmost Senecas represented half of the confederacy's 10,000 people. This tribe, which had suffered the greatest losses at Oriskany, along with the Cayugas, allied with the British. The smaller Oneidas and the Tuscarora, mostly sided with the Rebels. The Onondagas and the Mohawks were divided. The old Iroquois confederacy was torn apart, but the winner in this split was clearly the British.[4]

Another important military leader who took up the British cause was John Butler. Born in New London, Connecticut, in 1728, he soon accompanied his family to the Mohawk Valley where he gained a reputation as an interpreter for William Johnson in the many councils held with the Iroquois and other tribes in the 1750's and 1760's. He established his domain at Butlerville in close proximity to the Johnsons. In 1772, he was appointed a lieutenant-colonel of the Tryon County Militia and sided with the British under the influence of the Johnson family. He participated in St. Leger's campaign against Fort Stanwix in 1777 and soon thereafter was commissioned to raise his own regiment of provincial rangers. [5]

Butler and Brant proved to be an effective team in the years to follow, but not without controversy. The first major attack occurred in May 1778. Brant led a force of more than 300 Tories and Indians in a raid on Cobleskill. The raiders were confronted by the local militia and a detachment of Rebel regulars. Although more than twenty were killed on both sides, the Americans were overrun and the town destroyed.[6] Brant led additional raids at Springfield on Otsego Lake in July and German Flats, north of the Mohawk River, in September. At German Flats, the Americans employed a new defensive strategy. Alerted to the pending attack, the settlers took shelter in Forts Dayton and Herkimer. From there they watched as Brant's raiders destroyed all before them. Sixty-three houses, fifty-seven barns, three gristmills and a sawmill went up in smoke.[7]

The local militia units were finding it impossible to deal with these incursions. In the report of Captain Bellinger of the 4th Regiment of the Tryon County Militia to Governor George Clinton, he vented his frustrations.

> In my letter to Col. Klock, I beg'd him for God's sake
> to assist us with men, and if he had marched his men

directly, he might have been at the Flatts before it was attacked, and if he had sent 200 men, we might in all probability have saved a great many houses, and a great deal of Grain and Creatures.[8]

Colonel Jacob Klock, leader of the 2nd regiment of the Tryon County Militia, did not have the resources to respond. These militia units were a spent force after their defeat at Oriskany.

As a result, much of the defense of the frontier depended on the Albany County Militia under the leadership of Brigadier General Abraham Ten Broeck. Consisting of seventeen regiments, the Albany County Militia was responsible for the defense of settlements stretching from Saratoga on the east to the western reaches of the Mohawk Valley. At the beginning of the 1778 campaign, Ten Broeck had 4,783 men enlisted in his Brigade, including 358 in the 12th Regiment. The number of these available for duty was certainly lower, and the number of men that would actually turn out when called up was lower still.[9]

The militia strength was also weakened by the decision of the Continental Congress to draft militiamen into the Continental Army. In the winter of 1778, when Washington's forces at Valley Forge had been reduced to no more than 2000 effectives, Congress called on the states to draft members of the militia into service in the regular army. New York was required to assemble five battalions and rendezvous at Easton, Pennsylvania for a nine-month term of service. These troops would become known as Levy regiments.[10]

The militiamen of Ballston under the command of Lt. Colonel Gordon and Captains Collins and Stephen White, were constantly on the move. Typically they would serve for short periods, from a few days to a few weeks, and then return home to care for their farms and families. Thomas Barnum's service record is not unlike many other Middleline Road settlers. In his pension application written in 1832, Barnum often mistook the year of his participation, some of which are deleted from this summary, which is in chronological order.[11]

- One-half month under Col. James Gordon in the New York Militia and Captain Collins in pursuit of Tories

- One month under the same Captains at Palmerstown (Todays Wilton)
- One and a half months at Fort Edward under Captain Collins
- One-half month under Captain Steenbergh at Fort Edward
- One month between Fort George and Fort Ann obstructing the march of the British under Burgoyne in the month of July 1777
- One month under Captain Stephen White at Cherry Valley (1778)
- Half a month at Johnstown under Captain Collins
- Half a month under Captain Collins in the pursuit of the army landed at Lake Champlain and Lake George under the command of General Carleton. (October 1780)

While this record shows that militiamen were constantly being called into service, Governor George Clinton, who also served as a Brigadier General in the Continental Army, was displeased with the response of the militia units to the early 1778 raids. Clinton had ordered one-fourth of the command of both the Tryon and Albany County Militia to be sent to the frontier. Writing to Ten Broeck soon after the German Flats attack, he lamented that "not half of the Number of Militia Ordered for the protection of the Frontiers have been at any one time actually out on that service."[12]

∞

In addition to Brant's raids in the Mohawk Valley, John Butler was also active in taking the fight to the rebels. In July he led his Regiment of 200 Rangers and a large group of Seneca and Cayuga Indians to an overwhelming victory over militia units in the Wyoming Valley in Pennsylvania. The Indians showed no mercy—it was reported that 227 scalps were taken.[13] Although referred to as the Wyoming Massacre, those killed were militiamen, not civilians. Butler released those captured on parole with the proviso that they not take up arms again against the King. The rebels promptly violated this pledge, raising the ire of both Butler's Rangers and their Indian allies.

John Butler returned to Niagara, but his son Walter joined with Brant and Cornplanter, a Seneca war chief, in a raid that escalated the violence to another level. Walter Butler had recently escaped from confinement in Albany after being captured at German Flats the previous year. In November the three men led a party of 320 Indians, 150 Rangers and 50 men of the 8th Regiment in an attack on Cherry Valley.[14] The settlement was defended by the 7th Massachusetts Regiment under the command of Colonel Ichabod Alden. Fifteen soldiers, including Alden, were killed attempting to escape to the fort. While the Rangers invested the fort, the Senecas went on a rampage that Butler and Brant found impossible to prevent. The resulting carnage ended with the murder of thirty civilians.[15] Even the British were appalled. Richard Cartwright, John Butler's secretary, lamented the "acts of wanton cruelty committed by the bloodthirsty savages as humanity would shudder to mention."[16]

Militiamen from Ballston were familiar with Cherry Valley. A company of forty men under the command of Captain Stephen White in Lt. Col. Gordon's 12th Albany County Militia had served there earlier in the fall, clearing away the woods surrounding the fort.[17] At the critical time of the assault, however, the response of the militia was lacking. Four hundred men from the Albany Tryon County Militia marched to within two miles of Cherry Valley, when they were ordered to stop by Colonels Klock and Gordon. This hesitation prevented any realistic chance of engaging the attackers, who were able to get away unscathed.[18] Gordon returned to Fort Plank and from there issued an appeal to Colonel Goose Van Schaick to "march your Regt. up as quick as possible."[19]

Gordon was apparently in overall command of a detachment of the 12th Militia, which had been called up for service in the Mohawk Valley. Thaddeus Scribner in his pension application stated that he served at Fort Plank under Major Andrew Mitchell and Lt. Epenetus White, both of Ballston. When the alarm of the attack was received they marched immediately to Cherry Valley. The attackers had just withdrawn, leaving the arriving militia to bury the dead.[20] Gordon's neighbor Elisha Benedict Jr. deposed that he had "proceeded to Fort Planck at Canajoharie as a guard to the inhabitants at the time Cherry Valley was destroyed by the Indians" and that he "was at Cherry Valley the day after the massacre and guarded teams that picked up the dead in the neighborhoods for burial."[21]

Cherry Valley had implications for both sides. The British, clearly embarrassed by the behavior of their Indian allies, modified their strategy going forward. No longer would they conduct raids dominated by Indians. In future raids the reverse would be true. British regulars and Loyalists would be the larger force. Every attempt would be made to prevent another Cherry Valley.

The Americans had also learned their lesson. New York's Governor George Clinton expressed it clearly in a letter to John Jay just days after the massacre.

> Fatal Experience has more than sufficiently taught us the Impracticality of defending our extensive Frontiers by the Militia of the County and the small Proportion of regular Troop imployed in that service against an Enemy acting upon a desultory plan. It is of utmost importance that some more effectual Measures than have hitherto been pursued be adopted for the Defense of the Frontiers, and I am persuaded this can only be affected by Offensive Operations, thereby carrying the War into the Enemy's Country.[22]

General George Washington agreed. Engaged in a stalemate with the British forces occupying New York City, he devised a plan in the winter of 1779 to take the war directly to the Iroquois as suggested by Governor Clinton. The campaign was led by General John Sullivan, and supported by Governor Clinton's brother, Brigadier General James Clinton. The troops, over 4,500 strong, were not unreliable militia units, but seasoned veterans. The gathering of the troops and supplies for the expedition did not go unnoticed by the British Loyalists. John Butler noted that they were facing "some of the best of the Continental Troops commanded by the most active Rebel Generals, and not a Regiment of Militia among the whole."[23] In spite of Canadian awareness of the threat, Quebec's Governor Haldimand provided no additional troops until it was too late. He refused to believe that the Americans would launch such a large-scale invasion. On August 3 Haldimand ordered Sir John Johnson and 380 men to support Butler. They did not arrive in time to assist Butler and Joseph Brant, who were left to fend off the invaders with a combined force not exceeding 600 Rangers and Indians.[24]

The result was inevitable. Butler's force was overwhelmed at the only battle of the campaign at Newtown, near present-day Elmira, on August 29. From there Sullivan rampaged through the heart of the Iroquois Confederacy, destroying villages and crops throughout the Finger Lakes region. The Indians—warriors, women and children—fled before the advancing army, powerless to stop them. By the end of September, the campaign was over. Their homeland destroyed, the Iroquois retreated to Fort Niagara to spend a miserable winter, short of both food and adequate shelter. Although urged by the British to disburse to those villages untouched by the campaign, 2,900 Indians were still camped around the fort in late November.[25]

Sullivan's campaign had been successful to a point. The Iroquois settlements and crops were gone. The British forces had been pushed back to the Niagara frontier, incapable of launching attacks on the American settlements for the rest of 1779. However, the Loyalists under John Butler and Sir John Johnson, as well as Brant's Indian fighters, had survived to fight another day. Those days would come during the following year.

∞

Anticipating that the Loyalists and their Iroquois allies would be eager to come to terms with the victors of the 1779 campaign, General Schuyler sent four emissaries of the Mohawk and Oneida nations to seek peace. They delivered a condescending message to Guy Johnson at Fort Niagara. Aaron Hill, a leader of the Mohawks, responded to their entreaties.

> Did you not fight against us at Ft. Stanwix? Did you not go out to war against the King's people at Saratoga, the Highlands and other places? And did not some of you even join the Rebels who invaded our Country, and assist them to destroy us? And yet you have the assurance to come, while the Hatchet you employed against us is yet in your hands, and tell us that you have a regard for our Peace and Welfare. Deceitful Set![26]

There would be no peace. The four negotiators were thrown in jail. Raids of retaliation began early in 1780, as several small parties set out from Fort Niagara to resume their attacks. In May, Sir John Johnson led his King's Royal Regiment and Loyalists drawn from Jessup's King's Loyal Americans and McAlpin's American Volunteers, along with a contingent of Mohawks, south from Crown Point. This force totaling 528 men headed straight for Johnstown, where on May 21st they scattered the small contingent of Tryon County Militia men opposing them, capturing twenty-seven. They burned 120 barns, mills and houses, gathered up 143 local Loyalists and headed back to Crown Point.[27] A contingent of militia and rebel regular soldiers under Colonel Goose Van Schaick gave chase. They were joined by additional troops brought north by General James Clinton, brother of the governor, but arrived at Crown Point six hours after Johnson had embarked for Canada.[28]

Raids continued throughout the summer. In July, Joseph Brant led a party of 300 warriors in another futile attempt to capture Fort Stanwix. After a few days blockading the fort they gave up the attempt and withdrew.[29] Moving into the Mohawk Valley on August 2nd Brant overran Canajoharie killing seventeen, taking forty-one into captivity and completing the usual destruction of houses, barns and livestock.[30] The Albany County Militia was sorely challenged by all these incursions. Half of General Ten Broeck's brigade was ordered out in anticipation of further raids. Several regiments were stationed at Saratoga, including Schoonhoven's 12th and McCrea's 13th Albany County Militia. Others were held in reserve at Schenectady.[31] In June the State Legislature authorized the formation of a brigade of Levy troops drafted from the militia for a three-month enlistment under the command of Brigadier General Robert Van Rensselaer.[32]

October represented the culmination of the 1780 campaign. The raid on Ballston was a small excursion in the overall fall campaign of Governor Haldimand to seek retribution on the New York frontier. His strategy was to follow the old pathways of war—eastward from Lake Ontario, and southward from Lake Champlain, into the heart of rebel territory.

In late September Sir John Johnson left Oswego with a force of 900 men, including 150 British regulars, 150 Rangers led by John Butler, and 225 Loyalists from the King's Royal Regiment. They were joined by 265 Iroquois led by Joseph Brant.[33] After some delays this force headed southeast. They entered the Schoharie Valley from the south on October 17th and proceeded north. Failing to capture the three forts in the valley, they concentrated on destroying homes, farms and crops, much as Sullivan had done the year before. Reaching the Mohawk River near Fort Hunter they turned west, creating a similar path of destruction. Johnson's original strategy was to hook up with the second invading force coming southward from Canada and jointly attack Schenectady in a pincers movement. His late start foiled that plan.[34]

Entering the Mohawk Valley, the invaders were pursued by a force of Albany and Tryon County Militia, as well as elements of Levy Regiments, all under the command of General Robert Van Rensselaer. This force was deluded somewhat by the simultaneous threat from the north by Major Christopher Carleton and John Munro. One-hundred-fifty men from the 2nd Albany County Militia, based in Schenectady, had been sent north to defend against Munro at Ballston.[35] Other militia units were sent to Saratoga to defend against Carleton's incursions along the upper Hudson River.

Van Rensselaer's force caught up with Johnson at Klock's farm on October 19th and engaged them in a confused battle that ended when Johnson's men left the field as darkness descended. The invaders won the race to their boats hidden on Onondaga Lake and headed back to Oswego, escaping the pursuing rebels. They had made a wasteland of two valleys in the heart of rebel territory at the surprising low cost of nine killed, two wounded and fifty-three missing.[36] By the time Johnson's troops arrived back in Oswego on October 26, Carleton's raiders were already sailing down Lake Champlain, having completed their own expedition into rebel territory.

CHAPTER 8
The Ballston Raid

ajor Christopher Carleton was no stranger to war. Born into a military family, he was the nephew of Guy Carleton, the governor of Quebec during the early stages of the Revolutionary War. Carleton joined the British army as an ensign in the 31st Regiment in 1761 at the age of twelve. His military career took him to America where he met Sir William Johnson. Observing Johnson's immersion in local Iroquois culture, Carleton followed a similar path, taking an Indian wife and developing his own relationships with the local Indians.[1]

He returned to England, but in May 1776 he arrived back at Quebec City as part of the relief force that raised the siege of Quebec leading to the withdrawal of the Continental Army forces from Canada. Using his relationships with the Indians to his advantage, he may have returned to the Mohawk Valley incognito in the spring of 1778. In March the Marquis de Lafayette, while on his reconnaissance mission from General Washington, reported from Schenectady that "Major Carleton was some days ago disguised in this town and making preparations—two parties have gone on after him but I question much if they will be successful." They were not.[2]

In November 1778 while Brant and Walter Butler were conducting their infamous raid on Cherry Valley, Carleton led a contingent of 300 British army regulars, a small group of Loyalists and about 100 Indian allies on another raid. Carleton's force moved south along Lake Champlain to Crown Point and then east into Vermont. Brushing aside a small party of local militia, the invaders proceeded to destroy forty-seven houses and forty-eight barns along with a saw mill and grist mill. Altogether eighty prisoners were brought back to Canada. His excursion prepared him for his return visit along the Great Warpath two years later.[3]

The southward raid of October 1780 was the second part of the pincer movement to complement Sir John Johnson's raid through the Mohawk and Schoharie valleys. Carleton's force included 518 British regulars and 315 Provincials from various Loyalists regiments.[4] Among the Loyalist leaders were Major Edward Jessup, Capt. William Fraser, Capt. John Munro, and Capt. Joseph Anderson. Anderson had a long association with Munro. He purchased several parcels of land on the Vermont border in Pownall, Vermont in the early 1770's, in the same area as Munro.[5] Both had been brought before the Albany Committee on Conspiracies for recruiting Loyalists in 1777 and had been imprisoned in Connecticut, and both had escaped to join the King's Royal Regiment in Canada.[6] Earlier, in 1776, Anderson, acting as a spy within Benedict Arnold's army in front of Quebec, and had passed intelligence to Gov. Guy Carleton that helped lift the siege of that city.[7]

All these Loyalist leaders were familiar with the rebel territory they were about to enter. More importantly, they knew the people who lived there—their Tory friends and rebel enemies. From the former they could count on protection as they moved through the countryside. For the latter they sought revenge for the harassment they and their families had endured throughout the war at the hands of the Albany County Militia.

This contingent of 833 men left St. John's on the Richelieu River on September 28 in eight ships and twenty-six smaller bateaux and sailed south. On October 2 they camped at Valcour Island, the site of the naval battle with Benedict Arnold's navy four years before. Here they were joined by thirty Fort Hunter Mohawk warriors under the leadership of Lt. Patrick Langan from the Six Nations Indian Department and Mohawk war chief John Deserontyon. Known as "Captain John," he had been a long-time confidant of Sir William Johnson and had accompanied him on campaigns during the French and Indian War. He had joined the British cause early-on and assisted in the escape of both Guy and John Johnson to Canada. Seriously wounded in a skirmish near Fort Stanwix in September 1777, he recovered to participate in raids along the frontier.

On October 5 a party of 108 St. Regis Indians arrived at Carleton's

camp at Split Rock Bay on the west side of Lake Champlain, completing
the assembly of the raiding party which now totaled 970 men. The next
day Captain Munro led a detachment of 195 provincials and Indians
south from Bulwagga Bay, the same location used by John Johnson when
launching his spring campaign. This contingent consisted entirely of provincial troops and Indians, including Munro's and Anderson's companies
of the King's Royal Regiment, Fraser's Rangers and Deserontyon's Indians
led by Langan. Their destination was unknown to the officers remaining
with Major Carleton and was probably uncertain to Munro himself. They
set off on foot to the southwest, seeking opportunities to bring the war
to the rebels.[8]

Carleton's main body moved south along the lake past Fort
Ticonderoga, which had not been permanently occupied by either side
since Burgoyne's surrender. They moved into South Bay where they arrived at Skenesborough (Whitehall) on October 8. Counting their good
fortune at not having been discovered to this point, they settled in for a
good night's sleep. In the morning they proceeded south along the trail
past an abandoned blockhouse and soon arrived in front of Fort Anne.
This fort and its defenders were typical of the small, undermanned ob-
structions put in place along the frontier to protect the countryside from
invasions. Austin Wells, a sergeant in the Cambridge militia, provides a
description:

> Fort Ann was simply a picket fort without ditch or earthy
> embankment around it. It was square and enclosed about
> half an acre's space. Within the fort was a single barrack,
> one story high, some sixteen feet wide and thirty or forty
> feet long—a framed and clapboarded building. Captain
> Adiel Sherwood of the Kingsbury militia with Lieutenant
> Thomas Bradshaw of the same place had command of
> the fort during the summer of Seventeen Hundred and
> Eighty. It was garrisoned by drafts and volunteers from
> the surrounding towns serving a month by turns... I
> would not consent to be drafted, but went up as a vol-
> unteer with twelve men. The month expired and we
> returned, another file of men from Cambridge coming

up to supply our places. The number of the garrison was variable, between fifty and one hundred men were always there.[9]

The decrepit condition of the Fort was confirmed by the British. Openings in the logs were cut to fire through but "so ill was this done that those on the outside had an equal chance with the garrison as the holes were low enough to be fired into from the outside. Add to this that their gate had neither lock nor hinges, and so loosely was it fastened with a bar that some Indian trying to get into the fort pushed it down."[10] Needless to say, Captain Sherwood surrendered along with two lieutenants and 72 privates, all militiamen. Given the overwhelming odds his surrender seemed prudent, but later Governor Clinton informed General Washington that "the fort appeared to be surrendered through treachery or cowardness."[11] The fort was destroyed and the prisoners were taken in tow.

Carleton then turned northwest to descend on Fort George, but a small raiding party of King's Loyal Americans under the command of Lieutenant David Jones was sent south along the Hudson River. They destroyed everything in their path from Fort Edward to the hamlet of Saratoga (today's Schuylerville). Along the way at Fort Miller they burned the home of John McCrea, colonel of the 13th Albany Militia. McCrae was the brother of Jane McCrea who had been murdered and scalped by the Indians during the Burgoyne campaign. Jane had been David Jones fiancée. Jane and John McCrae's brother James lived in Ballston on 1250 acres that he had purchased in the Five-Mile Square, across the Middleline from James Gordon. Gordon's sister Sarah, recently arrived from Ireland, had married James' brother William in 1779. It is another example of the interrelationships among the participants in this struggle. It was personal.[12]

On the morning of October 11 Carleton's invaders advanced toward Fort George at the southern end of the lake. The fort's commander, Captain John Chipman, had no advance knowledge of the large force bearing down on him. He sent out a scouting party of forty-eight men under Captain Thomas Sill to assess the situation. Sill's men were soon surrounded by the Indians. The result was another bloody encounter at Bloody Pond. Twenty-seven troops were killed, including Sill, eight were captured, and thirteen fled into the woods.[13] This was the only action during the entire campaign that resulted in significant casualties.

Chipman was forced to surrender the fort along with forty-five of his men, all from Colonel Seth Warner's Continental Regiment. The prisoners were marched out and "the Savages were admitted to plunder the place, a thing they always look upon as their undoubted right."[14] It seems that Governor Clinton had a different view of Chipman's surrender than that of Sherwood. In the same letter to Washington he noted that Chipman "obtained a very honorable Capitulation before he was induced to surrender."[15] Clinton's frustration with the local militia units may have had an impact on his opposite views of the surrender of Fort Anne's militia and Fort George's continentals.

On October 12 Carleton's force, swollen by well over one hundred prisoners, began their trek northward along the west side of Lake George. The journey was difficult, crossing over the rugged mountains and around the bays. Arriving at Fort Ticonderoga on October 15 they were met by a detachment guarding their boats, which they boarded, arriving at Crown Point the next day. There they waited for word from Captain Munro who had not been heard from since he had left them ten days before.

According to a mid-19th-century account, eighteen months before Joe Bettys' demise in the spring of 1782, he may have played an important behind-the-scenes role in Captain John Munro's Ballston raid along the Middleline. This raid was more devastating to the community than the small incursions Bettys had led personally. On the morning of Monday, October 16, 1780, Hezekiah Middlebrook was driving some cattle from his homestead on Middleline Road near Ballston Center to a pasture he had further north when he met up with Joe Bettys. The chance encounter could have been deadly. Bettys was already known as an avowed enemy of the rebels, even though his most notorious raids were still in the future. Middlebrook was a leader of the local committee and well known for his support of the American cause. As Ballston neighbors, these adversaries had known each other before the war. For some reason this relationship defused the situation. Bettys suggested that Middlebrook return home, and even walked along the road with him before taking his leave through the forest. Nonetheless, Hezekiah was rattled by the experience. A later account of this alleged incident stated that "something in the Tory's manner impressed him with a sense of some impending danger". He was correct.[16]

In the days preceding Middlebrook's supposed encounter with Bettys, the Ballston area was on high alert for an invasion. Rumors abounded that the British, along with their Loyalist and Indian allies were about to descend on the frontier settlements. The constant raids in the Mohawk Valley over the previous three years always had the locals on edge. Small raiding parties were often spotted traveling down the Lake George-Lake Champlain corridor. Sir John Johnson's May raid, just twenty miles to the west, was fresh in the minds of the families along Middleline Road.

The seventeen regiments of the Albany County Militia were in constant motion during this period, being called out to respond to the numerous threats along the frontier. It is important to remember that the militia units were mostly farmers with minimal military training. Their first responsibility was to provide for their families, which required them to remain near home if at all possible. They were not pleased to be called up for long periods to garrison forts in the Mohawk Valley such as Fort Stanwix. They resisted being drafted into the Continental Army's Levy regiments, which often required their service for up to nine months. They were especially reluctant to remain on duty during harvest season in late summer, as we have seen with Thomas Barnum's experiences at the Battle of Saratoga. The men in Captain Collin's company of militia along Middleline Road would have shared the perspective of this account of their service in a mid-19th century account of the fall campaign.

> The Militia who were so discontented in garrison, would not be the less reliable for the public defense, and they gladly embraced the opportunity of guarding the minor posts that were scattered throughout the settlements, and nearer their own homes. Their discontent was in no degree inspired by cowardness, but by a natural, and perhaps pardonable anxiety to be with their families who were constantly in danger, and frequently driven by real

and false alarms to seek refuge in their blockhouses. It was manifestly the policy of the enemy to multiply these alarms by their small parties, scattered along the borders of the settlements, and to magnify the fears of the inhabitants.[17]

For the Ballston families, their blockhouse was the palisaded fort surrounding Rev. Eliphalet Ball's red meeting house on the south-west corner of the crossroads that later became known as Academy Hill, about one-half mile east of Middleline Road. The fort was similar to other "minor posts" on the frontier, constructed of oak logs with loop-holes for firing upon the enemy. In response to the alarms generated by Carleton's invasion to the north, this little fort was reinforced by troops of the 2nd Regiment of the Albany County militia from Schenectady, under the command of Major Abraham Switts.

Meanwhile the two Ballston companies of the 12th Regiment, led by Major Andrew Mitchell and Captain Collins, were ordered by Colonel Jacobus Van Schoonhoven to march to Fort Edward on Wednesday, October 11.[18] This unit returned to Ballston on Saturday, October 14 after viewing the British depart northward from Fort George on October 12.[19] During the week preceding Munro's attack, other members of the local militia maintained a defensive position along the high ground on Middleline Road. Referred to as Pierson's Ridge for its proximity to the cabin of Paul Pierson, it would later become known as Court House Hill. After several nights bivouacked on the ridge the men abandoned their post when Captain Collins' men returned with the news that Carleton's raid had ended. During this time each family took precautions against the possibility of an attack. For several nights the family of George Scott slept in the woods and secured their valuables in a chest they buried in the ground. They too had relaxed their guard after days of apprehension.[20]

Lt. Colonel Gordon, a member of the New York State Assembly since its formation in 1777, had been attending the fourth session of this body in Poughkeepsie. The Assembly had been called into session by Governor Clinton in early September 1780 to deal with the increasingly dire military situation in the state. Clinton was given expanded authority to draft men from the militia to serve for forty-five days, receiving the same pay and rations as Continental troops.[21] It was also during this session that the Assembly learned of the betrayal of General Benedict Arnold and his plan to surrender West Point to the British. The capture of Major André, his subsequent execution on October 2, and the escape of Arnold to the British lines in New York City, must have been on Gordon's mind as he rode back to his home on Middleline Road when the session ended on October 10. Arriving there on Friday the thirteenth, he would have become fully aware of the frantic response of his militia to Carleton's raid. He must have been relieved the next day when Captain Collins returned to report that Major Carleton and his men were last seen heading north along Lake George. Neither Gordon nor his neighbors along Middleline Road knew that another enemy force lurked nearby.

∞

Bulwagga Bay, separated from the main body of Lake Champlain by the peninsula of Crown Point, thrust southwest two miles in the wilderness. At its southern shore began an overland trail long frequented by natives traveling between Canada and the Mohawk Valley. This trail was the foot path alternative to the Great Warpath that followed Lakes Champlain and George and the Hudson River southward. Most recently, Sir John Johnson had improved this trail during his May invasion, turning sections of it into a roadway.[22] On October 7 Munro led his 200 men, fully loaded with supplies and ammunition, seven miles south, traveling east of Bulwagga Mountain. They probably camped in the vicinity of Penfield Pond where they buried their excess supplies for their use on the return trip. From there the path headed westward, most likely skirting Eagle Lake and Paradox Lake, much as Route 74 does today. Heading south along Schroon River they followed this interior trail west of the Schroon River and along the base of Crane Mountain reaching the Hudson River west of the later village of Warrensburg.[23] It was in that approximate location where, on October 9, they detached two men who had become injured and ill, along with a third man to assist them. Continuing south they reached the confluence of the Hudson and Sacandaga Rivers on the 11th.[24]

To this point the party would have been able to travel unimpeded by settlers since this area was essentially uninhabited. As they approached the Sacandaga they were entering into the old domain of the Jessup brothers. Edward Jessup was serving as leader of the provincial troops in Carleton's force and on that day he was engaged in the capture of Fort George, ten miles to the northeast. Jessup's enclave along the Hudson had been largely abandoned, its Loyalists constantly subject to raids by the local militia. If any locals remained in the area they would have welcomed Munro.

Making his way along the Sacandaga, Munro turned inland at the outlet of Daley Creek where he soon passed the Indian trail marker known as Tory Rock. Crossing the Kayaderosseras Mountains the invaders soon arrived at Lake Desolation.[25] Munro now had a decision to make. Several choices presented themselves. His primary objective may have been to coordinate with Sir John Johnson's raid in the Schoharie and Mohawk Valleys. Munro's presence could be used to draw American troops away from Johnson, while also causing some destruction of his own.[26] He had sent scouts to find Johnson and coordinate their plans but they had not returned. By October 12 runners from Carleton had come into Munro's camp, informing him of the British success at Fort Anne and Fort George, and their plan to retire northward back to Crown Point. At that point Munro's invading force was alone, and at risk for exposure and attack by the local militia who had already been alerted by Carleton's incursion.

Although interacting with Johnson may have been Munro's principal goal, there were impediments to this plan beyond just the mistiming. The principal settlement in that direction was Schenectady, a tempting target, but deemed too strong for his small force. Both militia and levy regiments were assembling there in anticipation of Johnson's raid to the west along the Mohawk. In addition, the rebels had recently built and manned a blockhouse along the Sacandaga to protect against just the sort of incursion that Munro was planning.[27] This blockhouse was manned on and off by up to thirty militiamen. Known to both the Indians and the Loyalists, it had been attacked as recently as April 1780 when a party of seven Indians was supposedly driven off by a single defender.[28]

Later in his report Munro described his dilemma as he concealed his force in the woods southeast of the Sacandaga River.

I can assure you that Consistent with the safety of the
men under my Command, I could not stay longer in the
Country, being within Twenty-five miles of Albany, Nine
miles of Schenectady and having received no intelligence
of Sir John Johnson, notwithstanding the appointed time
of our meeting was elapsed six days—Major Carleton
having returned to Crown Point, the Men in great want
of Provision.[29]

There are indications that his orders may have suggested an attack on
Saratoga before he was to join with Johnson. Saratoga remained the home
for Phillip Schuyler, who had rebuilt his mansion after it was destroyed
during the Battles of Saratoga. It remained a strategic outpost, and the fort
there was often manned by units of the Albany County Militia. Munro
decided against moving against that post.

My reason for not striking first at Saratoga as directed
was owing to the great number of Women and Children
which were lodged in the Barracks and having their husbands in my Detachment, would of course follow them,
and also not knowing that General Schuyler had arrived
there; these considerations induced me to get as near as
possible to Schenectady to join with Sir John Johnson in
which I was disappointed.[30]

Freeing their families would certainly had been enthusiastically supported by his Loyalist troops, but the burden of herding them back to
Canada through the wilderness was not a pleasing prospect.

Munro proceeded down the mountain from Lake Desolation to
Kayaderosseras Creek where his men set up camp, probably in the vicinity of the later village of West Milton.[31] While encamped in these woods
a third option presented itself. Munro sent William Fraser to scout his
old neighborhood around Ballston. An advance in that direction could
provide a double benefit. In addition to destroying a farming community with its mills and recent harvest, Munro and his party would have
the opportunity for some payback. Ballston was the home base for that

notorious company of the 12th Regiment of the Albany County Militia led by Captain Tyrannus Collins and Lt. Colonel James Gordon.[32] Munro made his decision. "I found it necessary to make a decent on Ballston, and proceed to join Major Carleton without loss of time."[33]

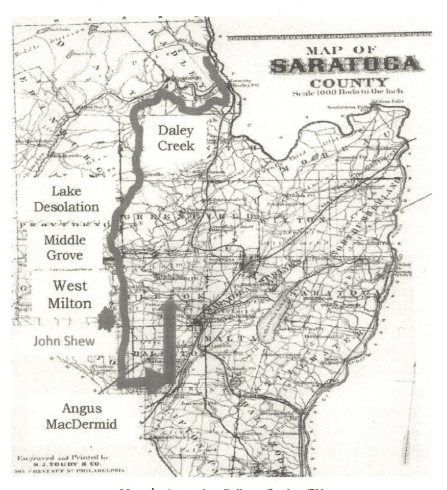

Munro's Approach to Ballston October 1780

∞

On Monday, October 16 Munro broke camp and began his march south along the path known as Paisley Street. The Scottish settlers in this area could be counted on for loyalty to the King.[34] Along the way Fraser returned from his scout with information that Ballston was well protected by local militia, including Switt's troops recently arrived from Schenectady. He may have also been able to tell Munro that both Gordon and Collins were back at home, having returned from their recent political and military journeys.

The party's approach was masked by the support of the local Loyalists. Serving as both guides and scouts, they were able to keep the invaders from being discovered throughout the day. However, as they approached the current Galway-Milton town line, they surprised and captured two men. These men were most likely acting as scouts for the militia, although they were quick to claim they were just two friends out hunting. Two of the Mohawks immediately recognized one of the men, with fatal consequences. The Indians were brothers, known as Aaron and David Hill, noted Mohawk warriors. The man they recognized was John Shew.

John's father, Godfrey Shew, had emigrated from Germany during the French and Indian War and served under Sir William Johnson. He eventually settled near Johnson's summer retreat known as Fish House on the Sacandaga. In spite of this close connection to the Johnsons, the Shews supported the rebel cause, and he and his sons joined the Tryon County Militia.

In June 1778 John had been captured along with his father and brother Jacob by these same Mohawk brothers, participants in a raid led by Lieutenant John Ross. On friendly terms before the war, John Shew had been allowed to remain among the Indians and was treated more like a brother than a prisoner. He immediately took advantage of his situation and escaped along with another captive. Now two years later, he was not given another chance. As his companion Isaac Palmatier watched, he was bound to a tree and dispatched by a tomahawk blow to the head.[35] Munro's raid had claimed its first victims – one dead, one captured.

As night fell the invaders continued south and entered the Town of Ballston along the path that became Hop City Road. Here they stopped at the cabin of Angus McDearmid, a recent immigrant from Scotland. The earliest account of this incident, provided by a McDearmid son-in-law, simply mentions that the soldiers crowded into the house for food and drink when the floor collapsed.[36] A slightly later account embellished the story.

About dusk they stopped at a Highland Scotchman's, one McDearmid. The Indians were highly delighted with a spinning wheel which Dame McDearmid was using. The house was filled so full with these untutored admirers of this ancient household appendage that the floor gave way precipitating all into the cellar.[37]

Leaving the McDearmids, the men headed down an embankment, crossing for the first time a stream called the Mourning Kill. Guided by James McDonald, a local Loyalist sympathizer, they generally followed a path, later named Devil's Lane, eastward until they reached the clearing of James Gordon at about midnight. There Munro divided his forces, sending William Fraser and his provincials across the Mourning Kill to the cabin of Captain Tyrannus Collins, the man responsible for Fraser's 1777 capture and imprisonment. Munro deployed the 130 soldiers of the King's Royal Regiment, dressed in their red uniforms, around the home of Gordon. These men were accompanied by the thirty Mohawks led by Langan and Deserontyon.[38] It was apparent that their mission was not random destruction. Having determined to attack Ballston, their first object was to target the leaders of the local Militia.

The invaders' animosity toward the most influential men of Middleline Road went back to the very beginning of the war. We have recounted the zealous approach taken by Gordon and Collins in tracking down Tories and making life miserable for their families. However, Gordon's partisanship extended beyond his military actions. As a member of the New York Assembly he had advocated for harsh treatment of captured Loyalists and had supported the 1779 Confiscation Act. That Act called for the banishment of many prominent men of New York who had sided with the British, and sentenced them to death without clemency if they returned. Among those named in the Act were Sir John Johnson, Guy Johnson, Edward and Ebenezer Jessup, and Isaac Low.[39] In his report on the raid, Munro cited Gordon's support of this law as justification for his actions against him.[40]

Gordon was asleep in his framed home with his wife Mary, the daughter of Eliphalet Ball, whom he had married in 1775, and Melinda his three-year-old daughter. They occupied a bedroom that stretched the full length of the south side of the house. Being a man of some means, the family was not alone. His household included two farmhands, Jack Galbraith, an Irishman, and John Parlow. Little is known of Galbraith. Parlow was the son of John Lawrence Parlow, a former associate of Gordon who had died in 1779 after being captured by the Oneidas. Apparently Gordon had taken in his fifteen-year-old son after his father's death.[41] At least four slaves were also part of Gordon's household — Nero, Jacob, Ann and Liz. Nero's origin is unknown but his exploits after the raid will be described later. Jacob had served in Burgoyne's army and had been taken prisoner by the Americans. He had been sold or given to Gordon, and Ann became his common-law wife.[42]

There may have been an additional person in the house. Most accounts of the raid do not mention James Gordon Jr. but there is much evidence that he existed. A James Gordon Jr. is included among the prisoners receiving pay for their time in Canada.[43] If he was taken in the raid he must have been at least a teenager, since younger children were left behind. Interestingly, there is a record of a marriage between a James Gordon and Margaret Garrick in 1764. James Jr. may have been a product of this earlier marriage.[44] Colonel Gordon never mentioned him and it is interesting that when his son Alexander died in 1793 at the age of nine, his gravestone indicated that he was the only son of James.

Gordon was startled awake by the sound of bayonets crashing through his bedroom window. Running into the hallway he was confronted by an Indian with hatchet raised, only to be saved from death by the intervention of Captain Munro. The family was herded outside into the cold. The entire household had been made captive with the exception of Liz, who fled into the adjoining woods. The Indian warriors had been accompanied by some of their women who proceeded to strip the cabin of anything of value, including the clothes of the family.[45] In order to not arouse the militia at the fort a mile away, Munro prevented the Indians from burning the home and barns, although Gordon's daughter Melinda later recalled that her mother had snuffed out a fire-brand that had been thrust into a bed in the kitchen. Her memories of this night remained with her, as did her memories of her father.

> He stood shivering in the cold, and Langdon took out of
> his knapsack a blanket coat and gave it to him. I recol-
> lect of being in my father's arms out of the door in the

moonlight, when he stood under the charge of Langdon. I recollect awakening some time afterwards by the side of a log heap, in company with my mother and Liz, where they had hid themselves.[46]

At the same time, Fraser and his thirty-four Loyalist rangers had crossed the Mourning Kill to Collins' log home. Tyrannus was there with his fourteen-year-old son Manasseh and his female slave. The rest of his large family—his wife Abigail and their seven young children—had returned to Richmond, Massachusetts, for safety. Tyrannus barred the door long enough to allow his son to escape through an upstairs opening in the logs, intended for a window.[47] Manasseh ran to the home of his sister Mary and her husband John Ball near the fort, alerting the Schenectady militia stationed there that a raid was in progress. Tyrannus, injured by the thrust of a tomahawk through the door, was captured along with his slave.[48]

Collins' nephew, Isaac Stow, Gordon's miller, was not so fortunate. Five of Fraser's men had crossed the Middleline to capture Stow, who was at home with his wife, Sarah, the daughter of Paul Pierson, and their ten-month-old daughter Clarinda. Stow was detained, but bolted to warn Gordon about the attack. It was too late for him to save Gordon and it turned out to be too late to save himself. The earliest description of what happened next was written succinctly by another captive of the raid. "I must not omit to mention one of my neighbors, Isaac Stow, who was inhumanly massacred for attempting to make his escape. An Indian sent his spear at him and struck it in his back, then caught it and held him, and smote his tomahawk into his head."[49] As his uncle and his employer looked on, he was scalped, dead at the age of twenty-five. His wife and daughter escaped by wading across the creek and hiding in the woods.[50]

The three parties of Munro's invasion force now reunited and moved north along the Middleline, coming next to the cabin of Thomas Barnum on the west side of the road near the intersection with today's Brookline Road. Barnum had moved to Ballston soon after marrying Achsah Benedict in 1772, and they had three small children. His family may have sought refuge in a safer location, since no mention is made of them. He was captured and his home pillaged. Barnum himself had been in the party of militia that had responded to the alarm during Carleton's raid, but had taken sick and returned home. He described his ordeal later in his pension application. "This declarant, although he had the fever and ague, was forced to march and carry his own looking glass naked and a pack on his back so heavy that when he sat upon a log he could not rise without help."[51] He was not alone. It was common practice during these raids that captives would be required to tote the spoils of war taken by the Indians. Apparently one of them had shown an interest in Barnum's mirror.

Across the road Barnum's mother Jerusha Starr Benedict was living with Elisha Benedict, Barnum's step-father. They had been married soon after the death of Thomas' father at the Battle of Lake George in 1755 and had four sons. The oldest, Caleb, aged twenty-two, served as an ensign in the militia under Captain Collins. Younger brothers Elisha, Jr, Elias and Felix served as enlisted men in the same company.

Although not actively serving at the time of the raid, father Elisha had participated in the invasion of Quebec in 1775 as a captain in the 2nd New York Continental Regiment. In early 1776 he was the commanding officer at Fort Chambly on the Richelieu River, leading a garrison of seventy-five men. It was during this time that the Americans realized they were losing the campaign to secure Canada for the revolution. Exacerbating the military defeat of Montgomery and Arnold in front of Quebec, the Canadian people were turning against the invaders. This was due in no small part to the harsh measures employed by General David Wooster, who assumed command after the death of General Montgomery in front of Quebec in December.[52]

Captain Benedict also appears to have come under criticism for his behavior at Chambly. Munro, in his report called him out, much as he had Gordon. "Captain Collins and Benedict were commanding Officers at Chambly, after taking possession of that part of the Province and had used Colonel Campbell and Major Dunbar very roughly."[53] John Campbell had been the Canadian Superintendent of Indian Affairs, and after leading the force that captured Ethan Allen in Quebec, had himself been taken prisoner in the surrender of the garrison at Fort St. John in November 1775.[54] Elisha Benedict's company had been assigned to Fort Chambly in January 1776 where Campbell had been imprisoned. Munro now had all three of these rebel officers under guard, along with three of Benedict's sons. The fourth son, Elisha, Jr. "escaped with only the clothing on his back."[55] Their slave Dublin was also captured. In an act that seemed to ignore Munro's concern about alerting the militia at the fort, the invaders pillaged the Benedict house and burned his barn.

The combined force proceeded up the road as it climbed up Pierson's Ridge. There were a number of cabins that straddled the hill and it may have been that Munro's forces spread out to surround the homes simultaneously to maintain the element of surprise. Most accounts mention the families raided one-by-one, but that may not have been the case. Little narrative detail of the attack on these hillside homes has been preserved.

At the foot of the hill to the east lived Edward Watrous who had just turned twenty-seven. He had married Susannah Pierson in 1777 and they had two children – two-year-old daughter Elizabeth and three-month-old son Edward. Once again, it is possible that his family had retreated to Richmond, the former home of Susannah's parents. Edward stayed on to protect his home and serve in the militia. He was captured and his home ransacked, but not burned.

Across the road at the crest of the hill lived Edward's father-in-law Paul Pierson, who at fifty-four was twice Edward's age and too old to serve in the militia.

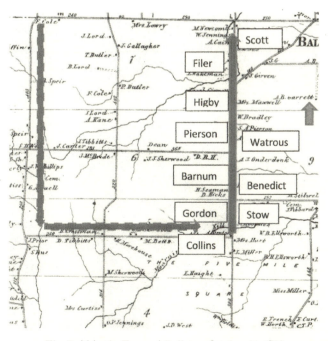

The Raid in the Town of Ballston October 16, 1780

He had five sons but only fifteen-year-old John was home at the time of the raid. He is the only Pierson listed on the rolls of the 12th Militia. All the others were in their twenties and may have remained in Richmond. Father and son were taken and the Indians did their part to grab everything of value, including the livestock, which was herded along the road as they proceeded northward.

Moving downhill the attackers came upon the home of John Higby, head of yet another family from Richmond. John had been married for twenty-five years to Mindwell Lewis and raised a large family. John's son Lewis, given his mother's surname, was at home and was captured along with his father. Higby's cabin was put to the torch, the first home to be burned. It may have been a case of over-zealous Indians or Munro may have felt that, shielded by the hill, he had put enough distance between his party and the fort to risk the destruction. Two of Higby's daughters no longer lived at the family home. They had married neighbors. If they were not yet aware of the raid and the destruction of their parent's home, they soon would be.

The burning of Higby's cabin may have been a godsend for the family of Jonathan Filer. An early account of their ordeal provides a description of one of the few bright spots for the families along the Middleline. You can sense the elation of the author in finally being able to relate a success story.

The Hawkins farm, where James Tibbets now resides (1858), was then occupied by Jonathan Filer. He heard the noise and saw the light of Benedict's burning barn and the rising flames from Higby's house, and suspecting the cause routed his family in all haste, and seizing what few effects he could carry, fled with them into the thick hemlocks that adjoined his clearing on the east. The enemy coming up, pillaged his premises and fired the house, and then passed on to the north. Filer's mother-in-law, Granny Leake, who had concealed herself near the house, as soon as they had retired, rushed from her hiding place, and succeeded in quenching the fire. The building, yet stands, an eloquent memorial of that fearful night, with its sides yet charred with the fire that, but for good Granny Leake, would have reduced it to ashes.[56]

There is mention in some accounts that a cabin adjacent to Filer belonging to Lemuel Wilcox was approached next. The story is told that Lemuel was away serving in the army and that his wife, Austie, daughter of John Higby, was overtaken by an Indian who used his knife to detach a gold necklace from her neck, then let her go.[57] Pension records tend to contradict this narrative. Lemuel was living in Middletown, Connecticut throughout the war and served in the Connecticut Line from 1777 to 1781, being present at the surrender of Cornwallis. Seeking a widow's pension in 1839, Austie deposed that she married Lemuel in 1786.[58] In 1780 she was only sixteen, and had probably not yet met Lemuel. One possibility is that the story is somehow conflated, and that the events described happened to her while still living with her parents.

The Filer house was on the next rise north of Pierson's Ridge. The road now descended until it approached a creek where James Gordon and George Scott, his brother-in-law, had built a saw mill in 1774. The road skirted the left bank of the creek until it left the stream to resume its northward track uphill across the current Milton Town line. At the saw-mill Munro detached fifty men, mostly rangers under the command of William Fraser, to cross the stream and approach the cabin of Scott. Presumably the main body continued north.

Scott was awakened by his barking dog and, seizing his gun, opened the door of his cabin, only to be confronted by Fraser whom he knew from his first years in the settlement. Fraser, apparently trying to save the life of his old acquaintance, shouted "Scott, throw down your gun or you are a dead man!" Not responding quick enough, three Mohawks who had accompanied the party let loose their tomahawks, striking Scott on his head. The Indians rushed in to scalp him but were stopped by Sargeant Staats Springsteen, who had apparently worked for Scott before the war.[59] Springsteen, born in Albany in 1755, came from a family long resident in the area. He and his brother Casper had joined Butler's Rangers in 1778 and were active recruiters of Loyalists for the British.[60] How he came to work for Scott is not known, but this relationship may have saved Scott's life.

The Indians proceeded to pillage the home, leaving Scott's wife Jane

(Gordon) to minister to her supposedly dying husband. Among the items taken from the home were wearing apparel, a beaver hat, a watch, silk stockings and several wigs George had brought from Ireland.[61] The sea chest used to secure their valuables in the woods, given to George by his brother John when they left Ireland, was also a causality of the raid.[62] Later, on the journey back to Canada, James Gordon spotted a wig worn by an Indian and assumed that his brother-in-law was dead. Fortunately, he was wrong. Scott recovered to live another five years. Their six-year-old son James fled into the woods, where he was eventually reunited with his mother.[63] James later recounted that he had recognized one of the Indians as an Oneida that had been in the party that had camped near his home in recent weeks. It is certainly possible that this party provided intelligence to Munro and eventually joined the raiding party.[64] No mention is made of Scott's three daughters, who were fifteen, thirteen and eight at the time. Perhaps they had also been hustled off to a safer location before the raid.

After this half-hour excursion, Fraser's detachment reunited with the main body and proceeded north, crossing Gordon's creek, and climbing up the hill into the current Town of Milton. At the crest of the hill lived George Kennedy and his twenty-two-year-old pregnant wife Mindwell (Higby). George was suffering from an injured foot, the result of an altercation with an axe. That did not exempt him from being taken, joining the growing number of captives. Their house was plundered and set afire, the second to be burned. Unlike her parents' home however, the Kennedy cabin was the first destroyed under orders from the officers who were leading the invasion. Far enough away from the fort now, the settlers along the northern section of the Middleline would suffer greater loss. Mindwell managed to escape into the woods, traveling south, crossing streams and suffering from the cold, until she came to the clearing of Samuel McCrea, a mile to the south. Two weeks later, her first-born child was delivered, and her husband was there to witness the event, as we shall see.[65]

Up the road from the Kennedys lived Jabez Patchen. Fifty-three years old, many of the children born of him and his wife Hannah (Squire) had moved out on their own. Two of his sons, Samuel and Squire, were serving in the militia and away from home. Once again, the women of the family are not mentioned as being present during the raid. Jabez was at home with his seventeen-year-old son Walter and his son-in-law Enos Morehouse, who had married his daughter Sarah in 1774. These men were able to escape through a back window, but Jabez was captured. His house was spared the flames.[66]

It's hard to imagine the scene as the raiders moved house to house, rounding up the men, scattering the few, frightened women and children who had stayed behind on the frontier with their husbands and fathers. All were forced out into the cold October night in their nightclothes, not able to retrieve more substantial clothing, which had already been claimed by the invaders. The Indians seem to have taken the lead in scouring the rooms for anything of value, forcing the captive men and their livestock to bear the burden of carrying their goods as they trudged along, prodded by their guards. As hard as it was for the settlers along the Middleline, it could have been much worse. From the stories retold in later years, several men had been saved from certain death by the forbearance of the officers in charge.

It was now about 4 AM, two hours before dawn. The next family to fall victim was that of Josiah Hollister, lying in a slight hollow along the east side of the road. This was his first year in Ballston, having moved from Sharon, Connecticut, with his wife Mehitable (Andrews) and their two young children, Samuel and Ruth. Loyalist soldiers burst through his door telling him to leave the house immediately before the Indians arrived. Josiah described what happened next in his journal.

> I took up my little son, my wife took the other child, and we left the house. They bade me give the child to my wife, but the child clung fast around my neck. I asked them to show some pity; "What can this woman do with two small children." One presented his gun to my breast and swore an oath that he would not be plagued with me any longer. My wife begged them to spare my life. Another struck up the muzzle of his gun and hauled me away to the guard. But judge what my feeling were at this time to see my house in flames, my wife and children turned out of doors, almost naked; myself hauled away among savages and men more inhuman than they.[67]

Josiah was related through marriage to Ebenezer Sprague, whose brother Jonathan had married Hollister's step-mother, Mary Chamberline, in 1773. It was Ebenezer who had helped Josiah get settled earlier that year, building a cabin just south of the Sprague home. Ebenezer was the patriarch of a large family. Three of his sons from his second marriage to Hannah St. John had joined the American cause and served in Gordon's 12th regiment. Although at sixty-nine Ebenezer was too old to serve himself, he was not too old to be taken captive along with two of his sons, John and Elijah. Together they stood and watched as their home went up in flames. His wife and teenage daughters may not have been among them. They may have been sent back to Sharon before the raid.

Two of George Kennedy's brothers, Thomas and John, lived on the west side of the road north of Sprague. Thomas was captured at the same time as the Spragues, but John lived farther up the road near the intersection of Middleline and Galway road. He was alerted by the flames from the homes and crops burning to the south and was able to escape into the woods with his wife Hannah (Olmstead). For some reason, the raiders passed by John's home without torching it.[68]

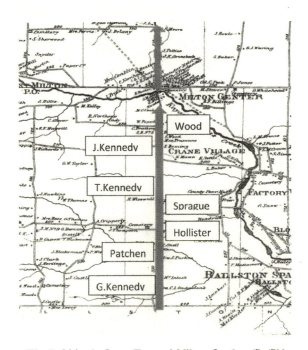

The Raid in the Later Town of Milton October 17, 1780

The last settlement along Middleline Road before it crossed the Kayaderossras Creek were a cluster of homes of the Wood clan, on the slight rise known as Milton Hill. Two of David Wood's five sons lived along the Middleline in the path of Munro's invaders. Stephen had married Ebenezer Sprague's daughter Hannah in 1769 and had two children, ten-year-old son Luther and five-year-old daughter, Cynthia. Although Stephen and his family were away visiting family in Connecticut, their house, barn, and 800 bushels of wheat were destroyed.[69] Stephen's younger brother, seventeen-year-old Enoch and his hired man Cyrus Fillmore were captured. Enoch had moved up from Sharon in August the previous year to join his father and brothers, and signed on to serve in Collins' company in the militia along with his cousin Elijah Sprague.[70]

Fillmore was also from Sharon and related to the Wood family. His uncle Nathanial had married Hepzibah Wood in 1767. Cyrus enlisted in the Connecticut Regiment of Colonel Charles Burrall in 1776. By 1778, at the age of twenty-one, he had moved to Ballston where he signed up to serve in the 5th New York Regiment under Colonel Lewis Dubois. The next year he accompanied that regiment in the Sullivan expedition against the Iroquois.[71] Cyrus' training in the army held him in good stead. Just as the Loyalists were moving off from the Wood property, Fillmore seized the opportunity to escape, as he later related.

> Just after leaving here, Fillmore, who was guarded by an Irishman, a regular soldier, in front, and a German soldier behind him, coming to a path that branched off from the road, suddenly plunged into it and ran for his life. The German inquired of the Irishman, "Shall I shoot?" The Irishman, missing his prisoner, replied, "Yes you damned fool!" and both fired at the fugitive. One ball whizzed through his ear-lock. Coming to a large hemlock tree that had fallen across the path, he secreted himself in its branches and thus escaped.[72]

Cyrus went back to Connecticut where he married Jemima Kneeland in September 1781. They returned to Saratoga County, and raised their family in Greenfield before moving to western New York. He filed for a pension in 1832, and in his wife's widow's application in 1847 it is mentioned that Cyrus was a relative of Millard Fillmore, a rising New York politician.[73] In fact, Cyrus and Nathaniel Fillmore, Millard's father, were cousins.[74] His widow could not have known that her husband's distant relative would become the thirteenth president of the United States just three years later.

∞

The Wood cabins were located in the last clearing along the road and were the last homesteads to go up in flames. Munro's men marched down the hill where they forded Kayaderosseras Creek. At that point they came to a halt along a little steam that crossed the road just north of today's Milton Center to consolidate their forces and assess their next move.[75] Still fearing that the militia from the Ballston stockade would be hot in pursuit, each prisoner was placed under the guard of two men. Munro supposedly ordered that if the militia approached, they were to dispatch their prisoners. The Indians in the party were certainly favorable to this order, if in fact Munro ever gave it. Consistent with the native code of honor they were expecting a reward for their assistance on the raid, and that often involved taking scalps.[76]

This brutal order seems at odds with the several actions of restraint shown by the invaders that saved the lives of Gordon, Scott and possibly others during the raid. Gordon in his memorandum of the raid does not mention this order, but his daughter Melinda in her later account relates the story.[77] All the accounts that mention it are certainly wrong on one point. With righteous indignation they reported that Munro was cashiered for this offense, but that never happened. In fact, his conduct during the raid met the approval of Governor Haldimand and he continued in the British service until the end of the war.[78]

Not wanting to linger at the creek any longer, the two hundred raiders, their thirty prisoners, and the confiscated livestock moved off, following the trail northward another ten miles until arriving at the base of Kayaderosseras Mountain, near present day Middle Grove. There they stopped and slaughtered the animals before climbing the mountain to camp for the night two miles beyond Lake Desolation.[79]

It was here that Munro displayed his own skill in dealing with the Iroquois in his party to solve a problem that had developed during the day's march. In this action he was ably assisted by his Indian advisor Patrick Langan and the lead warrior of the Mohawks, John Deserontyon (Captain John). It seems that four of the prisoners could not continue. George Kennedy's foot injury had so debilitated him that he allegedly begged to be put to death. For both Paul Pierson and Ebenezer Sprague, their age had caught up with them, and Paul's young son John also could not keep up. The Indian answer to this problem would have been instant death, but Munro proposed another solution. He suggested releasing the men, allowing them to return to their homes.

At the same time, to assuage the Indians, he allowed Captain John to select a number of men for adoption. Adoption was a long standing practice among the Iroquois to replace warriors lost in war. Deserontyon chose ten men — the four Benedicts, Thomas Barnum, John and Lewis Higby, Elijah Sprague, and Gordon's slave, Nero.[80] Even with this arrangement, on Wednesday morning, October 18, Munro released the four invalids five miles earlier than the pre-arranged location to forestall the Indians from dropping back to inflict their own justice.[81]

There are at least three reasons given for the lack of response to the raid by the local militia units stationed at the Ballston stockade. First, Gordon is said to have sent a messenger who met a militia force of 200 men commanded by Captain John Ball at the Milton meeting house. Upon hearing that pursuit would result in the deaths of the captives, the militia returned to the fort.[82] Second, as the four released men doubled back on the trail they were met by a group of men from Charlton who, hearing the same threat, retired as well.[83] Gordon, in his later account, mentioned that he had given a note intended for his wife to these four men, contents unknown.[84] In a third account, Munro gives credit to the local Loyalists in his report. "I am informed by persons that came in since, that they [the Loyalists] met a large body of militia pursuing us, when those guides informed them that my detachment consisted of five hundred men, they advised them to immediately turn back, which they accordingly did."[85]

A firsthand narrative from the pension records of a participant in the pursuit of the invaders, although written over fifty years later, may well be the most accurate account. David How had moved to Ballston with his family in 1773 at the age of twelve. Five years later he joined the militia and was sent to join the garrison at the Palmerstown blockhouse, in the current Town of Wilton, under the command of Captain Stephen White. Later in 1778 he was among the militiamen sent to the Mohawk Valley prior to the British and Indian attack at Cherry Valley. In October 1780, he participated in the abortive attempt to rescue his neighboring militiamen on the trail north of the burned out farms along Middleline Road.

> All the whigs able to bear arms in Ballston were called out to pursue the enemy. He the said David How and others volunteered and marched in pursuit to the Sacandaga Mountains near Lake Desolation when he and his associates met several prisoners returning home who had been released by the British on account of their inability, through age and infirmity, to march on the retreat. These prisoners, three of whom were Pierson, Kennedy, and Sprague, brought from Col. Gordon directions to the party in pursuit not to continue the pursuit, but to return to Ballston as the British officers had put the prisoners captured at Ballston into the custody of the Indians with orders to kill them if they should be attacked. The said How and his associates were ordered back and returned to Ballston.[86]

All three of these accounts may contain elements of the truth but, in any event, the chase was not sustained. The two-hundred-man British force and their thirty captives plunged on, following the old Indian trail northward.

For the families now left to carry on without their husbands and fathers, it would be a difficult time. In the days after the raid many of them gathered at the Ballston fort, or slept in the woods down the hill near the outlet of Ballston Lake. Each family made their own arrangements. Some moved in with relatives or neighbors in Ballston or surrounding towns. Others chose to move back to their family homes in New England. Jane Scott and her son James moved into a barn on the farm of Samuel McCrea and stayed there to the end of the war. All would wait in anticipation for word from their menfolk.

CHAPTER 9
Canada

L t. Colonel Gordon's recollection was that "nothing material happened until they arrived at Crown Point."[1] For Josiah Hollister, "nothing material" included little food. The slaughter of the cattle had provided enough meat to last three days. After that, the 200 Loyalists and Indians, as well as the thirty captives, survived on tea made by boiling hemlock branches. Their eight-day journey was an arduous one as they marched through the wilderness, crisscrossing the Hudson and Schroon rivers, often in waist deep water.[2] Most of the provisions they had stashed at the start of their campaign had been taken by others and the remainder was spoiled. Worn down by hunger and fatigue, they met up with Major Carleton's force on October 24.

Up to that point all the captives had suffered alike, regardless of their rank. With their arrival at Crown Point, 18th century social decorum called for deferential treatment for the captured officers. The militia rank and file drew one day's provisions, boarded the ship *Maria* and sailed to St. John, on their way to captivity in Montreal.[3] The *Maria,* now a conveyor of American prisoners northward along the Lake, had a much more glorious past. The schooner had seen action at Valcour Island in 1776 and had served as the flagship for General John Burgoyne during his 1777 invasion.[4] Meanwhile, Major Carleton was ordered to stay on Lake Champlain to guard against perceived rebel attempts to retaliate for the raids. While waiting at Crown Point, Gordon was invited to breakfast with Captain Munro, enjoyed lunch with William Fraser, and shared a drink of grog with his "old acquaintance" Major James Rogers. For dinner, Gordon and Captain Collins were invited aboard the *Carleton,* another survivor of Valcour Island, where they were joined by several other officers taken prisoner during Carleton's engagements at Fort Anne and Fort George. They were all invited to remain on board and continued to be treated with honor during the voyage north.[5]

For the others the trip was more harrowing. The men taken by the Indians for adoption were in constant fear for their lives during the journey. As they reached St. John's their captors had managed to secure enough liquor to get quite drunk and threatened to kill their new brothers. The ten captives were only held in an Indian town for two days before being brought to Montreal and sold back to the British.[6]

This was also the fate of Gordon's slaves. Patrick Langan, who had directed the Mohawk Indians during the raid, acting as an agent for the Indians, sold Nero to John Mittleburger, a Montreal tailor, in December for £60. However, Allan Maclean, Munro's Loyalist associate and now a general, claimed him as a prisoner of war. Nero later teamed up with Elisha Benedict's slave Dublin and escaped to Richmond, Massachusetts—two more refugees from Ballston that ended up there.[7]

Gordon's two other captured slaves, Jacob and Ann, were also sold by Langan to Montreal merchant Samuel Judah, for £24 and £60 pounds, respectively. Jacob claimed to be a free man who had served under Burgoyne at Saratoga and had been taken prisoner by the Americans. By some arrangement he came into the possession of Gordon. Jacob did not take his bondage well. In April 1781 he attacked his master and was committed to prison.[8] He eventually was released. Both men ended up back with Gordon and may have been among the seven slaves owned by him in 1790.[9]

Gordon's voyage to Montreal included a stop-over in Chambly, where he had the opportunity to meet with Colonel John Campbell, the same man that Munro accused of being mistreated by Tyrannus Collins and Elisha Benedict back in 1776.[10] Campbell was returning from yet another raid conducted simultaneously with the attack on Ballston. He had led a party of 300 Indians into Vermont on a remarkably similar mission, burning homes, destroying crops and capturing thirty-two settlers. Among the men taken was Zadock Steele whose path would soon cross with several of the Ballston captives.[11]

Lt. Colonel Gordon and Captain Collins, along with the eight enlisted men not given to the Indians, arrived in Montreal on October 31.[12] They were marched through the town to the north shore of the island where they were housed in the convent of the old French church. Variously referred to as the Recollet Convent and the Regal Church, this is almost certainly the current Church of the Visitation, located in the Sault-au-Recollet neighborhood of Montreal. Built around 1750 during the old French Regime, it is the oldest still-standing church in Montreal. Sixty-five men were crowded into two rooms, but at least they were sheltered from the elements for the first time since being forced from their homes.[13]

From there the privileges of rank again separated the prisoners. Officers in 18th century warfare were often treated as gentlemen and received special considerations not available to the common soldier. Often they were placed on parole, assigned to private homes of other gentlemen and given the freedom to move about the community. In return they pledged their honor not to take up arms against their opponents until exchanged. In contrast, "common soldiers did not qualify for parole because they were not gentlemen and could not be counted on to keep their word."[14]

The very next day, Gordon was visited by Robert Ellice. Ellice remembered Gordon from their business relationship after the French and Indian War, but they had chosen opposite sides at the start of the rebellion. Alexander Ellice had relocated to Montreal in 1776 and his brother Robert joined him two years later. There they continued to prosper in the fur trade business, becoming one of the largest merchandising firms in Canada.[15] Ellice had good news. He had interceded on Gordon's behalf with General Maclean and he was free to go home with him, upon payment of £3000 bail. This was a considerable sum, but Ellice paid it and Gordon was released into his custody. He stayed there only a week, however, before moving to a room in the home of a Mr. Levy. He began working for Levy, making up cans of tobacco, awaiting release.[16]

The enlisted men followed a different path. After remaining in the church for about a week, they were moved to a large stone building in the suburbs of Montreal where they were joined by those that had been taken in the simultaneous Vermont raid. Together they spent a long miserable winter along with two hundred other prisoners, guarded by a detachment of Hessians.[17] Zadock Steele, one of the Vermont prisoners, recalled the experience years later.

> Many of the prisoners as well as myself has only one shirt
> and were obliged to go without any while we washed that.
> We were allowed, or rather said to be allowed, one pound
> of bread and one pound of fresh beef per day. But, through
> the injustice and dishonesty of the person who dealt out
> our allowances, we were robbed even of a part of this
> humble pittance. We were kept almost totally without
> firewood, having scarcely enough to enable us to cook our
> meat. Pinched with hunger, half naked, and chilled with
> the cold, we were forced to have recourse to our beds,
> though they were the habitations of filthy vermin, tainted
> with the infections of mortal distempers, and scented with
> the nauseous smell of the dying and the dead.[18]

In this environment, the rank-and-file prisoners from Middleline Road spent their first winter in captivity. Often pressured to join the British cause, they refused. Josiah Hollister, in his recall of the harassment, wrote of his defiance. A Captain Jones came into his barracks and Hollister was ready for him.

> Jones saw me smile and said "There is a good natured
> looking man. I want a company of such men. Will you
> enlist? I answered "Yes". "Well, set down your name." I
> said, "I'll stay 'til I get home and then I will enlist very
> soon. I have not been used well enough to enlist here.
> Why, how have you been used?" "You came upon me
> in the night, hauled me out of doors, burned my house
> and turned my wife and children out. I will see you all
> hanged before I'll enlist to support such a government as
> that." They all gave a shout and Jones went out.[19]

In the spring of 1781, Hollister was among sixteen captives who developed scurvy and were transported to a hospital at Three Rivers where they were treated, recovered and returned to Montreal. On the anniversary of their capture, October 17, 1781, the Ballston men were among the prisoners relocated forty-five miles upriver to a more remote facility on an island in the St. Lawrence across from a blockhouse known as Coteau du Lac. The blockhouse on the mainland was manned by fifty soldiers from the King's Royal Regiment under the command of Captain Joseph Anderson whom the Ballston prisoners had first confronted during the raid that took them from their homes and families one year earlier.[20] In this inhospitable location they spent their second winter in captivity, where they would come face-to-face with an even more onerous individual from their past.

∞

From his first arrival, Lt. Colonel Gordon sought relief for his men and the other captives living in the deplorable conditions of their incarceration. In December he began a correspondence with the British officials that would continue for the next eighteen months. He brought to their attention the plight of his men and suggested that he be allowed to return to New York to secure provisions and money to sustain the prisoners. Gordon and other officers, including Tyrannus Collins, signed a petition which was sent to Frederick Haldimand, the governor in Quebec, asking that communications be opened with the Americans to seek funds to supplement the supplies provided by the British military.[21] In July Gordon appealed again to Haldimand to be allowed to return to Albany, noting that through his contacts there he would be able to secure supplies for his men. He noted that "my influence there would enable me to transact such a business more successfully than anyone at present in captivity here."[22]

Gordon's requests were denied. It seems that he had run afoul of his captors. The first indication of this was the recommendation of Captain Matthews, Haldimand's chief of staff, to deny Gordon's requests. In his letter of July 25 1781, Matthews indicated that "the abuses of indulgences daily manifested by the rebel prisoners does not warrant his Excellency's compliance with the requests of Colonel Gordon."[23]

Gordon's extended period of serving out his parole in the private home of businessman Levy in Montreal was about to end. Just as he was anticipating his departure for home, he was taken into custody and sent to prison in Quebec City. Upon his arrival there he dashed off a long letter to Haldimand citing the terms of his parole and demanding an explanation for the sudden change in his circumstances. He clearly was at a loss, lamenting that "I have not been guilty of the least breach of my parole since I have been a prisoner."[24]

Haldimand replied promptly, through Matthews, who simply told Gordon that "The sudden change in your situation proceeded from different accounts received from the colonies of your having held a conduct inconsistent with your parole." In the same letter, Matthews rubbed salt into the wound, indicating that both his former supporters in Montreal, General Maclean and businessman James Ellice, agreed with his imprisonment.[25] Matthews had told Maclean that Gordon was suspected of sending intelligence to his wife in his periodic letters to her.[26] Gordon's son, James, Jr., who had also been staying at the Levy house, was also held under suspicion in Montreal.[27] Gordon's hope of returning to his wife and family had been dashed.

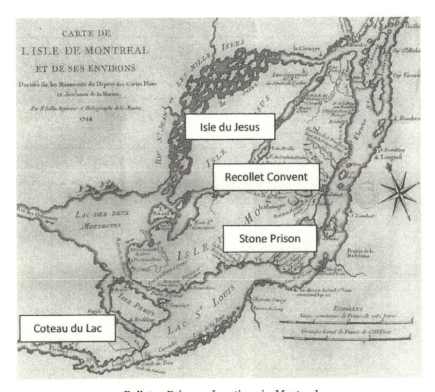

Ballston Prisoner Locations in Montreal

The situation was much worse for the enlisted men held on Prison Island at Coteau du Lac. The prison on the Island consisted of eighteen barracks housing twelve men each, a separate room for a hospital, as well as a block-house and a guardhouse.[28] When the prisoners first arrived they were allowed the liberty of walking around the entire twenty-acre island. Given the swift, cold current of the St. Lawrence, their Tory guards did not worry too much about their ability to escape. This did not prevent the inmates from making constant attempts, but most were either caught or died in the attempt. There is no evidence that the Ballston captives were among those that attempted to escape in the fall of 1781 before winter made it an impossible task. However, the change of seasons brought new danger. In addition to dealing with the winter weather, the prisoners had to contend with two commandants known for their cruelty. The first was a Tory named McDaniel, whose treatment of the captives caused them to rebel, refusing to do his bidding. For that some were shackled and put in confinement. Frustrated, McDaniel refused to allow the prisoners to build fires, increasing their suffering.[29]

McDaniel was finally relieved of his post, but his replacement proved to be even worse. While McDaniel's action seems to have been driven by contempt for the rebels and a mean streak often present among prison officials, his successor, James McAlpin, had a personal hatred for some of the prisoners. It is not hard to imagine the dread that must have over-come the Ballston prisoners when he arrived. McAlpin was the only son of Daniel McAlpin, the Loyalist commander of the American Volunteers whose family had been rounded up by Gordon's Ballston militia in 1777. He and his father had joined Burgoyne and fled to Canada where young McAlpin became an Ensign at the age of twelve. In 1780 he was appointed second lieutenant in a Loyalist company. Even though his immaturity was made known to Haldimand, he was given a commission in the King's Royal Regiment, and at the age of sixteen was placed in command of the prison at Coteau du Lac, overseeing thirty Loyalist soldiers. He was now in a position to inflict pain and suffering on the island's prisoners.[30]

McAlpin came to be aware that among the prisoners were some that had caused his family so much grief, and that only heightened his desire to seek retribution. In January 1782 the prisoners refused to follow his orders at which point he had them chained to posts in the barracks causing many to suffer severe frostbite. Zadock Steele related what happened next.

They were taken from the barrack chamber one by one, carried to the guard house and tortured in the most cruel manner. Some were surrounded with soldiers, armed with guns and bayonets pointing directly at them and so near as to render the prisoners unable to move without being pierced with the bayonets; while the infamous McAlpin whipped the prisoners and caned them till he had gutted his vengeance.[31]

Subject to this kind of mistreatment, the prisoners redoubled their efforts to escape. In June, five hazarded the dangerous journey. Two were captured and brought back to the island, but the abuse they had suffered led to an investigation and the court-martial of McAlpin. He was dismissed from the service and eventually returned to England with his mother.[32] Another casualty of his reign of terror was Captain Anderson. Criticized for letting McAlpin run amok he resigned his commission in December 1782, foregoing his half-pay status as a retired officer.[33]

The June breakout resulted in the construction of a picketed enclosure of the prisoner's barracks to prevent further escapes. Anticipating further abuse, and with no immediate prospects for release, the twelve men of one barracks devised a plan to tunnel under the stockade in a desperate bid for freedom. Among the prisoners in this room were two Ballston militiamen, Josiah Hollister and John Sprague, neighbors along Middleline Road. They had suffered all the injustices of enlisted men, imprisoned now for almost two years. They were joined in their nocturnal digging by ten other men, including Zadock Steele, the Vermont captive. It is fortuitous that both Hollister and Steele later wrote memoirs of their captivity, which provides much detail of their planned escape and eventual return to their homes and family.

The tunnel took eighteen days to complete, but for Hollister, it was work done in vain. He became sick and was unable to join the group in their escape. He was forced to stay behind as nineteen men burrowed their way to freedom on the night of September 10.[34] The escapees divided themselves into groups of four; each group escaped on a makeshift raft of logs lashed together by ropes made from their blankets. Steele's foursome included fellow Vermonter Simeon Belknap, Virginian William

Clark and John Sprague of Ballston. Their harrowing journey back to Vermont brought them close to death on a number of occasions. After traveling southeast for twenty-two days, crossing over Lake Champlain in another hand-made raft, they arrived at Pittsford fort, north of Rutland, on October 2. From there they traveled on to Bennington where Sprague and Clark left the others, heading westward toward home. In his memoir, Steele lamented that he never again heard from these men. But together they had shared an experience that they would never forget.[35]

A list of all American prisoners in Canada was compiled in July, 1782, two months before this escape. This list names sixteen of the twenty-five Middleline Road captives that had reached Canada. Of the remaining nine, the five slaves had been sold, and two of them, Gordon's man Nero and Benedict's man Dublin had previously escaped. John Parlow, Gordon's Loyalist servant, had been released. Three men - Jabez Patchen, John Higby and his son Lewis, had been released (or escaped) by September 1781.[36] The status of Gordon's hired man, John Galbraith is unknown.

Of the sixteen men still in custody, ten were held under various forms of house arrest in Montreal or the adjoining Isle du Jesus.[37] Two—James Gordon and Tyrannus Collins—were being held on the Island of Orleans near Quebec City, in similar circumstances. Four of the men had the misfortune to be imprisoned at Coteau du Lac.[38] The rationale for this distribution of the prisoners is not completely understood. In general, the officers certainly were provided the better arrangements, but some enlisted men also could be found living in Montreal homes. Some families were kept together (Elisha Benedict and his son Felix on the Isle du Jesus) while others were separated (Elisha Sprague in Montreal, his brother John, the escapee, at Coteau du Lac.) Table 3 in the appendix summarizes the disposition of the prisoners.

There is one more escape story to tell. After being placed in confinement in Quebec, Gordon continued to appeal to Haldimand. While his requests to return to New York continued to fall on deaf ears, he seized on Haldimand's willingness to allow money to be sent north in support of the prisoners. In September, Gordon wrote a letter to New York's Governor Clinton asking for his assistance to make this happen.[39]

The same month, in yet another letter to Captain Matthews appealing for his own release, Gordon suggested that his return to New York might increase his opportunity to be exchanged. Gordon prefaced his requests with his acknowledgement that Matthews had "always been particularly kind in paying attention to my different applications." Gordon and Matthews seemed to have gained a measure of respect for each other during their year of correspondence.

In the same letter he added that he was sharing quarters with "some militia officers here who had been brought prisoners this summer from the neighborhood where I formerly lived." Gordon was referring to the four men captured during the June 1781 raid on Ballston by John Walden Meyers.[40] Captain David Ramsey, Lt. Epenetus White, Lt. Henry Banta and his brother Ensign Christopher Banta remained Gordon's companions for the next several months at the provost prison in Quebec, where they were held in confinement. Life there appears to have been much different for these officers than the soldiers at Coteau du Lac. William Scudder, another captive who was under house arrest in Quebec, dined with Gordon at the prison several times. On New Year's Day they had "an excellent dinner, and the novelty of soft shelled walnuts, which is the first I have ever tasted in this province." In January of 1782 the Bantas, along with Scudder, were released on parole to the Isle du Orleans down river from the city.[41] Gordon and White were offered the same arrangement, but preferred to remain in Quebec City. Maybe the food there was just too good.[42]

The commonly held belief is that the Revolutionary War ended with the British surrender at Yorktown in October 1781, but it was not so evident at the time. The British army still controlled New York City, Charlestown and Savannah. General Washington led the victorious Continental Army back north to prevent General Clinton's army from considering any further offensive campaigns. In May 1782 the American negotiators—John Jay, John Adams, and Benjamin Franklin—arrived in Paris to begin the peace talks, but the preliminary Articles of Peace were not signed until November 1782.

For the 419 American prisoners still held in Canada in mid-1782 it was a difficult time. As word of the negotiations spread, expectations rose among the captives that the war would soon be over and they would be allowed to go home to their families. As the year dragged on the living conditions worsened, especially for the almost 200 prisoners at Coteau du

Lac.[43] We have already seen one example of this frustration—the desperate escape of Zadock Steele and eighteen other prisoners in September.

The Americans held in Quebec City certainly were living under better circumstances than their fellow militiamen imprisoned on the island near Montreal. Their parole gave them freedom to move around during the day, but subjected them to confinement at night.[44] However, their relationship with the British authorities once again turned sour. Captain Matthew's patience with these outspoken prisoners was running thin. After yet another appeal of their conditions, this time to the Continental Congress, the "rebel officers who have so long enjoyed their liberty upon parole, in their letter insinuated that they were not only in want and confinement, but in irons." He went on to cite the reaction of Haldimand. "Nothing but his Excellency's contempt for persons who would be capable of such ingratitude prevents his ordering them immediately into close confinement." He implied that this may still happen. "I have not yet learned the general's orders concerning Mr. Gordon and Mr. White, but shall not fail communicating them to you as soon as possible."[45]

This damning letter was written on May 27. On June 14 these two officers were moved to the Isle du Orleans, joining the two Banta brothers. Two months later these four men conspired to make their escape, as noted by Scudder.

> Saturday, August 24, 1782. My being particular to the day, month and year, is, that last evening Col. James Gordon Lieutenant White, Lieutenant Banter and Ensign Banter, made their escape or deserted. We suppose it was a matter which for some time had been under consideration. At any rate they are gone, and we suppose have broke their paroles, and embarked down the river.[46]

The harrowing journey undertaken by these four friends admits to their desperation. They crossed the St. Lawrence River in a stolen fisherman's boat and headed cross-country into Maine. After several days without food, Gordon was left behind in a weakened condition while the others sought help. Reaching a settlement, they returned to rescue their leader. After building a raft, they floated down the Kennebec River, reaching the coast at Passamaquoddy Bay. From there they made their way to Boston.[47]

It is ironic that these men who, as officers, having received much better treatment than their fellow enlisted men while confined, should suffer more in their final journey to freedom. The Lt. Colonel who had led his men both in war and captivity returned to civilization in November, 1782. He was soon followed by the men he had led. His captain, Tyrannus Collins, was exchanged in October and returned via Lake Champlain.[48] As fate would have it, the remaining Middleline Road captives arrived in Boston the same month as Gordon, on a much easier journey.

On October 16, 1782, Captain Law, a prison administrator, arrived at Coteau du Lac from Montreal to announce that the prisoners were to be released and allowed to return home. The next day, exactly two years after their capture, the four Middleline Road militiamen who remained on this island prison marched out with their fellow inmates. They traveled to Montreal where they were placed on board a ship bound for Quebec. It is probable that they were reunited with the other Ballston prisoners serving their parole in Montreal, and traveled down the St. Lawrence together. After being transferred to a larger vessel at Quebec, they set sail November 12, arriving in Boston fifteen days later.[49] Although they did not know it yet, the peace treaty had been signed in Paris during their voyage. Arriving on a Thanksgiving day, their return to American soil was not the end of their ordeal. Leaving the ship, they were on their own. They were released with only the clothes on their back, no food and no money to buy provisions. They were obliged to make their way home by relying on the charity of the people along the way.[50]

Josiah Hollister walked to Glastonbury, Connecticut, the home of the Hollisters for generations. He sold his coat for three dollars, which allowed him to obtain food and shelter at taverns along the route. At Glastonbury he was reunited with his uncles, Amon and Elijah Hollister. There he suffered one final blow, and it was a big one. After the raid his wife Mehitable and their two children, Samuel and Ruth, had returned to the home of her father in Litchfield. There she had been stricken with consumption and was near death. His uncles told Josiah he had to hurry if he was going to see his wife before she died. Stricken with grief, he rushed to her side. His pain is still evident in his journal written years later.

When we arrived she met us at the dore, all skin and bones, but O, my feelings at that time I cannot express nor can anyone have the least idea unless they have experienced the same. She told me her time was come; that she must soon leave the world; that it had been her longing desire to see me before she left the world, and that she desired to unite with me to return thanks to Almighty God that he had spared my life so that she might see my face once more in the land of the living.[51]

Mehitable died on January 27, 1783. In his journal, Josiah captured in verse the entire experience of the raid, his captivity and his return. The last stanzas recount her death

> She told me that her time had come,
> She must depart to her long home,
> Her Savior meet her soul in peace,
> Her troubled conscience was at ease.
>
> Says she, "these little children dear,
> Now I must leave them in your care,
> Be kind to them, keep them with you,
> For I must bid you all adieu."
>
> Her countenance grew pale and wan,
> Her strength decayed, her speech was gone,
> Her clay cold hands, she laid in mine,
> Her soul by death, she did resign.
>
> Her weeping friends around her stood,
> But not of them could serve for good,
> Her help was in the God of love,
> I trust she rests with Him above.
>
> May this not serve to harden me,
> Nay! By this awakened be,

It is a debt we all must pay,
We all must die and turn to clay.

Thanks be to God. His name be praised,
He has preserved me all my days,
Although he smote me with a rod,
Grant me a heart to praise my God. [52]

The other prisoners returned to a much more joyful homecoming. But for most of them they would not initially reunite with their families along Middleline Road. Their homes were destroyed, their nascent farms abandoned, their wives and children scattered. For most it meant a return to the towns of their birth in Massachusetts and Connecticut, at least for a time. There they could be supported by their extended family as they sought to rebuild their lives.

EPILOGUE
Life Goes On

For the Loyalists who participated in the Ballston raid there would be no home coming. Their new home would be in Canada. After the raid, John Munro had commanded the garrison at Coteau-du-Lac, preceding his fellow King's Royal Regiment Captain Joseph Anderson in that post. At the conclusion of the war he was placed on half-pay and traveled to England, seeking to receive compensation for his confiscated New York property. He was largely unsuccessful, receiving only £300 on his £10000 claim. Returning in 1788, he was appointed sheriff in the Loyalist settlement of Luneburg. There, along the St. Lawrence river he built and operated grist and sawmills to support his family. He entered politics and became a member of the Legislative Council of Upper Canada. Munro died in 1800 at the age of seventy-two.[1]

William Fraser, the neighbor, antagonist, and captor of James Gordon in 1781 attached his company to the Loyal Rangers commanded by Edward Jessup. He and his brother Thomas were stationed at the blockhouse on the Yamaska River east of Montreal where they continued to support scouting parties back into New York. After the war, William settled on a 700-acre tract in Edwardsburgh on the St. Lawrence River, awarded to him for his service. He became a prominent office holder and land owner. At his death in 1820 his estate included more than 13,000 acres. Considering that his first land purchase was 200 acres in Ballston, he certainly prospered in his new country.[2]

"Captain John" Deserontyon, the Mohawk warrior, continued to participate in raids in the Mohawk Valley. In June 1782 he led one of the last such raids, overrunning German Flats and destroying Ellice's Mills, owned by James Ellice, patron of James Gordon during his incarceration in Montreal.[3] After the war Deserontyon was compensated for his services to the Crown, receiving 3000 acres, a lump sum of £836 and an annual pension of £45. He was active in promoting the welfare of the small Mohawk settlement, a twelve-by thirteen-mile tract at the Bay of Quinte on the northern side of Lake Ontario. He died there in 1811.[4]

Joseph Anderson, whose resignation after the McAlpin court-martial deprived him of his pension, eventually settled in Kingston where he became Collector of Customs until his death in 1813. Christopher Carleton, the overall leader of the October 1780 raid, attained the rank of Lt. Colonel before his early death in Quebec City in 1787 at the age of thirty-eight.

Edward Jessup, who was the leader of the provincial forces that raided Fort Anne and Fort George under Carleton, was chosen to command a new Loyalist regiment, the Loyal Rangers, in November 1781. Also known as Jessup's Rangers, this unit was stationed at various posts along the border north of New York until being disbanded two years later. After the war his men were allotted land in townships along the St. Lawrence River. He, like Munro, journeyed to England to press his claim for compensation. He returned to Canada in 1788 and settled on his land grant of 1,200 acres in Augusta Township, across the St. Lawrence from present day Ogdensburg. He held several minor posts but age caught up with him and he was bedridden, afflicted with the palsy for several years before his death in 1816.[5]

∞

For the American captives, it is remarkable that all survived the war. It is also remarkable that most eventually returned to Ballston, after regrouping with their families in their Connecticut and Massachusetts enclaves. Some lived out their lives in Ballston and died there, while others were drawn westward to establish their families in the former lands of the Iroquois in central New York.

A review of tax records from 1787 as well as the 1790 census indicate that eighteen of the twenty-three free men captured in the raid were back living in Ballston five years after their return from Canada. Among the five who did not return to live there were Tyrannus Collins, James Gordon's captain, and Josiah Hollister, the author of the captivity journal. In addition, no record had been found confirming the return of three of the younger captives —Felix Benedict, Lewis Higby, and John Pierson.[6]

Of those that did return, Edward Watrous may have made the most important contribution to the development of Middleline Road in the years after the war. He returned to his home on the southern slope of the hill across the road from his father-in-law Paul Pierson and became an influential member of the community. He served as town supervisor from 1794 to 1796, and it was during his term that he offered to provide land for the erection of the county courthouse and jail on the crest of old Pierson's Ridge. It was a smart move for him. A small village grew up around the courthouse that at its height would contain approximately thirty-five buildings, including a tavern (still standing), a print shop for the town's first newspaper, as well as a blacksmith shop, lawyer's offices, stores and several residences.[7]

Others returned only to later move away from Ballston. Elisha Benedict and his son Caleb eventually relocated to the Bay of Quinte in Canada in the late 1790's where they both died soon after. It may have been that their time imprisoned in Canada had influenced their decision to return.[8] Several men eventually took advantage of the bounty land available to them and moved their families to central New York. Josiah Hollister, George Kennedy, Enoch Wood and Thomas Barnum all moved west in the years after 1800, spending their last years in towns with names harkening back to the Roman Republic—Marcellus, Camillus and Pompey.

Long-lasting bonds were formed by the shared experiences of war. In 1840, Elijah Sprague and Squire Patchen, son of Jabez, supported the pension claim of Enoch Wood. Their relationship went back over seventy years to their time together growing up in Sharon, Connecticut. Both recounted in detail the raid that had changed their lives sixty years earlier. All three had moved to Camillus in the Military Tract in the early years of the 19th century. Squire Patchen, six years older than Enoch, had known him thirty years in Ballston and another thirty years in Camillus. He ended his deposition in praise of his friend: "This informant further saith that the said Enoch Wood is a man of good reputation and had born a fair character through life and further saith not."[9]

By 1783 James Gordon was back at his home on Middleline Road, attempting to pick up the pieces of his life and business after two years in captivity. His wife Mary (Ball) had most likely gone to live with the Ball family during James' absence. Her mother Elizabeth had died in 1782 and her father Eliphalet had returned to Connecticut where he had remarried to Ruth Beecher in July 1783. Mary may have retreated to Richmond, a safe haven for both the Ball and Collins family during the last stages of the war. Her brother John continued to serve in the army, but his wife, the daughter of Tyrannus Collins, probably was in Richmond with her two young children.

In late July 1783 Gordon welcomed George Washington to his home during the General's tour of the battlefields at Saratoga, Lake George, Ticonderoga and Crown Point. After dinner, Lt Colonel Gordon escorted the Commander-in-Chief to Schenectady on his way back to his head-quarters at Newburg.[10] The year ended on a sad note for the Gordon and Ball families. In October, his father-in-law, Eliphalet Ball, returned to Ballston, bringing with him his youngest daughter, Betsey, who was very ill. She died at the Gordon home two months later at the age of fifteen.[11]

With the war over, Gordon went on to a successful career in politics. In an age when the well-placed gentry were expected to hold office as a public service, it was not unusual to hold more than one position at the same time. Throughout the 1780's after his return he served several terms as both town supervisor and New York State Assemblyman. After the Constitution was ratified, he was elected as a representative to the Second and Third Congress as a Federalist, supporting the policies of President Washington. During these early years, the geographic boundaries of the districts were constantly changing. Up for reelection in 1796, he was soundly defeated by John Williams based on returns from Washington County, an area where Gordon had little influence.[12] From there he went on to serve in the New York Senate from 1801 to 1805 before finally retiring from the political arena.

His business interests continued to thrive. Tax assessments during this period consistently indicated that he was among the wealthiest men in the town of Ballston. The 1790 census records list a large household of eleven men and women, plus seven slaves. Having only two children, the census indicates a large number of workers employed by Gordon and living on his property. In contrast, his son James, Jr, with a family of eight, continued to live on the fifty acres his father had given him. In 1800, the son the father never recognized, sold his small farm for $750 and moved away.[13] In his Will Gordon, Sr. mentions his daughter Melinda as his only child (His legitimate son Alexander died in 1793). This man who had often shown a paternalistic spirit toward his Middlleline Road neighbors in the first days of settlement, during the travails of war, and through their captivity in Canada, seems not to have extended that generosity to his first-born son.

Mary Gordon died in 1803 and soon thereafter Gordon leased his property in Ballston and freed his long-time slave Nero, who had shared with him in the experience of war and captivity. He moved to the home of his daughter Melinda Verplanck in Fishkill, New York but returned to visit friends in Ballston in the fall of 1809.[14]

His obituary in a local newspaper extolled his virtues upon his death in January,1810 at the age of 71.

> At all times when society called for his services, his sympathies were awake. If his county required it, he was ready to lend his aid. If the poor were distressed, he generously and without ostentation offered his purse. As a Christian he was exemplary; as a citizen, able in advice and experience; as a man, honest and upright; as a politician, sage and discreet. He died as he had lived, a sincere Christian, and friend to his species, regretted and lamented by his relatives, and all who were acquainted with his virtues.[15]

Life would go on along the Middleline, but without Gordon, Collins, the Benedicts, or Kennedys. And in spite of a promising start, the communities that developed along this roadway also vanished over time. In 1816 the Courthouse burned down and the community withered, to be replaced by the new village of Ballston Spa, growing around a mineral spring a few miles to the east.

Today no taverns, inns, mills or shops can be found along Middleline Road. Two hundred thirty-five years after the Ballston Raid, the land surrounding this road has reverted to its pastoral appearance. Large fields still separate older farmsteads and newer homes. Small woodlots still exist along the Gordon and Kayaderosseras Creeks, where large stands of white pine once stood. This land, long traversed only by Iroquois hunting parties, had seen pioneers carve out their homesteads, experience war and death, and recover to build a settled community in the heady days of the new republic, all in the course of one generation.

Appendix

TABLE 1- The Proprietors

	Original 1708		Distribution in 1771		Shares- a)
1	Nanning Harmanse	1	7,10	Evert Bancker & family	2/3
2	Johannis Beeckman	1	7,10	Helina Rutgers & family	2/3
3	Rip Van Dam	1	7,10	Adrian Renandet & family	2/3
4	Anne Bridges	1	12	Hon. William Smith	1/2
5	May Bickley	1	12	William Kelley	1/2
6	Peter Fauconnier	1	5	Cornelius Low	1/8
7	Adrian Hooghlandt	1	5	Cornelius Tiebout	1/8
8	Johannis Fisher	1	5,7,10, 11,12	Dirck Lefferts	1 5/6
9	John Tudor	1	11	Cornelius Clopper	1/2
10	Joris Hooghlandt	1	12	Peter Remsen	1/2
11	John Stevens	1		Thomas Clark	1/2
12	John Tatham	1	2	John Beekman	1/2
13	Sampson Broughton	1	13	Harmon Goveneur	1/3
			4	Rev Oglivie	1/4
			4	Mr. Lupton	1/4
				Philip Livingstone	1/12
			6	John Leake	1/8
				Isaac Low	1/4
			2	Johannis Beekman	1
			1	Nanning Fisher	1/2
			1	Peter Winne	1/2
			3	Van Dam family	5/6
	Total 1708 Shares	**13**		**Known 1771 Shares**	**11 3/16**

(a- Share allocation as determined by the Patent Trustees in 1771. Represents 11 3/16 of the 13 original shares. 1708 to 1771 mapping incomplete

Source: *Account and Sale of Land in Ballston and the 5029 Acre Tract,* Saratoga County Historians Office, Ballston Spa, NY

TABLE 2 – Selected Ballston Family Descendants

Surname	Given	Birth	Location	Death	Location	Marriage
Ball	Aling	1619	England	1680	New Haven, CT	Dorothy Tuttle
	John, Sr	1649	New Haven, CT		New Haven, CT	Sara Glover
	John, Jr	1685	New Haven, CT	1731	New Haven, CT	Mary Tuttle
	Eliphalet	1722	New Haven, CT	1797	Ballston, NY	(1) Elizabeth Van Flemen (2) Ruth Beecher
Barnum	Thomas, I	1625	England	1695		
	Thomas, II	1663	Norwalk, CT	1731	Danbury, CT	Sarah Judd
	Thomas III	1696	Danbury, CT	1762	Danbury, CT	Deborah Cornell
	Thomas IV	1730	Danbury, CT	1755	Lake George, NY	Jerusha Starr
	Thomas V	1749	Danbury, CT	1837	Pompey, NY	(1)Achsah Benedict (2)Martha Nigus
Benedict	Thomas	1617	England	1690	Norwalk, CT	Mary Bridgum
	James	1649	Southfield, NY	1717	Danbury, CT	Sarah Gregory
	Thomas	1694		1776		Abigail Hoyt
	Elisha	1736	Danbury, CT	1798	Canada	
Betts	Thomas I	1618	England	1688	Norwalk, CT	Mary Raymond
	Thomas II	1644	Guilford, CT	1717	Wilton, CT	Sarah Marvin
	John	1684	Norwalk, CT	1745	Norwalk, CT	Hannah Burwell
	Joseph	1717	Norwalk. CT	1804	Ballston, BY	Abigail Whitney
	Joseph	1750	Norwalk, CT	1782	Albany, NY	Abigail
Collins	John, I	1616	England	1670/1	Boston, MA	Susannah Colburn
	John II	1640	Boston, MA	1704	Guilford, CT	(1)Mary Trowbridge (2)Mary Kingsworth
	John III	1663	Guilford, CT	1751	Guilford, CT	Ann Leette
	John IV	1695	Guilford, CT	1760		Rachel Mix
	Tyrannus	1741	Guilford, CT	C1806	Northumberland, NY	Abigail Peck
Filer	George	1610	England	1681	East Hampton, NY	(1)Susannah Miller (2) Edith Snow

Surname	Given	Birth	Location	Death	Location	Marriage
	Samuel	1666	East Hampton	1733	East Hampton. NY	Abigail Osborn
	Thomas	1704	East Hampton	1748	East Hampton. NY	Jane Miller
	Jonathan	1747	Long Island City, NY	1822	German Flats, NY	Typhena Leek
Higby	Edward	1613	England	1699	Jamaica, NY	Jeddidiah Skidmore
	John	1658	Huntington, LI	1688	Middletown, CT	Rebecca Treadwell
	Edward	1684	Middletown,CT	1775	Westfield, CT	Rebecca Wheeler
	John	1707	Middletown,CT	1790	Stonington, CT	Sarah Candee
	John	1732	Middletown,CT	1821	Ballston, NY	(1)Mindwell Lewis (2) Lois Penfield
Hollister	John I	1612	England	1665	Wethersfield, CT	Joanna Treat
	John II	1644	Wethersfield,CT	1711	Glastonbury, CT	Sarah Goodrich
	Thomas	1672	Wethersfield,CT	1741	Glastonbury, CT	Dorothy Hills
	Josiah	1696	Glastonbury,CT	1749	Sharon, CT	Martha Miller
	Samuel	1723	Glastonbury,CT	1771	Sharon, CT	(1)Jemima Phelps (2) Mary Chamberlin
	Josiah	1754	Sharon, CT	1832	Mansfield, NY	(1)Mehitable Andrews (2) Naoim Bidwell
Middlebrook	Joseph, I	1610	England	1686	Bridgeport, CT	(1)Mary Bateman (2) Mary Odell (3) Hannah Wheeler
	Joseph, II	1650	Bridgeport, CT	1709	Bridgeport. CT	Sarah Williams
	Jonathan	1684	Bridgeport, CT	1754	Fairfield, CT	Martha Squire
	Michael	1712	Fairfield. CT	1791	Wilton, CT	Abigail Sommers
	Hezekiah	1740	Fairfield. CT	1832	Ballston, NY	(1)Phebe Nash (2) Sarah White
Patchen	Joseph	1610	England	1690	Fairfield, CT	(1)Elizabeth Iggledin (2) Mary Morehouse

Surname	Given	Birth	Location	Death	Location	Marriage
	Jacob, Sr	1683	Fairfield, CT	1749	Wilton, CT	Mary Hubbard
	Jacob, Jr	1701	Fairfield. CT	1764	Wilton, CT	Abigail Cable
	Jabez	1727	Fairfield, CT	1799	Milton, NY	Hannah Squire
Pierson	Henry, I	1618	England	1680	Southampton, NY	
	Henry, II	1652	Suffolk, NY	1701	Southampton, NY	Susannah Howell
	Josiah	1695	Sag Harbor, NY	1776	Long Island City, NY	(1)Martha Petty (2) Martha Halsey
	Paul	1726	Long Island City. NY	1802	Milton, NY	Elizabeth Hand
Sprague	Francis	1589	England	1670	Duxbury, MA	
	John, Sr	1630	Plymouth, MA	1676		Ruth Bassett
	John, Jr	1656	Duxbury. MA	1727	Lebanon, CT	Lois Abel
	John III	1690	Duxbury, MA	1760	Canaan, CT	(1)Mary Babcock (2) Hannah Burt
	Ebenezer	1711	Lebanon, CT		Ballston, NY	(1)Elizabeth Thatcher (2) Hannah St. john
Stow	John	1595	England	1643	Roxbury, MA	Elizabeth Bigg
	Thomas, Sr	1615	England	1680	Middletown, CT	Mary Griggs
	Thomas, Jr	1651	Middletown, CT	1730	Middletown, CT	Bethia Stocking
	Samuel	1681	Middletown. CT	1740	Middletown, CT	Ester Mould
	Isaac, Sr	1717	Middletown, CT	1773	Guilford, CT	Hepzibah Collins
	Isaac, Jr	1756	Guilford. CT	1780	Ballston, NY	(1)Phoebe Griswold (2) Polly Pierson
Watrous	Jacob	1605	England	1676	New London, CT	Hannah Collins
	Abraham	1644	Wethersfield,CT	1701	Saybrook, CT	Rebecca Clark
	Isaac	1680	Lyme, CT	1751		(1)Elizabeth Lord (2) Elizabeth Bronson
	Andrew	1717	Lyme, CT	1759	Lyme, CT	Dinah Wesrtcot
	Edward A	1753	Lyme, CT	1802	Ballston, NY	Susannah Pierson

Surname	Given	Birth	Location	Death	Location	Marriage
Wilcox	John I	1592	England	1651	Hartford, CT	
	John II	1622	England	1676	Middletown, CT	(1)Sarah Wadsworth (2)Catherine Stoughton
	Samuel, Sr	1658	Middletown, CT	1713	Middletown, CT	Abigail Whitmore
	Samuel, Jr	1684	Middletown, CT	1724	Middletown, CT	Ester Bushnell
	Jeremiah	1715	Middletown, CT	1760	Middletown, CT	Mary Stow
	Lemuel	1759	Middletown. CT	1839	Ballston, NY	Austie Higby
Wood	Edward	1578	England	1663	Long Island City, NY	
	Timothy	1622	England	1659	Jamaica, NY	Joanna Strickland
	Jonathan, Sr	1658	Jamaica, NY	1726	Norwalk, CT	Mary Titus
	Jonathan, Jr	1691	Jamaica, NY	1792	Wilton, CT	Elizabeth Monroe
	David	1718	Ridgefield, CT	1805	Ballston, NY	Dorothy Rockwell
	Enoch	1763	Sharon, CT	1847	Camillus, NY	(1)Sibble Sprague

TABLE 3 -Disposition of Settlers Affected by the 1780 Ballston Raid

Name	10-17-80 Status	Early disposition	Montreal Arrival -a)	Later Disposition	7-22-82 Prisoner List -b)	Dates Returned
John Shew	Killed	—	—	—	—	—
Isaac Palmatier	Captured		Date Unk		Coteau du Lac	12/82
James Gordon	Captured		10-31-80		Isle Orleans	Escaped 9/82
James Gordon Jr	Captured		10-31-80		Montreal	12/82
Jack Galbraith	Captured		Date Unk			Unk
John Parlow	Captured		Date Unk	Released	—	—
Nero Gordon (slave)	Captured	Indians	Date Unk	Sold, Escaped	—	—
Jacob Gordon (slave)	Captured		Date Unk	Sold	—	—
Ann Gordon (slave)	Captured		Date Unk	Sold	—	—
Tyrannus Collins	Captured		10-31-80		Quebec	10/82
Manasseh Collins	Escaped	—	—	—	—	—
Collins unk slave	Captured		Date Unk	Sold	—	—
Isaac Stow	Killed	—	—	—	—	—
Thomas Barnum	Captured	Indians	Date Unk	To British	Coteau du Lac	12/82
Elisha Benedict	Captured	Indians	Date Unk	To British	Isle Jesus	Unk
Calib Benedict	Captured	Indians	Date Unk	To British	Isle Jesus	11/82
Elias Benedict	Captured	Indians	Date Unk	To British	Montreal	12/82
Felix Benedict	Captured	Indians	Date Unk	To British	Isle Jesus	12/82
Elisha Benedict, Jr	Escaped	—	—	—	—	—
Dublin Benedict (Slv)	Captured		Date Unk	Sold, Escaped	—	—
Edward Watrous	Captured		10-31-80		Montreal	11/82
John Davis	Captured		10-31-80		Montreal	11/82
Paul Pierson	Captured	Released	—	—	—	—
John Pierson	Captured	Released	—	—	—	—
John Higby	Captured		Date Unk	Released 9/81	—	—
Lewis Higby	Captured		Date Unk	Released 9/81	—	—
Jonathan Filer	Escaped	—	—	—	—	—
George Scott	Wounded	—	—	—	—	—
George Kennedy	Captured	Released	—	—	—	—
Thomas Kennedy	Captured		10-31-80		Montreal	11/82
John Kennedy	Escaped	—	—	—	—	—
Jabez Patchin	Captured		10-31-80	Released 9/81	—	—
Josiah Hollister	Captured		10-31-80		Coteau du Lac	12/82
Ebenezer Sprague	Captured	Released	—	—	—	—
John Sprague	Captured		10-31-80		Coteau du Lac	Escaped 8/82
Elisha Sprague	Captured	Indians	Date Unk	To British	Montreal	12/82
Enoch Wood	Captured		10-31-80		Montreal	12/82
Cyrus Fillmore	Escaped	—	—	—	—	—

a) Haldimand Papers http://heritage.canadiana.ca Reel H-1738 B-183 Mss 21843, p.88
b) Haldimand Papers http://heritage.canadiana.ca Reel H-1738 B-183 Mss 21843, p.377-394

Abbreviations

AHN	America's Historical Newspapers
DCB	Dictionary of Canadian Biography
DHSNY	The Documentary History of the State of New York
DRCHNY	Documents Relative to the Colonial History of New York
FAA	Force's American Archives
HP	Haldimand Papers
MACC	Minutes of the Albany Committee of Correspondence
MCDDC	Minutes of the Committee for Detecting and Defeating Conspiracies
PCA	The People of Colonial Albany
PPGC	Public Papers of George Clinton
SWJP	Sir William Johnson Papers

End Notes

Chapter 1 Anne, by the Grace of God

1   Westbrook, Nicholas. *"Have we no longer a share in your history?" Preserving Old Minerley Road: le chemin des Iroquois,* Unpublished Essay, 2010, p.11

2   O'Callaghan, EB. *The Documentary History of the State of New York,* Albany, 1849, Vol. 1, p. 307

3   Cohen, Eliot A. *Conquered Into Liberty,* Simon & Schuster, New York, 2011, p. 22

4   Leisler's Rebellion, http://en.wikipedia.org

5   Bonomi, Patricia. *The Lord Cornbury Scandal,* University of North Carolina Press, Chapel Hill, 1998, p. 39

6   *Ibid.,* p. 5

7   *Ibid.,* p. 97

8   *Ibid.,* p. 3

9   Cronon, William. *Changes in the Land,* Hill and Wang, New York, 1983, p. 62

10 *The Colonial Laws of New York from 1664 to the Revolution, Vol. 1,* James B. Lyon, Albany, 1849, p. 40

11 McGrail, Francis, Jr. *The Kayaderosseras Patent: Colonial Land Ownership in Saratoga Co, New York,* Saratoga County Historians Office, Box 5, Unpublished, 1978, p. 5

12 Belinski, Stephan. *The People of Colonial Albany Live Here-Robert Livingston* http://www.nysm.nysed.gov/albany

13 *Calendar of N.Y. Colonial Manuscripts, Land Papers 1643-1803,* Albany, 1864, Vol. 3, p. 65

14 *Ibid.,* p. 76

15 Nammack, Georgiana. *Fraud, Politics and the Dispossession of the Indians,* University of Oklahoma Press, Norman, 1969, p. 54

16 Shannon, Timothy J. *Iroquois Diplomacy on the Early American Frontier,* Penguin Books, New York, 2008, p. 1

17   *New-York Historical Society Collections for* 1922, p. 359; in *McGrail,* Appendix A-1

18   McGrail. *The Kayaderosseras Patent,* p. A17

19   *New-York Historical Society Collections for* 1922, p. 360-364; in *McGrail,* p.11

20   Matson, Cathy. *Merchants & Empire-Trading in Colonial New York,* John Hopkins University Press, Baltimore, 1998, p. 61

21   *Ibid.,* p. 134

22   *Land Papers,* p. 78

23   Helffenstein, Abraham. *Pierre Fauconnier and His Descendants,* Philadelphia, 1911, p. 6

24   *Ibid.,* p. 17

25   *Ibid.,* p. 12

26   Bonomi. *Lord Cornbury Scandal,* p. 118

27   Matson. *Merchants and Empire,* p. 137

28   Scott, Kenneth. *The Slave Insurrection in New York in 1712,* NYS Historical Association Quarterly, Vol. 45-1, 1961

29   Lepore, Jill. *Slavery in New York, The Tightening Vise,* in Slavery in New York, Ira Berlin, Ed: New Press, 2005, p. 80

30   Hoagland, Cornelius N. *History and Genealogy of the Hoagland Family in America,* New York, 1891, p. 26

31   Adrian Hooglandt Family Tree records, http://home.ancestry.com

32   Rebushka, Alvin. *Taxation in Colonial America,* Princeton University Press, Princeton, 2008, p. 506

33   Hinderaker, Eric. *The Two Hendricks,* Harvard University Press, Cambridge, 2010, p. 129-131

34   Bonomi. *Lord Cornbury Scandal,* p. 86

35   Fox, Edith M. *Land Speculation in the Mohawk Country,* Cornell University Press, Ithaca, 1949, p. 6

36   Rebushka. *Taxation,* p. 506

37   Fox. *Land Speculation,* p. 7

38   *The Tudor Family of Barbados, Boston and New York City,* NEHGS Register, Vol. 103, Oct 2009, p. 372

39   Lepore, Jill. *New York Burning,* Random House, New York, 2005, Appendix C, p. 262

40   *New York Abstract of Wills Vol. IV 1744-1753,* New York Historical Society, 1895, p. 360

41   Indenture, provided by Lori Weiss

42   Woodward, E.M. *History of Burlington and Mercer Counties New Jersey,* Everts & Peck, Philadelphia, 1883

43   *New Jersey Calendar of Wills, Vol. 1 1670-1730,* Documents Related to the Colonial History of New Jersey Vol. XXIII, Patterson, 1895, p. 453

44 White, Barclay. *Early Settlements in Springfield Township*, Burlington County, N.J., address, January 4, 1870

45 *New Jersey Calendar of Wills, Vol. 1 1670-1730*, p. 453

46 William Johnson, *Cases of the Supreme Court of Judicature*, New York, 1883,Vol XIII, Jackson vs Haviland, p 229.

47 Palmer, Thomas. *Fieldbook of the Kayaderosseras Patent, Saratoga Co NY, 1774*, NYS Library Manuscripts and Special Collections, Albany, NY

48 Lee, Francis Bazley. *Genealogical and Memorial History of the State of New Jersey*, Lewis Historical Publishing Co., New York, 1910, p. 187

49 *Calendar of the Stevens Family Papers,* Stevens Institute of Technology Library, Ancestry,com

50 *Documents of the Assembly of the State of New York*, Vol. 18, 1917, Appendix D, First Presbyterian Church of New York City, p. 585

51 Witcraft, John. *Cornelius Janen Clopper and His Descendants*, Merchantville, 1938, p. 5

52 Johnson. *Cases of the Supreme Court of Judicature*, Vol XV, Jackson vs Gilchrist, p. 73

53 Mann, E.R. *The Bench and Bar of Saratoga County*, Waterbury & Inman, Ballston, 1876, p. 59

54 PCA. Beekman and Visscher biographies

55 *Kayaderosseras Patent Field Book-Twenty-One Lots of Land of the Share of Patentee Johannes Fisher, filed March 21,1775,* Saratoga County Historian's Office, Box 5

Chapter 2 This Extravagant Grant

1 Colden, Cadwallader. *State of the Lands in the Province of New York in 1732*, in *Documentary History of the State of New York*, O'Callaghan, E.B. ed., Weed, Parson & Co, Albany, 1850, p. 253

2 Brandow, John Henry. *The Story of Old Saratoga*, Albany,1919, p.32 ff

3 Jennings, Francis. *The Ambiguous Iroquois Empire*, W.W.Norton & Co., New York, 1984, p.162

4 Hinderaker. *The Two Hendricks*, p. 195

5 Shannon. *Iroquois Diplomacy*, p. 104,138

6 O'Callaghan, E.B. ed., *Documents Relative to the Colonial History of New York*, Weed Parsons & Co., Albany, 1855, Vol. VI, p. 866. Council at Albany, June 27, 1754

7 *Ibid.*, p. 851. Lt. Governor De Lancey to the Lords of Trade, July 22, 1754

8 *DRCHNY VII*, p. 77. Lords of Trade to Governor Hardy, March 19, 1756

9 Lustig, Mary Lou. *Privilege and Prerogative New York's Provincial Elite 1710-1776*, Fairleigh Dickinson University Press, Teaneck, NJ, 1995, p. 77

10   *Ibid.,* p. 85

11   *Ibid.,* p. 78

12   *Ibid.,* p. 119

13   *DRCHNY VII,* p. 881. Sir William Johnson to the Earl of Shelburne, December 16, 1766

14   O'Toole, Fintan. *White Savage William Johnson and the Invention of America*, State University of New York Press, Albany, 2005, p. 36

15   *Ibid.,* p 161

16   *DRCHNY.* VII, p. 436. Sir William Johnson Proceedings with the Lower Mohawk Indians at Ft. Johnson, March 20, 1760

17   *Ibid.,* p. 576. Sir William Johnson to the Lords of Trade, November 13, 1763

18   *Ibid.,* p. 674. Sir William Johnson to the Lords of Trade, October 30, 1764

19   *Ibid.,* p. 881. Sir William Johnson to the Earl of Shelburne, December 16, 1766

20   *Ibid.,* p. 876. Governor Moore to the Earl of Shelburne, November 8, 1766

21   Nammack. *Fraud, Politics and Dispossession,* p. 67

22   McGrail. *The Kayaderosseras Patent,* p. 47

23   Sullivan, James, Ed. *The Papers of Sir William Johnson,* The University of the State of New York, Albany, 1921, Vol. VI, p. 40. Kayaderosseras Proprietors to Sir William Johnson, 1767

24   McGrail. *The Kayaderosseras Patent,* p. 51

25   *SWJP. Vol. VI,* p. 173-174. Benjamin Kissam to Sir William Johnson, March 29, 1768

26   *DRCHNY,* VIII, p. 70. Governor Moore to the Earl of Hillsborough, May 12, 1768

27   McGrail, *The Kayaderosseras Patent,* p. 52

28   Bascom, Robert. *The Fort Edward Book,* James D Keating, pub, Fort Edward, 1903, p. 57

29   SWJP, Vol. XII p. 529-538, Indian Congress June 8-28, 1768, extracted in *McGrail* p. 53-59

30   *Ibid.,* Vol. VI, p. 274. John Morin Scott to Sir William Johnson, July 13, 1768

31   *Ibid.,* Vol. XII p. 572-78, Indian Congress, August 2-4, 1768. extracted in *McGrail,* p. 63-64

32   *Ibid.*

Chapter 3 Links and Chains

1   *The Colonial Laws of New York* p. 584

2   Dictionary of Canadian Biography, http://www.biographi.ca, William Smith, Jr.

3   *PCA.* John Glen, Jr.

4   *Land Papers* Vol XVI, p. 303

5   Yates, Austin. *Schenectady County. Its History to the Close of the Nineteenth Century*, New York History Company, 1902, p. 272

6   Hanson, Willis. *A History of Schenectady During the Revolution*, Heart of Lakes Publishing, Interlaken, 1988, p. 275

7   *Palmer Family of Plymouth, The American Genealogist*, 1956, Vol. 32, p. 39-45

8   *Annual Report of the Forest Commission for the Year 1893 Vol. I*, James B. Lyon. Albany. 1894. p. 136

9   *PCA*. Cornelius Cuyler

10   *New York Mercury, December 5, 1763*, America's Historical Newspapers http://www.americanancestors.org

11   *Field Book No. 1 of the Division of the Kayaderosseras Patent* 1771, Saratoga County Historian's Office, Ballston Spa, Box 3

12   Huntington, Elijah Baldwin. *History of Stamford Connecticut*, Stamford,1868, p. 424

13   The Society of Colonial Wars in the State of Connecticut, http: // colonialwarsct.org

14   Tuttle, George Frederick. *The Descendants of William and Elizabeth Tuttle*, Tuttle & Co., Rutland, 1883, p. 142

15   Kelley, Brooks Mather. *History of Yale University*, Yale University Press, New Haven, 1974, p. 51

16   Baird, Charles W. *History of Bedford Church*, Dodd,Mead & Co, New York 1882, p. 28

17   *Ibid.*, p. 60

18   Briaddy, Katherine Q. *Shadows, The Life and Times of Eliphalet Ball*, Ballston Spa, 1991, p. 32

19   *Ibid.*, p. 31

20   *Ibid.*, p. 33

21   Wyld, Samuel. *The Practical Surveyor*, 1725, with notes by David Manchey, re-printed 2005, http://www.colonialsurveyor.com

22   Life as a Colonial Surveyor, http://www.colonialsurveyor.com

23   Booth, John Chester. *History of Saratoga County*, extracted in *Centennial History of Ballston Spa*, Edward F. Grose, The Ballston Journal, Ballston Spa, 1907, p. 12

24   AHN. *The New York Gazette, November 28, 1774*

25   *Field Book No. 1, 1771*, p. 19

26   Lepore. *New York Burning*, p. 221

27   *Field Book No. 1, 1771*, p. 20

Chapter 4 The Five-Mile Square

1   *The New York Gazette*, March 23, 1771, America's Historical Newspapers, http://www.americanancestors.org

2   *Ibid.*, July 15, 1771

3   *Account and Sale of Land in Ballston and the 5029 Acre Tract Book B,* Saratoga County Historians Office, Ballston Spa, Box 4, p. 2

4   Kissam, Edward. *The Kissam Family in America,* Dempsey & Carroll's Art Press, New York, 1892, p. 15

5   Johnston, Henry, ed. *The Correspondence and Public Papers of John Jay 1763-1781,* Burt Franklin, New York, p. 9

6   Stevens, John Austin. *Colonial Records of the New York Chamber of Commerce 1768-1784,* J.F.Trow & Co., New York, 1867, p. 69

7   Cornelius Low House, http://en.wikipedia.org

8   *PCA,* Cornelius Cuyler

9   Stevens. *Chamber of Commerce,* p. 71-72

10 *Ibid.*, p. 74

11 AHN. *The New York Gazette,* June 30,1766

12 Witcraft, John R. *Cornelius Janen Clopper and his Descendants,* Dispatch Press, Merchantville, New Jersey, 1912, p. 2

13 The Peculiar People-A Christian Monthly Devoted to Jewish Interests, Vol. 5, No. 6, Sept 1892, p. 135

14 AHN. *The New York Mercury, April 10, 1758*

15 AHN. *The New York Gazette, Sept 3, 1759*

16 AHN. *New York Mercury, Jan 19, 1761*

17 AHN. *The New York Gazette, September 12, 1768*

18 Bergen, Tennis G. *Genealogy of the Lefferts Family,* Joel Munsell Pub., Albany, 1878, p. 66

19 An American Family Grows in Brooklyn, The Lefferts Family Papers at Brooklyn Historical Society, http://www.brooklynhistory.org

20 Bergin. *Genealogy of the Lefferts Family,* p. 34

21 Lepore. *New York Burning,* p. 221

22 Bergin. *Genealogy of the Lefferts family,* p. 35

23 *Field books of the Kayaderosseras:* John Tatham, New York State Library; May Bickley March 26 1771, New York Historical Society; John Stephens, Saratoga Room, Saratoga Springs Public Library,

24 *Account and Sale of Land, Book B,* p. 3, Saratoga County Historian's Office

25 Grose, Edward F. *Centennial History of Ballston,* Ballston Journal, Ballston Spa, 1907, p. 14

26 *Field Book No. 1. 1771,* p. 22

27 Saratoga County Deeds, Book 3, Page 389, Saratoga County Clerk's Office, Ballston Spa,

28 Briaddy. *Shadows* Appendix B, App 4

29 *The Colonial Laws of New York, Vol. V 1769-1775,* p. 319-322

30 *Ibid.*, p. 383-388

31 *Ibid.*, p. 772-773

32 Grose. *Centennial History*, p.15. Epenetus White, Dr. Elisha Miller and Elpihalet Kellogg

33 A Map of the Township of Ballston, ca 1772, Saratoga County Historians Office, Ballston Spa

34 *Account and Sale of Land, Book B*, p. 1

35 PCA. Gysbert Fonda

36 Grose. *Centennial History*, p 15.

37 *Account and Sale of Land, Book B*, p. 1

38 *Ibid.*, p. 2

39 Force, Peter. *American Archives – A Documentary History of the English Colonies in America, Fourth Series, Vol. II*, Washington, 1837, p. 1265

40 Stevens. *NY Chamber of Commerce*, p. 96

41 *Ibid.*, p. 103

42 John Tatem's lands allocated among Dirck Lefferts, Remsen and Daniel Campbell (NYS Library); John Stephen's lands allocated between Lefferts and Cornelius Clopper (Saratoga Room, Saratoga Springs Public Library); Johannis Fisher's/Vissher lands allocated between Johannes Vissher and John Beekman (Saratoga County Historian's Office)

43 Hansen. *Schenectady During the Revolution*, p. 4

44 *Letter Book of Daniel Campbell 1771-1801*, Transcribed by Elizabeth D. Shaver, 1982, Schenectady County Historical Society, Schenectady, p. 129

45 *Ibid.*, p. 165

Chapter 5 People of the Middleline

1 Bailyn, Bernard. *The Peopling of British North America – An Introduction*, Random House, New York, p. 93

2 Grant, Charles S. *Democracy in the Connecticut Frontier Town of Kent*, Columbia University Press, New York, 1961, p. 102

3 Mayer, Josephine. The *Reminiscences of James Gordon*, New York History, Vol. 17 No. 3 July 1936, p. 317

4 Meany, Joseph. *Merchant and Redcoat: The Papers of John Gordon Macomb*, http://archiver.rootsweb.ancestry.com/th/read/AMERICAN-REVOLUTION

5 Loescher, Burt Garfield. *Genesis, Rogers Rangers: The First Green Berets*, San Mateo, 1969, p. 165

6 Jacobson, Judy. *Detroit River Connections*, Genealogical Publishing Company, Baltimore, 1992, p. 29

7 Mayer,The *Reminiscences of James Gordon*, p. 316

8   Briaddy. *Shadows*, p. 35. The three Tories were John McIlmore, John Carey and Francis Hunter

9   Sylvester, Nathaniel, B. *History of Saratoga County, NY*, Everts & Ensign, Philadelphia, 1878, p. 256

10 Mayer. *The Reminiscences of James Gordon*, p. 322

11 Albany County Deeds, Albany Hall of Records, Book 9, p. 110

12 Selleck, Rev. Charles M. *Norwalk*, Norwalk,1896, map p. 39

13 Benedict, Henry. *The Genealogy of the Benedicts in America*, John Munsell Press, Albany, 1870, p. 9-20

14 Hall, Edwin. *The Ancient Historical Records of Norwalk, Conn*, James Mallory & Co., New York, 1847, p. 83

15 Bailey, James M. *History of Danbury, Conn 1684-1896*, Burr Printing House, New York, 1896, p. 25

16 Benedict. *Benedicts in America*, p. 285

17 Bailey. *History of Danbury*, p. 17

18 Ancestry.com. *U.S., Revolutionary War Pension and Bounty Records Warrant Application Files 1800-1900*, NARA microfilm publication M804, Thomas Barnum, roll no. 155, file W5788, p.1

19 Barnum, Patrick W. "Barnum Family Genealogy." http;/www.barnum.org,

20 Bailey. *History of Danbury*, p. 25

21 *Ibid.*, p. 43

22 *Ibid.*, p. 14

23 *Collections of the History of Albany Vol. 1*, J.Munsell, Albany, 1865, p. 225

24 Benedict. *Benedicts in America*, p. 289

25 Flick, Alexander C. *Minutes of the Albany Committee of Correspondence 1775 - 1779*, Vol. 1, University of the State of New York, Albany, 1925, p. 68,84

26 The Guilford Covenant of 1639, Hylbom Family Ancestry Project, http://hylbom.com

27 Smith, Ralph D. *Edward and John Collins and Their Descendants*, NEHGS Register, 1907 Vol. 61, p. 281

28 Connecticut State Library, Guilford Land Records, Reel #1426, Vol A-C, 1645-1715, p. 140,199

29 Guilford History Tours. http://www.historicguilford.org/hti/historic-walking-tours

30 Adams, Charles C. *Middletown Upper Houses*, The Stow Family, Grafton Press, New York, 1908

31 Field, David D., *Centennial Address: Society and the City of Middletown*, William B. Casey, Middletown, 1853, p. 163

32 Connecticut State Library, Middletown Land Records, Reel #2210, Vol. 1-2, p. 87

33 Smith. *Edward and John Collins*, NEHGS Register, 1907, Vol. 61, p. 285

34 Griswold, Mary. *Yesteryears of Guilford,* Shore Line Times Publishing Co., Guilford, Conn, 1938, p. 110

35 Talcott, Alvin. *Families of Early Guilford, Connecticut, Vol. II,* Genealogical Publishing Co., Baltimore, 1984, p. 1170

36 Smith. *Edward and John Collins,* NEHGS Register, 1907, Vol. 61. p. 285

37 Peck, Darius. A *Genealogical Account of William Peck,* Bryan & Goeltz, Hudson, 1877, p. 26

38 *Ibid.,* p. 8

39 Smith. *Edward and John Collins,* NEHGS Register, 1907, Vol. 61, p. 282

40 Bishop, Ira Elmore.*Bishop Families in America,* University of Wisconsin Press, Madison, 1967, Vol. 1, Introduction

41 Smith, Ralph D. *The History of Guilford, Connecticut,* Munsell Printer, Albany, 1877, p. 78

42 Mallary, R. Dewitt. *Lennox and the Berkshire Highlands,* G.P. Putman's Sons, New York, 1902, p. 5

43 *Vital Records of Richmond, Massachusetts to the Year 1850,* New England Historic and Genealogical Society, Boston, 1913, Richmond Births, p. 18

44 Main, Jackson Turner. *Society and Economy in Colonial Connecticut,* Princeton University Press, Princeton, 1985, p. 59

45 *Historical Statistics of the United States Vol. 2,* Bureau of the Census, Washington, 1975, p. 1168

46 Main. *Society and Economy,* p. 18

47 AHN. Connecticut Journal/Post Boy, New Haven, Connecticut, December 6,1771.

48 Talcott. *Families of Early Guilford,* Connecticut, Vol II

49 Ross, Peter. *The History of Long Island: Southampton NY,* Lewis Pub Co., New York, 1902

50 Pierson, Lizzie. *Pierson Genealogical Records,* Joel Munsell, Albany, 1878, p. 32

51 Mather, Frederic. *The Refugees of 1776 from Long Island to Connecticut,* J.B. Lyon Co, Albany, 1913, p. 1055

52 Smith, J.E.A. *History of Pittsfield,* Lee & Sheperd, Boston, 1869, p. 861

53 *Ibid.,* p. 319

54 Fitch, Asa. *Their Own Voices, Oral Accounts of Early Settlers in Washington County, New York,* Winston Adler, ed.,1983, Donald McDonald, p.19

55 Briaddy. *Shadows,* p. 39

56 Vaughan, Alden T. *New England Frontier,* University of Oklahoma Press, Norman, 1965, p. 133, 145

57 Caulkins, Frances. *History of New London, Connecticut,* New London, 1852, p. 43-46.

58 Bonsall, Grace. *Jacob Waterhouse of Wethersfield and New London, Conn.,* NEHGS Register, Vol 104, p. 186.

59 George Watrous, as quoted in *"Houses by the Water: The Waterhouse/Watrous Family in America"*, Leland Watrous, http://genealogy.com/ftm

60 Bonsall. *Jacob Waterhouse*, NEHGS Register, Vol. 104, p. 188

61 Lyme Births, Marriages and Deaths, NEHGS Register, 1880, p. 41

62 Walworth, Reuben. *Hyde Genealogy*, J. Munsell, Albany, 1864, p. 46

63 *Ibid.*, p. 26

64 Connecticut Church Record Abstracts 1630-1920, p. 129, Ancestry.com

65 Barbour Collection, Early Connecticut Marriages-Lyme, p. 137, Ancestry.com

66 Weeks, Harriet, *Descendants of Richard Hayes of Lyme, Connecticut*, Eagle Publishing Company, Pittsfield, 1904

67 Gillespie, C. Bancroft. *An Historic Record of the Town of Meriden*, Journal Publishing Co, Meridian, 1906, p. 230

68 Hawley, Emily C. *A Genealogical and Biographical Record of the Pioneer Thomas Skidmore,* 1911, p. 19

69 Higby, Clinton David. *Edward Higby and His Descendants,* T. R. Marvin & son, Boston, 1927, p. 38

70 Connecticut State Library, Middletown Land Records, Reel #2210, Vol 1-2, p. 69

71 *Ibid.*, p. 136

72 Higby. *Edward Higby and His Descendants*, p. 40

73 *Ibid.*, p. 62

74 Davis, Charles. *History of Wallingford*, Connecticut, Meriden, 1879, p. 49

75 *The Public Records of the Colony of Connecticut,* 15 Vol, FA Brown, Hartford, 1852, p. 375, http://home.ancestry.com

76 Dewey, Rev. Charles. *A History of the County of Berkshire, Massachusetts,* Pittsfield, 1829, p. 325

77 Price, Edward T. *Dividing the Land,* The University of Chicago Press, Chicago, 1995, p. 70

78 Clark, Elizabeth. History of Falls Village, Town Historian, http://webtown-hall.com

79 Connecticut Town Birth Records pre-1870, Barbour Collection, p. 42, Ancestry.com

80 The Fundamental Orders of Connecticut, http://connecticuthistory.org,

81 Nash, Elizabeth Todd. *Fifty Puritan Ancestors*, The Tuttle Morehouse & Taylor Co, New Haven, 1908, p. 47-50

82 Connecticut State Library, Middletown Land Records, Reel #2210, Vol. 1-2, p. 21

83 *Ibid.*, p. 46

84 Wilcox, John, Jr. A Compilation by the Society of Middletown First Settlers Descendants:(1654), http://home.ancestry.com

85 Manwearing, Charles. *A Digest of Early Connecticut Probate Records, Hartford District, Vol II 1700-1729,* Hartford, Conn, 1904, p. 8

86 *Ibid.*, p. 615

87 Ancestry.com. U.S. Revolutionary War Pension and Bounty Warrant Application Files 1800-1900, Lemuel Wilcox,

88 Everts,Louis H. History of the Connecticut Valley, Philadelphia, 1879, p. 810

89 Mather, Frederic Gregory. *The Refugees of 1776 from Long Island to Connecticut,* J.B.Lyon Co., Albany, p. 338

90 *Massachusetts Soldiers and Sailors of the Revolutionary War,* Wright & Porter Printing, Boston, 1899, p. 660

91 Ancestry.com. U.S. Revolutionary War Rolls 1775-1783, Jonathan Filer

92 Hail, Theodore. *Family Records of Theodore Parson Hamm, including accounts of the Scott-Gordon Families,* Wm C. Heath Printing Co., Detroit, 1892, p. 60-61

93 Olmstead, Henry King, *The Olmstead Family in America,* A.T. De Las Mare Co, New York, 1912, p. 198

94 Briaddy.*Shadows*, Autobiography of James Gordon, App-9

95 Heller, Daniel W. *The History of Ridgefield, Connecticut,* T.Donovan, Danbury, 1878, p. 21

96 Hollister, G.H. *The History of Connecticut*, Case Tiffany & Co., Hartford, 1855, p. 167

97 Selleck, Lillian. *One Branch of the Miner Family,* Donald Jacobus, New Haven, 1928

98 Anderson, Robert Charles. *Great Migration: Immigrants to New England 1634-35,* NEHGS, Vol. VII, p. 491-493

99 Selleck. *Norwalk,* p. 471

100 Hubbard, G. Evans. *Wilton Village: A History*, Wilton Historical Society, Wilton, 1971, p. 5

101 *Ibid.*, p. 19

102 Heller. *The History of Ridgefield*, p. 35

103 Shurtleff, Nathaniel. *Records of the Colony of New Plymouth* (PCR), Vol 1, Boston, 1851, p. 153, 156

104 *Ibid.*, Vol. 5, p. 53

105 Sprague, Warren Vincent. *Sprague Families in America,* The Tuttle Company, Rutland, 1913, p. 11

106 *Ibid.*, p. 13-17

107 Sedgwick, Charles F. *General History of the Town of Sharon*, Charles Walsh Pub, Amenia, 1898, p. 30

108 *Ibid.*, p. 157

109 Main. *Society and Economy*, p. 229

110 Boughton, James. *Bouton- Boughton Family,* Joel Munsell Sons, Albany, 1890, p. 10

111 Sprague. *Sprague Families in America,* p. 29

112 Albany County Deeds, Book 9, p. 393, April 13, 1774

113 Anderson,George Baker.*Our County and Its People-Saratoga County, NY*, Boston History Co, 1899, p. 47

114 Connecticut Department of Transportation – Rocky Hill-Glastonbury Ferry, http://www.ct.gov/dot/cwp/view

115 Adams, Sherman. *History of Ancient Wethersfield Connecticut*, Henry Stiles, ed., Grafton Press, New York, 1904, Vol. 1, p. 132

116 Hollister.*The History of Connecticut, Vol. 1*, p. 464

117 Case, Lafayette Wallace.*The Hollister Family of America*, Fergus Printing Company,Chicago,1886, p. 41

118 Adams. *History of Ancient Wethersfield*, Vol. 1, p. 277.

119 Case. *The Hollister Family of America*, p. 27

120 *Ibid.*, p. 26

121 National Register of Historic Places, John Hollister House, 14 Tyron Street, Glastonbury, Connecticut. http://www.mps.gov/nr

122 Adams. *History of Ancient Wethersfield, Vol.1*, p. 278

123 Case. *The Hollister Family of America*, p. 31,35

124 Adams. *History of Ancient Wethersfield Vol.1*, p. 205

125 Case. *The Hollister Family of America*, p. 60

126 *Ibid.*, p. 82

127 Hollister, Josiah. *The Journal of Josiah Hollister* in *History of the Bunn Family of America*, Ellis, James Alfred. Chicago, 1928, Appendix A, p. 314

128 *Ibid.*, p. 322-329

129 *Ibid.*, p. 329-334

130 Anderson. *The Great Migration Begins*, Vol. V, p. 382

131 Jacobus, Donald Lines. *History and Genealogy of the Families of Old Fairfield*, Fairfield,1930, p. 465

132 *Ancestry and Descendants of Gershon Morehouse,Jr,* http://.americanrevolution.org/morehouse.html

133 Jacobus. *Families of Old Fairfield*, p. 465

134 The Ancestry of Lorenzo Ackley and his wife Emma Bosworth, http://home.ancestory.com

135 Anderson. *The Great Migration Begins,* Vol. I, p. 300

136 Hubbard, *Wilton Village: A History*, p. 71

137 Legett, Grace Patchen. *The History and Genealogy of the Patchin-Patchen Family*, The Patchin-en Family Association, Waterbury, 1952, p. 190

138 "Samuel Squire", Witch Trials, http://home.ancestory.com

139 Legett. *Patchin-en Family*, p. 191

140 Hubbard. *Wilton Village: A History*, p. 162

141 Schenck, Elizabeth Hubbell. *The History of Fairfield Connecticut*, New York, 1889, p. 2

142 Shattuck, Lemuel. *History of the Town of Concord from Its Earliest Settlement to 1832,* Boston, 1835, p. 14

143 Schenck. *History of Fairfield,* p. 66

144 Jacobus. *Families of Old Fairfield,* p. 409

145 Middlebrook, Louis F. *Register of the Middlebrook Family,* Hartford, 1909, p. 22

146 *Abstract of Fairfield County Probate Records, Vol. 3, 1675-1690,* p. 215, USGenWeb Project, Fairfield Co, CT, http://www.ctgenweb.org/county/cofairfield/pages/ probate

147 Middlebrook. *Register of the Middlebrook Family,* p. 19-21

148 *Ibid.,* p. 354

149 *Ibid.,* p. 39-41

150 Hubbard. *Wilton Village: A History,* p. 118

151 "Middlebrook Farm",The Wilton Bulletin, September 26,1984

152 Middlebrook. *Register of the Middlebrook Family,* p. 48

153 Hubbard. *Wilton Village: A History,* p. 137

154 Smith, Ralph D. *The History of Guilford, Connecticut,* J. Munsell Printer, Albany, 1877, p. 13

155 Reynolds, Cuyler. *Hudson-Mohawk Genealogical and Family Memoirs,* Lewis Historical Publishing Company, New York, 1991, Betts, Vol. II p. 643

156 Benedict. *Benedicts in America,* p. 95

157 Selleck. *Norwalk,* p. 226

158 Reynolds. *Hudson-Mohawk Memoirs:* Betts p. 644

159 Hall. *Norwalk,* p. 103

160 Reynolds. *Hudson-Mohawk Memoirs:* Betts p. 644

161 Selleck. *Norwalk,* p. 236

162 Hubbard. *Wilton Village: A History,* p. 27-30

163 Joseph Bettys 1717-1804, Family Tree file, http://home.ancestory.com

164 Connecticut State Library, Norwalk Land Records, Book 13, p. 428

165 *Account and Sale of Land, Book B,* p.3

166 Albany County Deeds, Book 11, p. 272

167 *Revolutionary Reminiscences,* in The Family Magazine, JA James & Co, Cincinnati, 1840, p. 15

Chapter 6 Rebels and Loyalists

1 Berleth, Richard. *Bloody Mohawk, The French and Indian War & American Revolution on New York's Frontier,* Black Dome Press, Delmar, 2009, p. 51-57

2 Selesky, Harold E. *War and Society in Colonial Connecticut,* Yale University Press, New Haven, 1990, p. 168

3 Connecticut Provincials http://www.Kronoskaf.com

4   Marston, David P. *Swift and Bold: The 60th Regiment and Warfare in North America 1755-1765*, McGill University, Montreal, 1997, p. 51

5   *Ibid.,* p. 24

6   Fraser, J. *Skulking for the King,* The Boston Mill Press, Erin Ontario, 1985, p. 31

7   Dorrough, Richard. *Kneel Before the King,* http://www.saratoganygenweb.com/loyalist.htm,

8   The 48th Foot in the French and Indian War, http://www.kronoskaf.com/syw/index.php?title=48thfoot

9   Will of Cornelius Brouwer of Schenectady, NY, http://brouwergenealogy.blogstop.com

10   *DCB.* John Munro

11   Corbett, Theodore. *No Turning Point-The Saratoga Campaign in Perspective,* University of Oklahoma Press, Norman, 2012, p. 49

12   Aldrich, Lewis Cass. *History of Bennington County, Vermont,* D. Mason & Co., Syracuse, 1885, p. 50-52

13   Corbett. *No Turning Point,* p. 20

14   *PCA.* Philip Schuyler

15   Sylvester. *History of Saratoga County, New York,* p. 260

16   Corbett. *No Turning Point,* p. 19

17   Jesup, Henry Griswold. *Edward Jessup and His Descendants,* John Wilson and Son, Cambridge, 1887, p. 204

18   *Ibid.,* p. 211

19   *Ibid.,* p. 207-8

20   Breen, Timothy H. *American Insurgents American Patriots,* Hill and Wang, New York, 2010, p. 152

21   Force, Peter. *American Archives – A Documentary History, Fourth Series, Vol. II,* Washington, 1837, p. 517

22   *Ibid.,* p. 741

23   Intolerable Acts. https://en.wikipedia.org/wiki/

24   *Articles of Association,* http://www.ushistory.org/declaration/related/assoc74.htm

25   *Ibid.*

26   Breen. *American Insurgents,* p. 168-170

27   *FAA. Vol. II,* p. 968, 992

28   Lustig. *Privilege and Prerogative,* p. 168

29   Stevens. *Chamber of Commerce,* p. 85,96

30   Fraser. *Skulking for the King,* p. 25, 82,

31   Fryer, Mary. *John Walden Meyers-Loyalist Spy,* Dundurn Press, Toronto, 1983, p. 65

32   Sullivan, James. *Minutes of the Albany Committee of Correspondence 1775-1778,* The University of the State of New York, Albany, 1923, Vol. 1, p. 56

33 *Ibid.*, p. 85

34 *Ibid.*, p. 91

35 *Ibid.*, p. 192

36 *Ibid.*, p. 249

37 *DCB.* Daniel Claus

38 Hanson. *Schenectady During the Revolution*, p. 45-50

39 *Ibid.*, p. 50

40 Corbett. *No Turning Point*, p. 89

41 *MACC.* p. 228

42 Fraser. *Skulking for the King*, p. 65

43 Cohen. *Conquered into Liberty*, p. 156

44 *MACC.* p. 393

45 *Ibid.*, p. 410

46 *Ibid.*, p. 431

47 *Ibid.*, p. 715

48 *Ibid.*, p. 756

49 Fraser. *Skulking for the King*, p. 44

50 Force, Peter. *American Archives – A Documentary History, Fifth Series, Vol. III,* Washington, 1853, p. 1391

51 *MACC.* p. 690

52 *Ibid.*, p. 839

53 Potter-MacKinnon, Janice. *While the Women Only Wept,* McGill-Queens University Press, Montreal, 1993, p. 74

54 Corbett. *No Turning Point*, p. 145

55 MACC. p. 935

56 Fraser. *Skulking for the King*, p. 38

57 Booth, John Chester. *History of Saratoga County 1858,* Saratoga County Historical Society, Ballston Spa, NY, Unpublished, p. 85. Ballston names also cited in Grose's Centennial History, p. 19

58 Fraser. *Skulking for the King,* p. 40

59 Corbett. *No Turning Point*, p. 137

60 Cain, Alexander R. *I See Nothing But The Horrors of a Civil War,* 2014, p. 32-37

61 *Ibid.*, p. 153

62 *Ibid.*, p. 334

63 Luzader, John. *Saratoga, A Military History of the Decisive Campaign of the American Revolution,* Savis Beatie LLC, New York, 2008, p. 291

64 Nathanial Bacheller letter to his wife, October 9, 1777, transcribed by Eric Schnitzer, Saratoga National Historical Park, January 28, 2016

65 Wilkinson, James. *Memoirs of My Own Times,* Abraham Small, Philadelphia, 1816, Vol. 1, p. 270

66   Carrington, Henry B. *Battles of the American Revolution*, A.S. Barnes & Co, New York, 1876, p. 348

67   *The Public Papers of George Clinton*, Wynkoop Hallenbeck Crawford Co., New York, 1900, Vol. II, p. 456

68   Ancestry.com. U.S., *Revolutionary War Pension and Bounty Records Warrant Application Files 1800-1900*, Thomas Barnum, roll no. 155, file W5788, p.3

69   PPGC. p. 447

70   Paltsits, Victor. *Minutes of the Commissioners for Detecting and Defeating Conspiracies, Albany County Sessions, 1778-1782*, Albany, 1909, Vol.1, p. 82

71   *Ibid.,* p. 207

72   *Ibid.,* p. 81

73   https://en.wikipedia.org/wiki/Christopher_Alexander_Hagerman,

74   Sylvester. *History of Saratoga County*, p. 250

75   Watt, Gavin K. *The British Campaign of 1777, Vol 2 The Burgoyne Expeditions*, Global Heritage Press, Milton, 2003, p. 266

76   *Account and Sale of Land, Book B*, p. 3, Saratoga County Historian's Office

77   *MACC.* p. 334

78   *MCDDC.* p. 622

79   1787 Tax List for the Town of Ballston, compiled by Lynn Calvin, Saratoga County Historian's Office

80   *MCDDC.* p. 436

81   Paltsits. *Schenectady Minutes, Conspiracies*, p. 1100

82   *MCDDC.* p. 103,173,189,344

83   Corbett. *No Turning Point*, p. 258

84   Lovelace, David. *Tory Spy*, Heritage Books, Westminster, Maryland, 2009, p. 81-85

85   The family was generally named Betts in Connecticut records, Bettys in Ballston local histories and Bettis in the minutes of the Committee of Conspiracies

86   Garden, Alexander. *Anecdotes of the American Revolution*, A.E. Miller, Charleston, 1828, p. 167

87   Bratton, John. *The Gondola Philadelphia and the Battle of Lake Champlain*, Texas A&M University Press, College Station, 2002, p. 145

88   *Ibid.,* p. 139

89   *Ibid.,* p. 146

90   Battle of Valcour Island. https://en.wikipedia.org/wiki/

91   Beaty letter to Gov Haldimand, October 2, 1781 in *American Historical Magazine*, Vol IV, The National Americana Society. New York, 1909, p. 424-425

92   Simms, Jeptha. *The Frontiersmen of New York*, Geo. C. Riggs,, Albany, 1883, p. 589

93   Beaty letter, p. 426

94   Booth. *History of Saratoga County*, p.104 (specific names vary in some other accounts)

95   Library of American History, *Revolutionary Anecdotes,* UP James, Cincinnati, p. 212

96   Lovelace. *Tory Spy,* p. 131

97   Fryer. *John Walden Meyers,* p. 139

98   Garden. *Anecdotes of the American Revolution,* p. 170. Detailed accounts of Bettys' capture can be found in the Grose, Sylvester and Booth Histories.

Chapter 7 War on the Frontier

1   Cohen. *Conquered Into Liberty,* p. 240-245

2   Taylor, Alan. *The Divided Ground,* Vintage Books, New York, 2006, p. 51

3   Graymont, Barbara. *The Iroquois in the American Revolution,* Syracuse University Press, Syracuse, 1972, p. 138

4   Taylor. *The Divided Ground,* p. 4

5   *DCB.* John Butler

6   Graymont. *Iroquois,* p. 166

7   *PPGC. Vol. IV,* No. 1771, p. 49

8   *Ibid.,* p. 48

9   *Ibid., Vol. II,* p. 780

10   *Ibid., Vol. II,* p. 812

11   Ancestry.com. U.S., *Revolutionary War Pension and Bounty Records Warrant Application Files 1800-1900,* Thomas Barnum, roll no. 155, file W5788, p.10

12   *PPGC. Vol. IV,* p. 54

13   Cruikshank, Ernest. *The Story of Butlers Rangers and the Settlement of Niagara,* 1893, in Butler's Rangers, Leonaur, 2011, p. 51

14   Graymont. *Iroquois,* p. 184

15   Cherry Valley Massacre. https://en.wikipedia.org/wiki/

16   Cartwright, R.E. *Life and Letters of Richard Cartwright,* Toronto, 1876, p. 33

17   Ancestry.com. U.S., *Revolutionary War Pension and Bounty Records Warrant Application Files 1800-1900,* Thomas Barnum, roll no. 155, file W5788, p.2

18   Watt, Gavin. *The 1778 Campaign,* draft - chapter 5 *Returning to the Mohawk Region,* pre-publication. 2016

19   *PPGC. Vol. IV,* p. 287

20   Ancestry.com. U.S., *Revolutionary War Pension and Bounty Records Warrant Application Files 1800-1900,* Thaddeus Scribner, roll no. 2141, file W1499, p.2

21   *Ibid.,* Elisha Benedict, roll no. 211, file S12183, p.3

22   *PPGC. Vol. IV,* No.1918, p. 289

23   Graymont. *Iroquois,* p. 209

24   *Ibid.,* p. 214

25   *Ibid.,* p. 222.

26 *Ibid.,* p. 228
27 Watt, Gavin, *Burning of the Valleys,* Dundurn Press, Toronto, 1997, p. 78
28 Hough, Franklin. *The Northern Invasion of October 1780,* New York, 1866, p. 29
29 Watt. *Burning of the Valleys,* p. 81
30 *Ibid.,* p. 30
31 *Ibid.,* p. 27
32 *Ibid.,* p. 32
33 *Ibid.,* p. 164
34 *Ibid.,* p. 162
35 *Ibid.,* p. 335
36 *Ibid.,* p. 337

Chapter 8 The Ballston Raid

1   Watt. *Burning of the Valleys,* p. 93
2   *PPGC, Vol. II,* p. 852
3   Carleton Raid. https://en.wikipedia.org/wiki/
4   Watt. *Burning of the Valleys,* p. 95
5   Fraser, Alexander. *Bureau of Archives for the Province of Ontario,* L.K.Cameron, Toronto, 1905, p. 424
6   Joseph Anderson Biographical Sketch, http://home.ancestory.com
7   Watt, Gavin K. *Poisoned by Lies and Hypocrisy,* Dundurn Press, Toronto, 2014, p. 132
8   Cometti, Elizabeth. *The American Journals of Lt. John Enys,* Syracuse University Press, Syracuse, 1976, p. 37
9   Fitch. *Their Own Voices,* Austin Wells, p. 101
10 Cometti. *Enys Journal,* p. 44
11 *PPGC. Vol. VI,* p. 354
12 Watt. *Burning of the Valleys,* p. 102
13 *Ibid.,* p. 104
14 Cometti. *Enys Journal,* p. 46
15 *PPGC. Vol. VI,* p. 354
16 Booth. *History of Saratoga County,* p. 93
17 Hough. *The Northern Invasion of 1780,* p. 34
18 Watt. *Burning of the Valleys,* p. 122
19 Briaddy. *Shadows,* p. 102
20 Scott, James. The Raid on Ballston 1780 – Memoranda of Reminiscences, 1846, in *The Bulletin of the Fort Ticonderoga Museum,* Vol. VII, no.4, July 1946, p.15
21 Hough. *The Northern Invasion of 1780,* p. 41

22   Murray, Eleanor. The Invasion of Northern New York, 1780, in *The Bulletin of the Fort Ticonderoga Museum*, Vol. VII no.4, July 1946, p. 9

23   *Ibid.*

24   Sylvester. *History of Saratoga County*, p. 70

25   Stone. *Reminiscences of Saratoga*, Worthington Co., New York, 1880, p. 413 fn

26   Fraser. *Skulking for the King*, p. 65

27   Watt. *Burning of the Valleys*, fn 141, p. 286

28   http://freepages.genealogy.rootsweb.ancestry.com/ ~godfreyshewfamily/

29   Munro Supplementary Report, November 20, 1780, Haldimand Papers, Reel 1652, p. 268.

30   *Ibid.*

31   Booth. *History of Saratoga County*, p. 92

32   Watt. *Burning of the Valleys*, p. 120

33   Munro Supplementary Report, November 20, 1780

34   Booth. *History of Saratoga County*, p. 93

35   Simms. *The Frontiersman, Vol. II*, p. 479

36   Simms, Jeptha. *History of Schoharie County and the Border Wars of New York*, Munsell and Tanner, Albany, 1845, p. 264

37   Booth. *History of Saratoga County*, p. 93

38   Watt. *Burning of the Valleys*, p. 124

39   http://archives.gnb.ca/exhibits/forthavoc/html/NY-Attainder.aspx?culture=en-CA

40   Cruikshank, Ernest and Gavin Watt. *The Kings Royal Regiment of New York*, Global Heritage Press, Milton Ontario, 2006, p. 59

41   *Ibid.*, p. 289 n174

42   Mackey, Frank. *Done with Slavery – The Black Fact in Montreal 1760-1840*, McGill-Queens University Press, Montreal, 2010, p. 126

43   Briaddy. *Shadows*, Appendix K, App 72

44   *Marriage Licenses Issued by the Province of New York Prior to 1784*, Weed, Parsons & Co., Albany,1860. p. 156

45   Booth. *History of Saratoga County*, p. 94

46   Grose. *Centennial History*, Mrs. Waller's Story, p. 40

47   Scott, James. Memoranda of Reminiscences, 1846, in *The Bulletin of the Fort Ticonderoga Museum*, Vol. VII, no. 4, July 1946. p.16

48   Booth. *History of Saratoga County*, p. 93

49   Hollister, *Journal*, p. 335

50   Watt. *Burning of the Valleys*. p. 126

51   Briaddy. *Shadows*, p. 103

52   Wooster, David. *Genealogy of the Woosters in America*, M. Weiss Printer, San Francisco, 1885, p. 88

53   Munro's November 20 Report, in *The Kings Royal Regiment*. p. 59

54   Watt. *Lies and Hypocrisy*, p. 197n8

55   Ancestry.com. U.S., *Revolutionary War Pension and Bounty Records Warrant Application Files 1800-1900*, Elisha Benedict, roll no. 211, file W12183, p.3

56   Booth. *History of Saratoga County*, p. 95

57   Briaddy. *Shadows*, p. 105

58   Ancestry.com. *U.S., Revolutionary War Pension and Bounty Records Warrant Application Files 1800-1900*, Lemuel Wilcox, roll no. 2575 file W22663

59   Booth. *History of Saratoga County*, p .95

60   Upper Canada Land Petition of Staats Springsteen, August 14, 1795, http://home.ancestory.com

61   Scott. *Memoranda of Reminiscences, 1846*, p.18

62   Hall, Theodore P. *Family Records of Theodore Parsons Hall*, W.C Heath Printing Co. Detroit, 1892, p. 65

63   Scott. *Memoranda of Reminiscences, 1846*, p.18

64   *Ibid.*

65   Booth. *History of Saratoga County, p. 96*

66   *Ibid.*

67   Hollister. *Journal*, p. 335

68   Booth. *History of Saratoga County*, p. 96

69   *Ibid.*

70   Ancestry.com. *U.S., Revolutionary War Pension and Bounty Records Warrant Application Files 1800-1900*, Enoch Wood, roll no.2626, file W9030

71   *Ibid.*, Pension records of Cyrus Fillmore

72   Booth. *History of Saratoga County*, p. 97

73   Ancestry.com, Pension records of Cyrus Fillmore

74   Nathaniel Fillmore 1771-1863, Family Tree in Ancestry.com,

75   Stone. *Reminiscences of Saratoga*, p. 419

76   Watt. *Burning of the Valleys*, p. 132

77   Grose. *Centennial History*, p. 39-40

78   Munro's November 20th Report, in *The King's Royal Regiment*, p. 59

79   Booth. *History of Saratoga County*, p. 98

80   Booth. *History of Saratoga County*, Gordon's Memorandum p. 99

81   Munro's October 24th Report, in *The King's Royal Regiment*, p. 57

82   Scott. Memoranda of Reminiscences, 1846, p.23

83   Stone. *Reminiscences of Saratoga*, p. 423.

84   Grose. *Centennial History*, p. 39

85   Munro's November 20th Report, in *The King's Royal Regiment*, p. 58

86   Ancestry.com. *U.S., Revolutionary War Pension and Bounty Records Warrant Application Files 1800-1900*, David How, roll no. 1339, file S23706, p.2

Chapter 9 Canada

1   Booth. *History of Saratoga County,* Gordon's Memorandum, p. 99

2   Hollister. *Journal,* p. 337

3   *Ibid.*

4   Ketchum, Richard M. *Saratoga Turning Point of America's Revolutionary War,* Henry Holt and Company, New York, 1997, p. 132

5   Booth. *History of Saratoga County,* Gordon's Memorandum, p. 99

6   Briaddy. *Shadows,* p. 103

7   Fiske, David. *History Lesson: Nero, Courageous Slave from Ballston,* The Saratogian, February 10, 2013

8   Mackey. *Done with Slavery,* p. 126.

9   1790 US Census Records, Town of Ballston, http://home.ancestry.com

10   Booth. *History of Saratoga County,* p. 100

11   Watt. *Burning of the Valleys,* p. 149

12   Haldimand Papers, http://heritage.canadiana.ca/view/oocihm.lac. Reel H-1738, mss 21843, B183

13   Booth. *History,* p.100; Briaddy. *Shadows,* p. 103; Hollister. *Journal,* p. 337

14   Burrows, Edwin G. *Forgotten Patriots,* Basic Books, New York, 2008

15   *DCB.* Alexander Ellice

16   Booth. *History of Saratoga County,* p. 100

17   Hollister. *Journal,* p. 337

18   The Captivity of Zadock Steele, in *Indian Narratives,* Tracy and Brothers, Claremont, 1854, p. 225

19   Hollister. *Journal,* p. 338

20   Watt, Gavin. *I Am Heartily Ashamed,* Dundurn Press, Toronto, 2009, p. 26

21   *HP.* Reel H-1738, mss 21843, B183, p. 106-109. James Gordon to Capt. Law, December 19, 1780

22   *Ibid.,* p. 153-155. James Gordon to Capt. Law, July 18, 1781

23   *Ibid.,* p. 160. Capt. Mathews to Capt. Law, July 25, 1781

24   *Ibid.,* p. 165. James Gordon to Governor General Frederick Haldimand, July 31, 1781

25   *Ibid.,* p. 168. Capt. Mathews to James Gordon, August 2, 1781

26   Watt, Gavin. *A Dirty, Trifling Piece of Business,* Dundurn Press, Toronto, 2009, p. 219

27   *Ibid.,* p. 238

28   Watt. *I Am Heartily Ashamed,* p. 81

29   Steele. *The Captivity of Zadock Steele,* p. 228-230

30   Cain. *Horrors of a Civil War,* Appendix F, p. 123

31   Steele.*The Captivity of Zadock Steele,* p. 235

32   Fraser. *Skulking for the King,* p. 60

33   *Watt. I Am Heartily Ashamed,* p. 258

34   Hollister. *Journal,* p. 344

35   Steele. *The Captivity of Zadock Steele,* p. 249-267

36   Briaddy. *Shadows,* Appendix K, p. 72

37   *HP.* Reel H-1738, mss 21843, B18; The ten under house arrest were the four Benedicts, Edward Watrous, James Gordon, Jr., John Davis, Elisha Sprague, Thomas Kennedy and Enoch Wood

38   *Ibid.,* The four held at the island prison at Coteau du Lac were Thomas Barnum, Josiah Hollister, John Sprague and Isaac Palmatier. A fifth prisoner from Ballston, Samuel Patchen, was captured in 1781

39   *Ibid.,* p. 188. James Gordon to Gov. George Clinton, September 22, 1781

40   *Ibid.,* p. 185. James Gordon to Capt. Mathews, September 22, 1781

41   Scudder, William. *Journal of William Scudder, An Officer in the Late New York Line, 1794,* p.154, http://quod.lib.umich.edu/

42   *HP.* Reel H-1738, mss 21843, B18; p. 224

43   Ibid., Return of the Rebel Prisoners, June 24, 1782, p. 239

44   Grose. *Centennial History,* p. 41

45   *HP.,* Reel H-1738, mss 21843, B18; p. 225 Capt. Mathews to Richard Murray, May 27, 1782

46   Scudder. *Journal,* p.213

47   Grose. *Centennial History,* p. 41

48   *Revolutionary War Rolls, 1775-1783,* NARA M246, roll 0135, Tyrannus Collins, Prisoner at Quebec

49   Hollister. *Journal,* p. 352

50   Briaddy. *Shadows,* p. 103

51   Hollister. *Journal,* p. 354

52   Briaddy. *Shadows,* p. 113. The full poem is transcribed there

Epilogue Life Goes On

1   *DCB.* John Munro

2   *Ibid.,* William Fraser

3   Watt. *I am Heartily Ashamed,* p. 211

4   *DCB.* John Deserontyon

5   *Ibid.,* Edward Jessup

6   1787 Tax list, Town of Ballston; 1790 Census, *Shadows,* Appendix O

7   *Lost to History: Archaeology of a Frontier Community,* New York State Museum, October 2002, p.4

8   Stone, *Reminiscences of Saratoga,* p. 416fn

9   Ancestry.com. *U.S., Revolutionary War Pension and Bounty Records Warrant Application Files 1800-1900*, Enoch Wood, roll no.2626, file W9030

10   Briaddy. *Shadows*, p. 152

11   *Ibid.*, p. 168

12   A New Nation Votes, http://elections.lib.tufts.edu,

13   Saratoga County Deeds, Book B, p. 147, Saratoga County Clerk's Office

14   *The Reminiscences of James Gordon*, p. 324

15   *Independent American, January 23, 1810*, Ballston Spa, New York, Vol. II, Issue 18 p. 3

Bibliography

A New Nation Votes. n.d. http://elections.lib.tufts.edu. 2015.

Account and Sale of Land in Ballston and the 5029 Acre Tract. Ballston Spa: Saratoga County Historians Office, 1774.

Adams, Charles C. *Middletown Upper Houses*. New York: Grafton Press, 1908.

Adams, Sherman. *History of Ancient Wethersfield Connecticut*. New York: Grafton Press, 1904.

Albany County Deeds. Albany: Albany Hall of Records, 2014.

Aldrich, Lewis Cass. *History of Bennington County Vermont*. Syracuse: D.Mason & Co., 1885.

Allen, Thomas B. *Tories - Fighting for the King in America's First Civil War*. New York: Harper Collins, 2010.

"America's Historical Newspapers." n.d. *American Ancestors.org*. 2015.

Anderson, George Baker. *Our County and its People-Saratoga County, N.Y.* Boston: Boston History Company, 1899.

Anderson, Mark R. *The Battle for the Fourteenth Colony*. Hanover: University Press of New England, 2013.

Anderson, Robert Charles. *The Great Migration: Immigrants to New England 1634-1635*. Boston: New England Historical Genealogical Society, 2010.

—. *The Great Migratrion Begins: Immigrants to New England 1620-1633*. Boston: New England Historical Genealogical Society, 1995.

Bailey, James M. *History of Danbury Connecticut 1684-1896*. New York: Burr Printing House, 1896.

Bailyn, Bernard. *The Peopling of British North America- An Introduction*. New York: Random House, 1986.

Baird, Charles W. *History of Bedford Church*. New York: Dodd, Mead & Co, 1882.

Banner, Stuart. *How the Indians Lost Their Land*. Cambridge: Harvard University Press, 2005.

Barclay, Florence. "Palmer Family of Plymouth." *The American Genealogist* (1956): Vol 32.

Bascom, Robert. *The Fort Edward Book*. Fort Edward: James D. Keating, 1903.

Belinski, Stephan. *The People of Colonial Albany*. n.d. 2015. <http:/www.nysm.nysed.gov>.

Benedict, Henry. *The Genealogy of the Benedicts in America*. Albany: John Munsell Press, 1870.

Bergen, Tennis G. *Genealogy of the Lefferts Family*. Albany: Joel Munsell, 1878.

Berleth, Richard. *Bloody Mohawk - The French and Indian War & American Revolution on New York's Frontier*. Delmar: Black Dome Press, 2009.

Bickley, May. *Field Books of the Kayaderosseras*. New York: New York Historical Society, n.d. Map.

Bishop, Ira Elmore. *The Bishop Familes in America*. Madison: University of Wisconsin Press, 1967.

Bonomi, Patricia. *A Fractious People*. New York: Columbia University Press, 1971.

—. *The Lord Cornbury Scandal*. Chapel Hill: University of North Carolina Press, 1998.

Bonsall, Grace. "Jacob Waterhouse of Wethersfield and New London Connecticut." *New England Historical Genealogical Register* (1950): Vol 104.

Booth, John Chester. *History of Saratoga County*. Ballston Spa: Saratoga County Historical Society, Unpublished, 1858.

Boughton, James. *Bouton-Boughton Family*. Albany: Joel Munsell Sons, 1890.

Brandow, John Henry. *The Story of Old Saratoga*. Albany, 1919.

Bratton, John. *The Gondola Philadelphia and the Battle of Lake Champlain*. College Station: Texas A&M University Press, 2002.

Breen, Timothy H. *American Insurgents American Patriots*. New York: Hill & Wang, 2010.

Briaddy, Katherine Q. *Shadows The Life and Times of Eliphalet Ball*. Ballston Spa, 1991.

Burke, Thomas E. Jr. *Mohawk Frontier The Dutch Community of Schenectady, New York, 1661-1710*. Albany: State University of New York Press, 1991.

Burrows, Edwin G. *Forgotten Patriots*. New York: Basic Books, 2008.

Cain, Alexander R. *I See Nothing but the Horrors of A Civil War*. San Bernardino, 2014.

Calendar of New York Colonial Manuscripts, Land Papers 1643-1803. Albany, 1864.

Calhoon, Robert M. *The Loyalists in Revolutionary America*. New York: Harcourt Brace Jovanovich, 1965.

Calvin, Lynn. *1787 Tax Lists for the Town of Ballston*. Ballston Spa: Saratoga County Historians Office, 2015.

Carrington, Henry B. *Battles of the American Revolution*. New York: A.S. Barnes & Co., 1876.

Cartwright, R.E. *Life and Letters of Richard Cartwright*. Toronto, 1876.

Case, Lafayette Wallace. *The Hollister Family of America*. Chicago: Fergus Printing Company, 1886.

Caulkins, Frances M. *History of New London, Connecticut*. New London, 1852.

Clark, Elizabeth. *History of Falls Village*. Town of Canaan Historian, 2015. Web site.

Cohen, Eliot A. *Conquered into Liberty*. New York: Simon & Schuster, 2010.

Colden, Cadwallader. *The Colden Papers*. New York: New York Historical Society, 1922.

—. "The State of Lands in the Province of New York." 1732. Colden Papers.

Collections of the History of Albany. Albany: J. Munsell, 1865.

Cometti, Elizabeth. *The American Journals of Lt. John Enys*. Syracuse: Syracuse University Press, 1976.

Corbett, Theodore. *No Turning Point-The Saratoga Campaign in Perspective*. Norman: University of Oklahoma Press, 2012.

Countryman, Edward. *A People in Revolution*. New York: W.W. Norton & Company, 1981.

Cronon, William. *Changes in the Land*. New York: Hill and Wang, 1983.

Cruikshank, Ernest and Gavin Watt. *The King's Royal Regiment of New York*. Milton, Ontario: Global Heritage Press, 2006.

Cruikshank, Ernest. *The Story of Butler's Rangers and the Settlement of Niagara in Butler's Rangers*. Leonaur, 2011.

Davis, Charles Henry. *History of Wallingford, Connecticut*. Meriden, 1870.

Dewey, Rev. Charles. *A History of the County of Berkshire, Massachusetts*. Pittsfield, 1829.

Dictionary of Canadian Biography. n.d. http://www.biographi.ca/en/index.php. 2015.

Dorrough, Richard. *Saratoga GenWeb-Kneel Before the King*. n.d. http://www.saratoganygenweb.com/loyalist.htm. 2015.

Ellis, James Alfred. *The Journal of Josiah Hollister in the History of the Bunn Family of America*. Chicago, 1928.

Field Book of the Division of the Patent of the Kayaderosseras. Ballston Spa: Saratoga County Historians Office, 1771.

Fiske, David. "Nero, Courageous Slave from Ballston." *The Saratogian* (February 10, 2013). Newspaper Article.

Fitch, Asa. *Their Own Voices-Oral Accounts of Early Settlers in Washington County, New York*. New York: Winston Adler, 1983.

Flick, Alexander C. ed. *Minutes of the Albany Committee of Correspondence 1775-1779*. Albany: University of the State of New York, 1925.

Force, Peter,ed. *American Archives Fourth Series, Containing a Documentary History of the English Colonies in North America. Vol II*. Washington: M. St. Clair Clarke and Peter Force, 1837.

—. *American Archives: Fifth Series, Containing a Documentary History of the United States of America*. Wahington: M. St. Clair Clarke and Peter Force, 1853.

Fox, Edith M. *Land Speculation in the Mohawk Country*. Ithaca: Cornell University Press, 1949.

Fraser, Alexander. *Bureau of Archives for the Province of Ontario*. Toronto: L.K.Cameron, 1905.

Fraser, J. *Skulking for the King*. Erin Ontario: The Boston Mill Press, 1985.

Fryer, Mary. *John Walden Meyers-Loyalist Spy*. Toronto: Dundurn Press, 1983.

Garden, Alexander. *Ancedotes of the American Revolution*. Charleston: A.E. Miller, 1828.

Gillespie, C.Bancroft. *An Historic Record of the Town of Meriden*. Meriden: Journal Publishing Co., 1906.

Grant, Charles S. *Democracy in the Frontier Town of Kent*. New York: Columbia University Press, 1961.

Graymont, Barbara. *The Iroquois in the American Revolution*. Syracuse: Syracuse University Press, 1972.

Griswold, Mary. *Yesteryears of Guilford*. Guilford: Shore Line Times, 1938.

Grose, Edward F. *Centennial History of Ballston Spa*. Ballston Spa: The Ballston Journal, 1907.

Guilford Land Records 1645-1715. Hartford: Connecticut State Library, 2015.

Haldimand Papers - Heritage Canadiana. n.d. http://heritage.canadiana.ca/view/oocihm.lac.

Hall, Edwin. *The Ancient Historical Records of Norwalk, Connecticut*. New York: James Mallory & Co., 1847.

Hall, Theodore. *Family Records of Theodore Parson Hamm, Including Accounts of the Scott-Gordon Families*. Detroit: Wm C Heath Printing Co., 1892.

Hamilton, Edward P. *Fort Ticonderoga - Key to a Continent*. Boston: Little, Brown and Company, 1964.

Hanson, Willis. *A History of Schenectady During the Revolution*. Interlaken: Heart of Lakes, 1988.

Hawley, Emily C. *A Genealogical and Biographical Record of the Pioneer Thomas Skidmore*. 1911.

Helffenstein, Abraham. *Pierre Fauconnier and His Descendants*. Philadelphia, 1911.

Heller, Daniel W. *The History of Ridgefield, Connecticut*. Danbury: T. Donovan, 1878.

Hess, Peter J. *People of Albany The First 200 Years*. Albany, 2009.

Higby, Clinton David. *Edward Higby and his Descendants*. Boston: T.R. Marvin & Son, 1927.

Hinderaker, Eric. *The Two Hendricks*. Cambridge: Harvard University Press, 2010.

Historical Statistics of the United States Colonial Times to 1970. Washington: US Dept of Commerce Bureau of the Census, 1975.

Hoagland, Cornelius N. *History and Genealogy of the Hoagland Family in America*. New York, 1891.

Hoff, Henry B. "The Tudor Family of Barbados, Boston, and New York City." *New England Historical Genealogical Society Register* (vol 163-4 October 2009).

Hollister, G.H. *The History of Connecticut.* Hartford: Case Tiffany & Co., 1855.

Hough, Franklin. *The Northern Invasion of October 1780.* New York, 1866.

Hubbard, G.Evans. *Wilton Village: A History.* Wilton: Wilton Historical Society, 1971.

Huntington, Elijah Baldwin. *History of Stamford, Connecticut.* Stamford, 1868.

Jacobson, Judy. *Detroit River Connections.* Baltimore: Genealogical Publishing Co., 1994.

Jacobus, Donald Lines. *History and Genealogy of the Familes of Old Fairfield.* Fairfield, 1930.

Jennings, Francis. *The Ambiguous Iroquois Empire.* New York: W.W. Norton & Co., 1984.

Jesup, Henry Griswold. *Edward Jessup and his Descendants.* Cambridge: John Wilson and Son, 1887.

Jodoin, Mark. *Shadow Soldiers of the American Revolution.* Charlston: History Press, 2009.

Johnson, Henry. *The Correspondence and Public Papers of John Jay* XE "Jay, John" *1763-1781.* New York: G. P. Putnam's Sons, 1890.

Johnson, James M. *Key to the Northern County - The Hudson River Valley in the American Revolution.* Albany: State University of New York Press, 2013.

Johnson, William. *Supreme Court of Judicature in the State of New York.* Albany, 1883.

Kammen, Michael. *Colonial New York- A History.* New York: Oxford University Press, 1975.

Kayaderosseras Patent Field Book - Twenty-one Lots of land of the Share of Patentee Johannes Fisher. Ballston Spa: Saratoga County Historians Office, 1775. Document.

Kelley, Brooks Mather. *History of Yale University.* New Haven: Yale University Press, 1974.

Ketchum, Richard M. *Divided Loyalties - How the American Revoltion Came to New York.* New York : Henry Holt and Company, 2002.

—. *Saratoga Turning Point of America's Revolutionary War*. New York: Henry Holt and Company, 1997.

Kissam, Edward. *The Kissam Family in America*. New York: Dempsey & Carroll's Art Press, 1892.

Lee, Francis Bazley. *Genealogical and Memorial History of the State of New Jersey*. New York: Lewis Historical Publishing Co., 1910.

Lefferts, Family Papers. *Brooklyn Historical Society An American Family Grows in Brooklyn*. 2015. http://www.brooklynhistory.org.

Legett, Grace Patchen. *The History and Genealogy of the Patchin-Patchen Family*. Waterbury: The Patchin-en Family Association, 1952.

Lepore, Jill. *New York Burning*. New York: Random House, 2005.

Lepore, Jill. "The Tightening Vise." Berlin, Ira. *Slavery in New York*. New York: New Press, 2005.

Library, Stevens Institute of Technology. "Calendar of the Stevens Family Papers." 2015. *Ancestry.com*.

Livingston, William. Milton M Klein,ed. *The Independent Reflector*. Cambridge: Harvard University Press, 1963.

Loescher, Burt Garfield. *Genesis, Rogers Rangers:The First Green Berets*. San Mateo, 1969.

Lost to History: Archaeology of a Frontier Community. Report. Albany: New York State Museum, 2002.

Lovelace, David. *Tory Spy*. Westminster: Heritage Books, 2009.

Luzader, John. *Saratoga, A Military History of the Decisive Campaign of the American Revolution*. New York: Savis Beate LLC, 2008.

"Lyme Births, Marriages and Deaths." *New England Historical Genealogical Register* (1884).

Mackey, Frank. *Done with Slavery - The Black Fact in Montreal 1760-1840*. Montreal: McGill-Queens University Press, 2010.

Main, Jackson Turner. *Society and Economy in Colonial Connecticut*. Princeton: Princeton University Press, 1985.

Mallart, R. Dewitt. *Lenox and the Berkshire Highlands*. New York: G.P.Putnam's Sons, 1902.

Mann, E.R. *The Bench and Bar of Saratoga County*. Ballston Spa: Waterbury and Inman, 1876.

Manwearing, Charles. *A Digest of Early Connecticut Probate Records - Hartford District*. Hartford: Genealogical Publishing Co, 1904.

Marriage Licenses Issued by the Province of New York Prior to 1784. Albany: Weed, Parsons and Co., 1860.

Marston, David P. *Swift and Bold: The 60th Regiment and Warfare in North America 1755-1765.* Montreal: McGill University, 1997.

Massachusetts Soldiers and Sailors of the Revolutionary War. Boston: Wright and Potter, 1899.

Mather, Frederic. *The Refugees of 1776 from Long Island to Connecticut.* Albany: J.B.Lyon Co., 1913.

Matson, Cathy. *Merchants and Empire-Trading in Colonial New York.* Baltimore: John Hopkins University Press, 1998.

Mayer, Josephine. "The Reminiscences of James Gordon." *New York History* (1936): Vol 17 no 3.

McGrail, Francis, Jr. *The Kayaderosseras Patent: Colonial Land Ownership in Saratoga County, New York.* Ballston Spa: Unpublished, Saratoga County Historians Office, 1978.

Meany, Joseph. *Mechant and Redcoat: The Papers of John Gordon Macomb 1757-1760.* Fordham, 1990. PhD Dissertation.

"Middlebrook Farm." *The Wilton Bulletin* (1984). Newspaper Article.

Middlebrook, Louis F. *Register of the Middlebrook Family.* Hartford, 1909.

Middletown Land Records. Hartford: Connecticut State Library, 2015.

Murray, Eleanor. "The Invasion of Northern New York, 1780." *Bulletin of the Fort Ticonderoga Museum vol VII no. 4* (July 1946): 3-12.

Nammack, Georgiana. *Fraud, Politics and the Dispossession of the Indians.* Norman: University of Oklahoma Press, 1969.

Nash, Elizabeth Todd. *Fifty Puritan Ancestors.* New Haven: The Tuttle Morehouse and Taylor Co., 1908.

O'Callagan, E.B. *The Documentary History of the State of New York.* Albany: Weed Parsons & Co., 1849.

O'Callagan, E.B. *Documents Relative to the Colonial History of New York.* Albany: Weed Parsons & Co, 1855.

Olmstead, Henry King. *The Olmstead Family in America .* New York: De Las Mare Co., 1912.

O'Toole, Fintan. *White Savage.* Albany: State University of New York Press, 2005.

Palmer, Thomas. *A Map of the Township of Ballston.* Ballston Spa: Saratoga County Historians Office, 1772. Map.

—. *Field Book of the Kayaderosseras Patent, Saratoga Co New York.* Albany: New York State Library Manuscripts and Special Collections, 1774. Document.

Paltsits, Victor. *Minutes of the Commissioners for Detecting and Defeating Conspiracies-Albany County Sessions 1778-1782.* Albany, 1909.

Peck, Darious. *A Genealogical Account of William Peck.* Hudson: Bryan & Goeltz, 1877.

Pierson, Lizzie. *Pierson Genealogical Records.* Albany: Joel Munsell, 1878.

Potter-MacKinnon, Janice. *While the Women Only Wept.* Montreal: McGill-Queens University Press, 1993.

Price, Edward T. *Dividing the Land.* Chicago: The University of Chicago Press, 1995.

Rebushka, Alvin. *Taxation in Colonial America.* Princeton: Princeton University Press, 2008.

"Revolutionary Reminiscences." *The Family Magazine* 1840.

Reynolds, Cuyler. *Hudson-Mohawk Genealogical and Family Memoirs.* New York: Lewis Historical Publishing Co., 1991.

Roberts, James A. *New York in The Revolution as Colony and State.* Albany: Weed-Parsons, 1897.

Ross, Peter. *The History of Long Island: Southampton NY.* New York: Lewis Publishing Co., 1902.

Saratoga County Deeds. Ballston Spa: Saratoga County Clerks Office, 2015.

Schenck, Elizabeth Hubbel. *The History of Fairfield Connecticut.* New York, 1889.

Scott, James. "The Raid on Ballston 1780- Memoranda of Reminiscences 1846." *The Bulletin of the Fort Ticonderoga Museum vol. VII no. 4* (July 1946): 12-24.

Scott, Kenneth. "The Slave Insurrection in New York in 1712." *New York State Historical Association Quarterly* (1961): vol 45-1.

Scudder, William. *Journal of William Scudder, An Officer of the Late New York Line.* 1794.

Sedgwick, Charles F. *General History of the Town of Sharon.* Amenia: Charles Walsh, 1898.

Selesky, Harold E. *War and Society in Colonial Connecticut.* New Haven: Yale University Press, 1990.

Selleck, Lillian. *One Branch of the Miner Family*. New Haven: Donald Jacobus, 1928.

Selleck, Rev Charles M. *Norwalk*. Norwalk, 1896.

Shannon, Timothy J. *Iroquois Diplomacy on the Early American Frontier*. New York: Penguin Books, 2008.

Shattuck, Lemuel. *History of the Town of Concord from its Earliest Settlement to 1832*. Boston, 1835.

Shaver, Elizabeth. *Letterbook of Daniel Campbell 1771-1801*. Schenectady: Schenectady County Historical Society, 1982. Transcription.

Shurtleff, Nathaniel. *Records of the Colony of New Plymouth*. Boston: W. White, 1855.

Simms, Jeptha. *History of Schoharie County and the Border Wars of New York*. Albany: Munsell and Tanner, 1845.

—. *The Frontiersman of New York*. Albany: Geo. C. Riggs, 1883.

Smith, J.E.A. *History of Pittsfield*. Boston: Lee & Sheperd, 1869.

Smith, Ralph D. "Edward and John Collins and Their Descendants." *New England Historical and Genalogical Register* (1907): Vol 61.

—. *The History of Guilford Connecticut*. Albany: J Munsell, 1877.

Sprague, Warren Vincent. *Sprague Families in America*. Rutland: The Tuttle Company, 1913.

Steele, Zadock. *The Captivity of Zadock Steele in Indian Narratives*. Claremont: Tracy and Brothers, 1854.

Stephens, John. *Field Books of the Kayaderosseras*. Saratoga Springs: Saratoga Springs Public Library, n.d. Map.

Stevens, John Austin. *Colonial Records of the New York Chamber of Commerce 1768-1784*. New York: JF Trow & Co., 1867.

Stone, William L. *Reminiscences of Saratoga*. New York: Worthington Co., 1880.

Sullivan, James. *Minutes of the Albany Committee of Correspondence 1775-1778*. Albany: The University of the State of New York, 1923.

—. *The Papers of Sir William Johnson*. Albany: The University of the State of New York, 1921.

Sylvester, Nathaniel Bartlett. *History of Saratoga County New York*. Philadelphia: Everts & Ensign, 1878.

Talcott, Alvin. *Families of Early Guilford, Connecticut*. Baltimore: Genealogical Publishing Co., 2010.

Tatham, John. *Field Books of the Kayaderosseras*. Albany: New York State Library, n.d. Map.

Taylor, Alan. *The Divided Ground*. New York: Vintage Books, 2006.

The 48th Foot in the French and Indian War. n.d. http://www.kronoskaf.com. 2015.

The Colonial Laws of New York from the Year 1664 to the Revolution. Albany: James B. Lyon, 1849.

The Public Papers of George Clinton. New York: Wynkoop Hallenbeck Crawford Co., 1900.

The Public Records of the Colony of Connecticut. Hartford: FA Brown, 1852.

"U.S Revolutionary War Pension and Bounty Warrant Application Files 1800-1900." n.d. *Ancestry.com*. 2015.

Upper Canada Land Petition of Staats Springsteen August 14, 1795. n.d. Ancestry.com. 2015.

Vaughan, Alden T. *New England Frontier*. Norman: University of Oklahoma Press, 1965.

Vital Records of Richmond, Massachusetts to the Year 1850. Boston: New England Historical Genealogical Society, 1913.

Walworth, Reuben. *Hyde Genealogy*. Albany: J.Munsell, 1864.

Watrous, Leland Rice. *Genealogy.com Houses by the Water: The Waterhouse/ Watrous Family in America*. n.d. http://www.genealogy.com/ftm/w/a/t/Leland-R-Watrous/index.html. 2015.

Watt, Gavin K. *A Dirty, Trifling Piece of Business*. Toronto: Dundurn Press, 2009.

—. *draft -The 1778 Campaign, Chapter 5 Returning to the Mohawk Region*. pre-publication, 2016.

—. *I Am Heartily Ashamed*. Toronto: Dundurn Press, 2009.

—. *Poisoned by Lies and Hypocracy*. Toronto: Dundurn Press, 2014.

—. *The British Campaign of 1777 Vol. 2 The Burgoyne Expeditions*. Milton: Global Heritage Press, 2003.

—. *The Burning of the Valleys*. Toronto: Dundurn Press, 1997.

Weeks, Harriet. *Descendants of Richard Hayes of Lyme, Connecticut*. Pittsfield: Eagle Publishing Co., 1904.

Westbrook, Nicholas. "Have we no longer a share in your history? Preserving Old Minerley Road: le chemin des Iroquois." 2010. Report.

White, Barclay. "Early Settlements in Springfield Township." Address. 1870.

White, Lorraine Cook. *The Barbour Collection of Connecticut Town Vital Records*. Baltimore: Genealogical Publishing Co., 1994.

Wilkinson, James. *Memoirs of My Own Times*. Philadelphia: Abraham Small, 1816.

Witcraft, John. *Cornelius Jansen Clopper and his Descendants*. Merchantville: Dispatch Press, 1912.

Woodward, E.M. *History of Burlington and Mercer Counties, New Jersey*. Philadelphia: Everts and Peck, 1883.

Wooster, David. *Genealogy of the Woosters in America*. San Francisco: M. Weiss, 1885.

Wyld, Samuel and David Manchey. *The Practical Surveyor 1725*. The Invisable College Press, 2001.

Yates, Austin. *Schenectady County - It's History to the Close of the Nineteenth Century*. New York: New York History Company, 1902.

Index

K

L

M

James Richmond is retired, with a life-long interest in Genealogy and American History. He has published several articles on the New England roots of the Richmond family, as well as articles on local history relating to locations in Saratoga County, New York. Jim also lectures on local history at libraries, historical societies and educational institutions. "War on the Middleline" is Jim's first full-length book. He resides in Ballston Spa, New York with his wife Diane and is the father of three adult children.